Diane Ghirardo
was educated in California at San Jose
State University and Stanford University, where she
obtained her PhD. Since 1984 she has been a Professor of
Architecture at the University of Southern California in
Los Angeles. She has lectured widely, and served on archi-
tectural juries; she was a founding editor of the magazine
Archetype, and executive editor of the *Journal of Architectural
Education*. Her extensive publications include *Building New
Communities: New Deal America and Fascist Italy* (1989),
Out of Site: A Social Criticism of Architecture (1991),
and *Mark Mack* (1994).

WORLD OF ART

This famous series
provides the widest available
range of illustrated books on art in all its aspects.
If you would like to receive a complete list
of titles in print please write to:
THAMES AND HUDSON
30 Bloomsbury Street, London WC1B 3QP
In the United States please write to:
THAMES AND HUDSON INC.
500 Fifth Avenue, New York, New York 10110

Printed in Singapore

DIANE GHIRARDO

ARCHITECTURE
AFTER MODERNISM

166 illustrations, 40 in color

THAMES AND HUDSON

For my parents,
Margaret Madden Ghirardo and Joseph Ghirardo

© 1996 Thames and Hudson Ltd, London

First published in the United States of America in
1996 by Thames and Hudson Inc., 500 Fifth Avenue,
New York, New York 10110

Library of Congress Catalog Card Number 96-60260
ISBN 0-500-20294-x

Printed and bound in Singapore

Contents

Acknowledgments

As is the case with most authors, I received help from many people in various ways while this book was underway. Nikos Stangos of Thames and Hudson and Robin Middleton of Columbia University demonstrated remarkable patience in waiting for the final manuscript. Francesca Rogier, Howard Smith, John Uniak and Sally Nicholls all helped locate photographs at various points. Robin Middleton, Denise Bratton and Margaret Crawford read and commented most helpfully on different versions of the book. Stephen Fox of the Anchorage Foundation and Rice University in Texas subjected the manuscript to a particularly rigorous reading, and even though I clung stubbornly to some points, many of his suggestions have been incorporated into the text. In editing the final manuscript, Emily Lane not only saved me from some errors but also contributed her acute insights to many of the issues, in particular the section on London's Docklands. To Emily go very special thanks. Aaron Hayden attentively rendered the book's arguments visually.

Students in a graduate seminar at Rice University in the spring of 1995 sharpened my thinking on the issue of public space, and audiences at lectures at the University of Houston, University of British Columbia, Rice University, and University of California, Berkeley, offered provocative critiques. Diane Beckham, Ireen Brooks and Christine Hess of the Association of Collegiate Schools of Architecture and Valezra Earl of the University of Southern California provided logistical support at key moments. Morris Adjmi, Barbara Allen, Armando and Marina Antonelli, Justin Antonin, Lee Buckley, Frances Chamberlain, Mike Davis, Faiza Al-Hassoun, Richard Ingersoll, Carlos Jiménez, Lars Lerup, Sandra Macat, Mark Mack, Karen McCauley, John McRae, Vince Pecora, Nicole Pertuiset, Margaret Power, and Sophie Spalding, offered friendship and stimulating discussions about art, architecture and Postmodernism and other important matters while I was researching and writing. Wil Bailey, Brad Brown, Richard Loring and Brad Surber of Archetype beautifully reassembled my home following the 1994 Northridge earthquake.

I wrote this book during two of the most difficult years of my life. The love and support of Rachel, Joe, Natasha, JoAnn, Ferruccio, Vittoria and Carlo Trabalzi and of my parents sustained me.

Introduction

The period following 1965 ushered in an approach toward architecture that came to be known as Postmodernism, initially in the United States, and ultimately elsewhere in the industrialized world. Postmodernism is a diverse, unstable concept that has denoted particular aesthetic approaches in literary criticism, art, film, theater, and architecture, not to mention in fashion and armed battle. In 1995, *The New York Times* defined the war in Bosnia as a "Postmodern War," in which civilians and armed forces can no longer be distinguished, highly sophisticated weaponry plays almost no role, and little informal groups, such as militias or tribal groups, replace states. Such wars are intractable and difficult to end through negotiation because central authority no longer exists.

Within the domain of philosophy and political science, Postmodernism can also refer to epistemology, or particular modes of thought and knowledge, or even specific characterizations of the political economy and social conditions of the late 20th century. That it is unstable as a category is one of its inherent features in aesthetics and epistemology, for theorists of Postmodernism have ascribed to it a rejection of the possibility for unity of form or ideology. The definition of what Postmodernism means varies from field to field, even from writer to writer. In architecture its connotation has changed considerably between 1970 and 1995. Remarkably, few of the insights in political economy or sociology made their way into architecture, particularly those of Postmodernism's economic and social equivalent, post-Fordism (see below, p. 37). Instead, theories of knowledge and of aesthetics from other disciplines infiltrated architecture over the last quarter-century virtually without regard to other, arguably more significant, forces.

Postmodernism in these fields shares certain common features, such as the rejection of a unitary world view as embodied in what are called master narratives, meaning grand explanatory systems, including those of most religions or political groups, or of Karl Marx or Sigmund Freud. Where the forces of modernization in the early 20th century tended to obscure local, regional and ethnic differences, Postmodernists focus

7

precisely on those differences and bring to the fore that which had been marginalized by dominant cultures. Perhaps this is best exemplified by the renewed emphasis on ethnic and feminist studies in order that attention be given to voices that have not traditionally been heard. There are variants of Postmodernism in other disciplines that have had an impact on architecture, such as Post-Structuralism and Deconstruction, which I will discuss later in this Introduction.

Postmodernism in architecture is most commonly understood as a stylistic phenomenon. Yet it should be understood first in the context of what the movement opposed, and second in what it affirmed. The very term—Postmodernism—indicated the distinction enthusiasts for the new approach intended in the early 1970s: an architecture differentiated from and following in the wake of Modernism, which many had begun to assert was anachronistic. The best scholarly accounts of this transformation in architecture have been published by Kenneth Frampton, Mary McLeod, Magali Sarfatti Larson, and Heinrich Klotz.

To a significant extent, as both Frampton and McLeod note, the early polemicists on behalf of Postmodernism and against the Modern Movement offered a caricature of what they opposed, both Modernism's formal elaboration and its underlying social and political premises. Exempt from this critique would be a building such as Louis Kahn's Salk Institute in La Jolla, California (1959–65), which seems to many to transcend the worst flaws of 1960s Modernism in the United States, especially the fetishization of structure and technology. Sited majestically overlooking the Pacific Ocean, the Salk Institute evidenced the full range of Kahn's formal interests: integrated mechanical and service systems set on separate floors between the laboratories, the exploration of "voids expressed positively." Kahn responded to the relatively simple program by proposing a spatial division of functions, with studios set apart from the labs for study and solitary research and separate meeting rooms. He rendered the service aspects of the program clear and clean while at once celebrating the site and his virtuoso treatment of reinforced concrete.

The Modern Movement enjoyed its richest flowering and attained its historic prestige during the decades between the two World Wars, when it was born in a spirit of renunciation of the old world, a commitment to addressing mass housing needs, and an enthusiasm for exploring the architectural potential of materials and technologies often disdained by the previous generation. It claimed the energy of talented, committed architects throughout Europe, even if it represented the ideas of a relatively marginal and socially homogeneous group of architects and resulted in only a modest number of buildings.

8

1 Louis Kahn, Salk Institute, La Jolla, California, 1959–65.

Although marked by different emphases—on the one hand, a techno-logical determinism, on the other the idea of aesthetic self-expression—the ideas of most Modernist architects retained as an underlying constant a belief in the power of form to transform the world, even if it was usually linked to some vague broader goals of social reform. Through modern architecture's sleek machined surfaces and structural rationalism, architects passionately believed that housing and other social problems could be solved. Such assumptions formed the ideological underpinnings of Le Corbusier's urban projects for Paris, Marseilles and North Africa, but also of his smaller villa projects, such as the Villa Savoye.

By the mid-1930s, in many places the tenets of the Modern Movement were being eclipsed by modernity interpreted as a monumental classicism, spurred in part by the interests and patronage of governments in Soviet Russia, Nazi Germany, Fascist Italy, and the United States. Undeterred by this and by the exile of major German exponents of Modernism such as Ludwig Mies van der Rohe, Walter Gropius and Erich Mendelsohn, and buoyed by the avid support of major hist-orians such as Sigfried Giedion, Nikolaus Pevsner and Henry-Russell Hitchcock, and finally by the postwar building boom, the Modern Movement acquired a mythical significance far greater than its actual accomplishments before World War II.

The Modern Movement was fueled not only by new technologies and intergenerational rivalry, but also by quite specific conceptions of the role of the architect and the source of architectural form. Mary McLeod and Alan Colquhoun fruitfully explored the various strands of thought characteristic of the Modern Movement on the question of how architectural form is generated. On the one hand, some architects emphasized functionalism and the generation of form by a sort of biotechnical determinism. On the other, architects emphasized intuition and the genius of the architect as formgiver. The leading early Modernists—Le Corbusier, Mies van der Rohe and Gropius—managed to combine the two apparently opposed conceptions, but they were exceptions. A split between these two understandings of Modernism became quite visible in architecture in the 1960s. McLeod argued that architects such as Eero Saarinen and Jørn Utzon viewed design as a highly personal means of self-expression, although their architecture might be understood best as explorations in the expressive possibilities of construction, materials and program. Other commentators such as Cedric Price and Tomás Maldonado emphasized the almost autonomous generation of form. What united both, however, was a relative indifference to history and tradition, and both positions drew their own groups of followers.

Modernism took on a new life after World War II, particularly in the United States, where Modern Movement aesthetics, sleek, machine-like, and unornamented, converged with such technologies as the steel frame and glass curtain walls to produce cost-effective skyscrapers and suburban office parks and shopping centers. At the same time, the notion of the architect as exalted purveyor of form began to dominate schools and then the profession.

Reduced costs and speedier construction made Modernist buildings appealing to developers and city administrators, who seized the opportunity to revamp town centers in the 1950s and 1960s as the middle class took flight to the suburbs. As part of major campaigns to "revitalize" urban areas that were being depopulated, cities undertook sweeping urban renewal programs, with affordable rental housing and lower income groups (especially racial and ethnic minorities) shunted aside on behalf of the gleaming glass boxes that Le Corbusier and Mies van der Rohe had first envisioned more than a quarter of a century earlier. Governments, banks, corporations and cultural institutions such as museums adopted modern architecture as their signatures in generally well-constructed buildings. But architects gained increasing prestige for producing buildings for developers concerned chiefly with rapidity, cheapness and spectacular effect.

2 Albert C. Martin & Associates, Arco Towers, Los Angeles, California, 1973.

3 John Portman Associates, Hyatt Regency Atlanta, Peachtree Center, Atlanta, Georgia, 1967: the atrium.

As Modernist aesthetics drifted from the margins to the mainstream, and as the world came to terms with the atrocities of Nazi Germany, the A- and H-bombs and the imminent possibility of nuclear destruction, the oppositional political positions articulated by some of the major interwar exponents of Modernism disappeared, especially in the United States. Bereft of faith in the possibility of transforming the world, the earlier utopian hopes and dreams, however misguided and partial, were supplanted by a fundamentally bland affirmation which, in the United States, came to be associated not with rebellion but with the power of capitalism. Mies van der Rohe's 860–880 Lake Shore Drive towers in Chicago (1948–51) and his Seagram Building in New York (1958) set the stage for the many lean and gridded urban skyscrapers that went up over the next fifteen years, with contributions in the United States from other firms such as Skidmore, Owings & Merrill (SOM), Pereira and Associates, John C. Portman, Jr., Johnson/Burgee, Albert C. Martin & 2 Associates, Kohn Pederson Fox, and Welton Becket Associates. Portman's Hyatt Regency Atlanta, Peachtree Center, in Atlanta, Georgia (1967), 3 exemplifies the innovations introduced by an ambitious architect turned developer. Promoted as the heart of an inner city revival, Peachtree Center abandoned the Modernist slab hotel typology and introduced a grand interior atrium rising up twenty-two stories. In a design reproduced in countless subsequent hotels by Portman and others, the individual rooms overlook the atrium and the glass-encased elevators that sweep visitors up to a revolving restaurant topped by a blue glass dome.

As Portman's skyscraper hotels so tellingly demonstrate, corporate capital had by the 1950s and 1960s forged much the same kind of alliance with modern architectural aesthetics that it had with Keynesian economics, in effect expunging the left-wing connotations and recuperating both for different purposes. During the 1930s the American business community had opposed John Maynard Keynes's project for massive compensatory spending on the grounds that it was fiscally unsound and potentially threatening to the political and social order. By the end of World War II, however, business had fashioned a new consensus on deficit spending by devising a conservative, investment-oriented model of Keynesianism that served its own ends. With this new partnership, United States capital began to penetrate every corner of the globe; architectural emblems of modernity accompanied other American cultural debris such as Levi's and Coca-Cola to Europe, Asia, Africa and Latin America, where they displaced indigenous traditions and testified to the hegemony of American capital and institutions.

From the 1950s forward, the confluence of economic interests and aesthetics spread rapidly from the United States and became the quintessential expression of corporate capitalism in far-flung reaches of the globe. The dream of standardization that had animated some segments of the Modern Movement was realized with a vengeance in commercial building, and by the mid-1960s a backlash began to form. The task of repeating steel frames and curtain walls turned out to be not terribly taxing, and even less demanding of creativity. While such large corporate firms as Skidmore, Owings & Merrill and C. F. Murphy Associates followed the lead of Mies van der Rohe and produced high quality if sober and imitative buildings, other groups pursued variants on the Modern Movement of a quite different type, hyper-celebrations of the supposedly liberating possibilities of endless technological development. Buckminster Fuller in the United States, the Archigram group in England, Superstudio in Italy and the Japanese Metabolists were the most prominent examples. Fuller's personal investigations into technologically sophisticated and utilitarian designs, preferably to be mass-produced, dated back to the late 1920s. He retained a sense of reality in his projects and a recognition of the need to propose viable solutions to real social problems. But Archigram, Super-studio and to a lesser degree the Metabolists swept away any tedious connection with reality. With a series of splashy publications and cartoon-like, science-fiction images, they made their marks without taking seriously questions such as how things would be built, how they would last over time, and what the social implications might be for the people who were destined to occupy their fantastic cities. Almost no one took Super-studio and Archigram seriously, least of all the developers and bankers who were responsible for commissioning and financing projects designed in Modernist style. Nonetheless, taken together they signaled the demise of the appeal of rationalist Modernism, a reaction against a building style that came to be seen as boring, indifferent to the surroundings and to the discipline's own historical traditions to boot.

The most serious assaults on the Modern Movement had lasting impacts. Four books published within less than a decade signaled the forthcoming change: Jane Jacobs's *The Death and Life of Great American Cities* (1961), Robert Venturi's *Complexity and Contradiction in Architecture* (1966), Aldo Rossi's *The Architecture of the City* (1966), and Hassan Fathy's *Architecture for the Poor* (first published as *Gourna: A Tale of Two Villages* in 1969).

Although their effect was felt at different times in different cultures owing to dates of translation and publication, and although other seminal books also appeared, together these four suggest the dimensions of the changes in attitudes toward architecture.

Jacobs challenged the planning ideas of Le Corbusier and other Modern Movement designers, as well as the Garden City program of Ebenezer Howard, popularized in the United States by Clarence Stein, as inappropriate for cities. Celebrating the heterogeneity of urban neighborhoods and old buildings, Jacobs used her own district in New York as a means of unearthing the diversity and liveliness possible on city streets, which she contrasted with the deadening regularity of low-income housing projects that killed the street. Unlike most architectural critics of the time, Jacobs acknowledged the connection between development money and urban change, financial practices and the decay of cities.

Some of her most telling arguments demonstrated how designers followed the ideology of Modern Movement planning rather than their own instincts about urban neighborhoods. The hidden order of the unredeveloped street, Jacobs argued, sustained a rich and varied urban life and improved security to boot. Some of her emphases—on the lived experience of architecture, the rituals and patterns of daily life, the network of human relationships that constitute our experiences of cities and which modern architecture and planning ignored—only slowly began to bear

4 Frank Gehry, Loyola Law School, Los Angeles, California, 1981-84.

fruit. Contemporary cities should not undergo further devastating urban renewal according to the misguided principles of the Modern Movement, she concluded, but rather should be nourished as the vital and engaging places they were in reality.

With gradual acceptance of Jacobs's ideas came a renewed appreciation for visual variety in the cityscape. Urban designers began to juxtapose different elements rather than seek a continuous uniform screen, and to accept the value of the existing and varied elements in cities. The new aesthetic preference carried down even to the construction of the individual building complex, achieving full fruition much later in a project such as Frank Gehry's Loyola Law School in Los Angeles (1981-84), where the juxtaposition of disparate, brightly colored volumes hinted at a diverse urban fabric. For the University at Castellanza (1990) Aldo Rossi did not invent heterogeneity, but discovered and enhanced it. For the campus, he simply took over and transformed an abandoned textile plant, accepting the diverse structures as valid.

Hassan Fathy's book detailing the construction of the village of New Gourna in Egypt during the 1930s at the same time chronicled his

14

attempt to resist the importation of foreign building technologies, which he believed failed on many accounts to meet the needs of rural Egypt. Apart from decrying the exorbitant cost of such systems and the technical expertise that put them out of reach of the average Egyptian, let alone the poor, Fathy also lamented the loss of traditional building methods and cultural competence that this tidal wave of foreign technology implied. In addition to resisting the overwhelming influence of Western building styles and methods, Fathy called into question the notion of the architect as principally a designer, arguing instead for seeing the architect as carrier and safeguard of tradition, and building as the expression of culture rather than of the will or ego of an individual. It is a sad irony that despite his dogged insistence that his building methods and approaches could most benefit the peasantry, Fathy ended up with few exceptions designing for the wealthy in traditional styles, largely as nationalist expressions of resistance against Western power. Despite its engaging architecture, the village of New Gourna also failed to entice residents away from making their livings from tomb robbing.

Fathy's book signaled a pervasive resistance to Western Modernism and an often contentious confrontation with colonial legacies in many non-Western countries. New Gourna also evidenced profound conflicts in values and a host of underlying political and social issues only partially addressed by the architect in a way that is emblematic of many government building projects throughout the world. Geoffrey Bawa's Parliament Complex, Sri Jayawardhanapura, Kotte, Colombo, Sri Lanka   5

5 Geoffrey Bawa, Parliament Complex, Sri Jayawardhanapura, Kotte, Colombo, Sri Lanka, 1982.

6 Geoffrey Bawa,
Lunuganga Gardens,
Bentota, Sri Lanka,1950.

(1982), confronted and transcended both Modernism and tradition in a building designed to house the parliament in a country deeply divided by ethnic and religious differences.The commission itself involved transferring the parliament to a remote, relatively inaccessible site precisely so as to limit confrontations among warring factions. Set as an island surrounded by lakes, it refers to indigenous traditions of island temples, but also to the fortresses of colonial powers that successively hit the country. The landscaping is particularly sensitive, although on a far larger scale
6   than some of Bawa's extraordinary projects such as the Lunuganga Gardens at Bentota, Sri Lanka (1950). Through the use of multivalent imagery and direct appeals to traditions in the roof and the crafting of the timber members, Bawa sought to produce a civic building that embraced the traditions of all factions—an aspiration easier to realize in the building than in the society.

16

The Ju'er Hutong Courtyard Housing Project at Beijing in China, begun in 1987 and still ongoing, embodies ideas similar to those advanced by Fathy, but with a collaboration among architects, residents, and government. Planned and designed at the Institute of Architectural and Urban Studies at Tsinghua University with Professor Wu Liangyong as chief architect, the project's principal objective was to rehabilitate the housing in an inner city neighborhood so as to improve the physical environment while integrating modern living requirements and cultural continuity. It also envisioned serving as a model for housing reform, and for developing ways of incorporating university research into local projects. Designers had to confront such problems as overcrowding, dilapidated housing, temporary housing following the 1976 earthquake, and poor ventilation. The rehabilitated neighborhood incorporates modern amenities within the old framework by adapting traditional typologies, but also by working in close cooperation with residents.

Robert Venturi's approach differed from that of Jacobs in that he specifically addressed what he saw as the vacuous buildings produced by followers of the Modern Movement, independent of their social underpinnings or economic imperatives. His agenda directly engaged strategies for individual buildings and for urban design projects, especially those produced by a small class of elite architects. While spending two years in Italy with a Rome Prize fellowship admiring the wonders of antiquity and the Renaissance, Venturi discovered the rich possibilities of architectural history. Following the lead of Gropius at the Bauhaus, historical studies had been excised from the curricula of most schools of architecture in the United States (although not at Venturi's alma mater, Princeton). Venturi saw this as a tremendous loss for architects, for only this lack could explain their continuing fascination with the dull glass boxes and tedious constructs of Modernism. Opposing "orthodox modern architecture," Venturi celebrated "messy vitality over obvious unity," richness over clarity of meaning, and, in a much quoted passage, "both–and" instead of "either–or." He also insisted that the complexities of contemporary life did not permit simplified architectural programs, therefore except for single-purpose buildings, architects needed to address multifunctional programs. In this book and a later one written with Denise Scott Brown and Steven Izenour, *Learning from Las Vegas* (1972), Venturi adopted a position not unlike that of Jacobs when he urged architects to take into consideration and even to celebrate what already existed rather than attempt to impose a visionary utopia out of their own fantasy.

Although most of his examples of architecture that expressed the ideas he prized were drawn from Italy between 1400 and 1750, he also

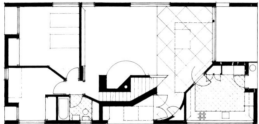

7, 8 Venturi and Short Architects (Robert Venturi with Arthur Jones), Vanna Venturi House, Chestnut Hill, Pennsylvania, 1964: facade and plan.

included buildings by Le Corbusier, Alvar Aalto and Louis Kahn, suggesting that it was not Modernism per se that he opposed, but rather unimaginative versions of it. Venturi's first attempt to confront these issues was the design for his mother's house, the Vanna Venturi House at Chestnut Hill, Pennsylvania (1964), where he experimented with historical allusions on the facade while developing a complex and intriguing interior, following the Guild House (1960), a senior citizens' apartment building in Philadelphia. In each case, the design embodied principles as outlined in *Complexity and Contradiction*: an emphasis on the facade, on historical elements, on the complex play of materials and historical allusions, and on fragments and inflections.

Italian architect and theorist Aldo Rossi's *Architecture of the City* confronted not United States cities ravaged by urban renewal but European cities suffering the effects of wartime destruction and postwar redevelopment. Like Jacobs and Venturi, Rossi rejected what he termed naive

18

functionalism, the notion advanced by some Modernist architects that "form follows function." His specific targets were architects who celebrated technological determinism and who disdained the rich complexity of cities, not just their buildings but their histories, urban forms, street networks, and personal stories. Rossi too turned back to the past, to the European city, in order to identify first how cities grew and were transformed over time, and second, how building types participated in the morphological evolution of the city. Studying the structural elements of the city, Rossi proposed not a style but a mode of analysis and an approach to urban housing, design and change that took into account particular histories, patterns of change and traditions. Building types formed one of the solid bases for his approach to design, but for Rossi building types were understood as rooted in the specific customs and habits of particular cities or parts of cities rather than abstract constructs independent of historical conditions. He called not for repetitions but for creative adaptations based upon considered analyses of individual cities. Rossi subsequently developed his ideas in the San Cataldo Cemetery at Modena (begun 1980) and the Borgoricco Town Hall (1982), drawing 9 upon rural, urban and vernacular traditions for his designs. The Town Hall, for example, set in a field with houses scattered about in the surrounding farmland, recalls a Venetian villa but consists of the compact, highly differentiated forms of an urban civic building.

9 Aldo Rossi, project for the Town Hall, Borgoricco, Italy, 1982: perspective view from the south.

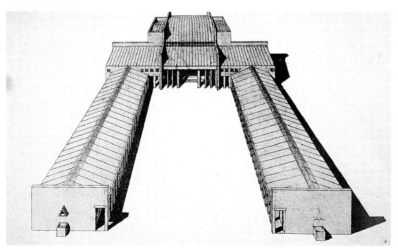

It is useful to compare the positions of Venturi and Rossi more closely because the differences in their views are echoed in subsequent architecture in Europe and the United States. For both, architecture's challenge transcends and at the same time encompasses the idiosyncrasies of individual architects, and it was on the basis of this historic mission that both writers criticized architecture and urbanism in the period after World War II. Both also turned to the architectural past as a tool for returning architecture to its historic public responsibilities. The differences in their positions can be attributed largely to their respective contexts. The millennial tradition of urban cultural continuity in Europe allowed Rossi to bypass the 19th-century emphasis on architectural history as a succession of styles. This urban continuity concomitantly embodied a significant social dimension: new buildings confirmed and extended longstanding traditions, which also included the notion that governments were obliged to provide housing and other services to citizens. The broad frame of these cultural traditions could accommodate considerable invention, as well as personal interpretations, while maintaining general cultural significance.

Venturi adopted eclecticism as a tool with which to perform a critique of American Modernism, in a society where broad cultural experience is shaped by individual sensibilities rather than a millennial urban tradition. The political culture that so dominates Europe is replaced in the United States by a culture of commerce and advertising. Rossi's description of the city as the defining socialization experience in Europe is, by contrast, in Venturi's United States, the culture of communication. Instead of unifying socially, or reflecting political identity, or reinforcing individual identities, culture in the United States consists of alternative symbols with which individuals are invited to define themselves. Venturi's turn to commercial advertising as the framework upon which to erect Postmodern architecture therefore encourages a pessimistic architecture that collapses historical references into deflated images and ambiguous spatiality. American Postmodernism therefore has been bound up with visual codes and a vision of the public only as otherwise indistinct consumers.

Likewise, the aesthetic preferences of Postmodernism in the United States lent themselves to far more cartoon-like trivialization and packaging than did those of Modernism. Perhaps more tellingly, this version of Postmodernism could not advance alternative possibilities for architects to participate professionally in the world of building. Critiques of contemporary conditions in exclusively architectural terms likewise failed to challenge the notion that architecture is to blame for the shortcomings and problems in the built environment. Although Jacobs criticized architectural and planning decisions, and she proposed architectural and planning alternatives, her critique comprehended far more, and a far more nuanced understanding of the causes of urban degradation.

While Jacobs's study only gradually exerted an influence on planners and architects, and Fathy likewise slowly drew adherents to his approach in the Islamic world, Venturi and Rossi quickly attracted a group of like-minded architects. Despite differences, Vittorio Gregotti, Giorgio Grassi and Ticino school architects Mario Botta, Bruno Reichlin and Fabio Reinhardt, in a loose grouping known as the Tendenza, followed Rossi in rejecting the universalizing impulse of Modernist rationalism and in valuing historical sources. They claimed, with varying degrees of credibility, to recover and emphasize local building traditions and materials, and to respect historic urban fabrics. Rossi's lean, taut architecture based on geometric volumes and abstract vernacular traditions set the agenda for the other northern Italian and Ticinese architects. Perhaps because Italian vernacular buildings are largely unornamented, their own designs, at least until the early 1980s, depended less upon the evocation of aristocratic historical styles through ornament than did those of American Postmodernists.

The modest little Vanna Venturi House heralded a trend that soon found a following in housing design in the United States. Venturi and his partner Denise Scott Brown argued throughout the 1970s and 1980s that the architect's task was to express meaning to the general public, whether in the design of a house or a civic building. For Venturi and Scott Brown, "the people" became mobile bearers of meaning, appealed to as authorities in *Learning from Las Vegas* (1972) or in arguments to defend their decorative programs. When the people took the form of design review boards, however, they were disparaged as idiots and buffoons.

Michael Graves and Robert A. M. Stern also sought to address popular taste in startlingly pastel and boldly historicizing designs. In reality their work, like that of Venturi's office, appealed to the sensibilities of architectural cognoscenti rather than mass audiences. Despite their polemical and populist assertions, the eclectic feasts produced in the name of populism seem instead little more than the triumph of the architects' personal taste and their ability to convince a class of wealthy clients to accept it, particularly since the recondite historical allusions inevitably could be deciphered only by a small, elite body of clients and other architecture buffs.

By the early 1970s, the design strategies Venturi advocated had acquired a name—Postmodernism—and a list of prominent followers, including Charles Moore as well as Robert Stern. In Moore's Burns House at Santa Monica, California (1974), and Stern's contemporary

10

10 Charles Moore, Burns House, Santa Monica, California, 1974.

11 Robert A. M. Stern, Lang Residence, Washington, Connecticut, 1974.

Lang Residence in Washington, Connecticut, the architects offered equally populist claims for designs that essentially advanced a narrowly aestheticizing and historicizing agenda. Dominated by pastel hues and brash collages of thinly applied skins emblazoned with historicizing elements, these splashy confections ignited the enthusiasm of upwardly mobile young professionals for designs for their own houses, and also in particular of the developers of mini-malls and strip shopping centers in the United States. In Southern California entire neighborhoods of exuberantly historicizing speculator-built homes inspired by these designers seemed to crop up overnight. The 1980 Venice Biennale organized by Paolo Portoghesi signaled that the movement had spread beyond the United States, not only to Europe, with designs by Portoghesi in Italy, Christian de Portzamparc in France, and Ricardo Bofill in Spain, but also to the Far East, with work by Takefumi Aida and Arata Isozaki in Japan, particularly the Okanoyama Graphic Arts Museum at Nishiwaki, Hyogo (1982–84), with its massive concrete pillars at the quasi-temple front, galleries strung out like carriages on a train, rusticated podium, and pastel tones. This marked a striking contrast to Isozaki's earlier, sleekly machined and Modernist Gunma Prefectural Museum of Modern Art at Takasaki (1974), an aluminum-paneled essay of variations on the cube.

As Isozaki's designs reveal, the openness to tradition did not invariably issue in puffed-up versions of classicism. In the United States,

12 Arata Isozaki, Gunma Prefectural Museum of Modern Art, Takasaki, Japan, 1974.

13 Hans Hollein, Austrian Travel Agency, Opernringhof, Vienna, Austria, 1978.

14, 15   Arquitectonica's Spear Residence in Miami, Florida (1976–78), with its bold chromatic scheme emphasizing dramatic interior volumes, marked an effort to wed vital Caribbean chromatics with cool Modernism. Hans Hollein in Austria adopted a different approach which emphasized highly crafted, almost jewel-like designs with a willingness to problema-

13   tize the very subject of his architecture, as in the Austrian Travel Agency in Vienna (1978).

The so-called return to history boasted even more ardent supporters than the Postmodernists during the 1970s and 1980s. Quinlan Terry, Alan Greenberg and Leon Krier called for a return to academic classicism. In a variety of settings, Krier argued for a return not only to classical architecture but to pre-20th-century principles of town planning. Part of the appeal of his program for a new architecture and urbanism was the wholesale avoidance of everything that had happened to cities, architecture, capital accumulation or finance since the Industrial Revolution. Krier's deft elimination of discord rendered his perky little sketches of an integral world as appealing as Disney cartoons, and no less indifferent to the complexities of the modern world. The urban principles Krier articulated received a more substantive development in the hands of such architects as Elizabeth Plater-Zyberk, Andrés Duany and Stephanos Polyzoides. As they developed a following, they founded an organization, Congress on New Urbanism, in 1993 to advocate urban and suburban design on a far more modest scale with greater visual variety and greater tolerance for diverse styles than was found in Modernist planning.

24

14, 15 Arquitectonica, Spear Residence, Miami, Florida, 1976–78.

16 Cees Dam, Town Hall, Almere, Netherlands, 1986.

16, 17 Bound up with these urban plans, however, were a set of nostalgic, separatist social images that were met with contempt by many critics and architects—and by enthusiasm among middle-class clients. Perhaps the most successful effort at a new town, but outside of the tenets of the New Urbanism, is Almere in the Netherlands, near Amsterdam on the Zuider Zee, planned by Teun Koolhaas, with its Town Hall designed by Cees Dam and apartments by Herman Hertzberger and other notable architects. Pedestrian-scaled but responsive to other forms of transport from bicycles to motorcars, Almere aspires to be a livable city that respects traditional Dutch patterns of living and working, architectural traditions but also modern transformations. Certainly one of the significant differences lies not in the architecture but in the Netherlands' commitment to decent, low-cost housing for all of its citizens: Almere lacks the spatial segregation by class and income that is too characteristic of planned residential communities in the United States.

In the 1970s, Postmodern designers delivered a crescendo of broadsides (and some buildings) against what amounted to a caricature version of Modernism. They ignored the exponents of Modernism during the 1920s and 1930s who had attacked bourgeois and elitist architectural institutions, and they derided Modernist hopes that social change would accompany innovative aesthetics. To be sure, the belief that new architectural forms were sufficient to improve the world now appears naive at best. Nonetheless, Postmodernists who disparaged the Modernists'

26

utopian goals through form fell into at least two major errors. On the one hand, over time from the late 1970s through the 1980s they abandoned any aspirations for social change not just through form, but altogether. Although in some cases Postmodernists forged alliances with preservationists to preserve housing stock, these instances were relatively uncommon; during the building boom of the heady 1980s, alliances with other forces to improve housing were the exception rather than the rule. Concerns about ecology or the appropriateness of building in geologically inappropriate areas suffered even greater marginalization. Throughout Europe and the United States, too many brash Postmodernist designs of the 1980s seemed to embody no dreams beyond wealth and power.

The second error was that the opponents of utopian Modernism still celebrated the power of architecture to convey meaning, as in the works of the populist-oriented Postmodernists, or to render critiques of contemporary society through form, as the case of such an architect as Peter Eisenman with his series of numbered houses. Paradoxically then, they reasserted the power of form, along with that of themselves as architects, at the same time that they were scoffing at the utopian aspirations of early Modernists. Perhaps the fundamental continuity between Modernist and Postmodernist architects derives from the reassertion of the power of form, and hence the primacy of design, to the exclusion of other strategies for improving cities and living conditions. Design certainly ought to be a component of any urban program, but not one that can be fruitfully isolated.

17 Teun Koolhaas, a street in Almere, planned in 1970.

Despite spirited attacks on their predecessors and their own celebrations of historical styles, the designers responsible for the new wave of buildings seemed unable to come up with a richer theory—that is, something other than anti-Modernism—to undergird their own practices. In the United States and Europe, the debates about Postmodernism through the 1970s were joined exclusively on the level of style, and in some cases the explicit rejection of any social concerns. Those who sustained a commitment to Modernism often did so by claiming the high moral ground, usually linking their positions with the only partially true tales of the suppression of Modernism by totalitarian regimes during the 1930s. They also advanced claims of the greater tectonic logic of their designs, more honesty in the expression of structure, and a greater faithfulness to the imperatives of contemporary materials and technologies. In the United States during the 1970s, a branch of this group, known as the "Whites," included Peter Eisenman, Richard Meier, Michael Graves and Charles Gwathmey, who adhered fairly strictly to the pure, sleek architectural aesthetic of Modernism. The "Greys," on the other hand, Venturi, Moore and Stern, as we have seen increasingly rejected the white look in favor of historical styles and architectural elements. Other historicizing positions were advanced in Europe by Paolo Portoghesi, Quinlan Terry and Leon Krier. Even though their disputes occupied many pages of architectural publications throughout the 1970s, like the Modernists of the 1930s their debates were marginal to the actual processes of commissioning, financing and constructing buildings.

18   The Portland Building at Portland, Oregon (1980), by Michael Graves—who during the 1970s gradually abandoned the Whites for the increasingly pastel-hued Grey camp—figures as a prototype for the assimilation of Postmodernism by the American architectural mainstream. Graves won the competition for a new city administration building in part thanks to the presence of an advocate, Philip Johnson, on the design jury. Onto a simple cubic block raised high on a podium and punctuated by small square windows, Graves added swags, an inverted pyramid pattern outlined in the revetment, enlarged architectural elements such as keystones, and the molded plaster figure of Portlandia sweeping over the entrance. Like Robert Venturi, Graves had also won a Rome Prize that enabled him to study Italian architecture firsthand. When he abandoned the Whites, it was to incorporate a highly mannered, if not precious, interpretation of classical and Italianate decorative elements into symmetrically configured designs such as the Portland Office Building.

18 Michael Graves, The Portland Building, Portland, Oregon, 1980.

The unusually bold and richly chromatic decorative scheme explicitly referred to Italian architectural history, and gave rise to heated polemical battles over the appropriateness of the style and the colors in the context of an attractive city center.

20   Frank Gehry's house in Santa Monica (1978), although more provocative in the unorthodox use of materials and jerry-built imagery, triggered far less controversy. Indeed, some critics dismissed it as junk architecture. Perhaps the modest size of the house contributed to its acceptance, but Gehry did not advance a theory of architecture or take up a polemical position remotely like that of Graves. Although both buildings were on the West Coast of the United States, Graves as a Princeton professor, a lapsed member of the New York Five, and a standard fixture in the East Coast-based architectural press, generated controversy within the profession in ways Gehry never has.

From the vantage of the mid-1990s, the indifference displayed in these debates to much beyond aesthetic issues is striking. With some notable exceptions, architects and most of their publications ignored the consequences of downtown skyscraper development, suburban growth, shanty constructions on the peripheries of major international cities, office park construction and matters such as ecology, toxic materials and environmental degradation that conditioned the transformation of the landscape

19   throughout the world. The headquarters of the NMB (now ING) Bank in Amsterdam (1984) by Anton Alberts and Max van Huut, on the other hand, came from one of many small, serious and local firms concerned about their communities. Ten units clad in brick celebrate Dutch

19 Anton Alberts and Max van Huut, NMB (now ING) Bank Headquarters, Amsterdam, Netherlands, 1984.

20 Frank Gehry, Gehry House, Santa Monica, California, 1978.

building traditions, and a passive solar system addresses ecological concerns. Not least of the building's assets are that it presents varied facades to the street, and opens a pleasant plaza on the site. All too often the major protagonists in the architectural debates actively disparaged those who raised concerns about such matters. Seduced by the easy money available in the vast monopoly game that was the Reagan–Thatcher era, it was easy to yield eagerly to the dictates of mindless expansion, for architects as for others. Just as Modernists formulated theories to undergird their technological and formal visions, so too did some of the Postmodernists of the 1980s seek a theoretical framework within which to locate their socially indifferent, self-referential designs. In the absence of ideas from within architecture, they turned to other disciplines.

Following World War II, research in the humanistic disciplines of anthropology, philosophy and literary criticism turned toward problems of language. Issues under consideration involved analysis of the historical, scientific and philosophical structures of what was loosely referred to as "the West"—a coherent entity distinguishable geographically and philosophically. Beginning in the 1960s, and springing from the writings first of anthropologist and Structuralist Claude Lévi-Strauss, and then of Michel Foucault and Jacques Derrida, two movements took shape, Post-Structuralism and Deconstruction. Both came to have a direct impact on discussions about architecture, and then on the building process itself. While the movements have most strongly affected architectural discourse and practice in Western Europe and the United States, their influence also extended to other areas of the world. Nonetheless, it is important to bear in mind the very strong Eurocentric bias of Postmodernism in this and earlier versions.

One of the most important areas in which Post-Structuralism and Deconstruction had something to offer the world of architecture concerned the questions of meaning and how individuals order the world. In the absence of a compelling social vision, and under the impetus of the demand of historicizing Postmodernists that architecture express meaning and communicate, Postmodernists who found they could not bring themselves to embrace historical eclecticism for architectural inspiration found a way out by adopting theoretical insights from Post-Structuralism and Deconstruction.

To understand this, we need to consider the aspect of Structuralism that had the most powerful impact on architecture. Among other things, Structuralists sought an understanding of how meaning is produced. Lévi-Strauss characterized meaning and the mechanisms that produce it as being independent of any pre-existing ideas, and certainly beyond the control of the individual. This then necessitated studies that sought to go beyond the subject to what was claimed to be a universal set of mechanisms, in short, mechanisms that are unchanging regardless of the particularities of individuals.

In architecture, this led to an equally insistent focus on meaning: significantly, it was not a matter of analyzing how meaning is produced,

32

21 Johnson/Burgee, AT&T Building, New York, 1978–84.

but rather of vesting the architect with the responsibility for designing buildings that radiated meaning. During the late 1970s and early 1980s, structures scripted with recognizable historical motifs, such as Johnson/ Burgee's AT&T Building in New York (1978–84) or Graves's Portland

21, 18

Building, were held to convey meaning simply by virtue of their appropriation of recognizable historical symbols. In the translation, then, the idea of meaning narrowed so that it was understood to be the province not of society in general, or even of the patron, but of the architect, rendering it grounded and not universal, as the Structuralists had sought.

One aspect of the focus on meaning surfaced in narratives of loss in the work of Alberto Pérez-Gómez and Manfredo Tafuri. Although their ideas were couched in terms of defiant contemporaneity, these theorists followed in the footsteps of some of the most nostalgic architectural theorists of the 19th century, from A. W. N. Pugin and John Ruskin to William Morris, in proposing the Middle Ages as the last moment of a true architecture, less because of aesthetic preferences than because of a desire to recover an idealized, simpler world of ordered hierarchies, reciprocal resonsibilities, and social harmony. Apart from seriously misreading medieval history, and despite their own social or religious activism, these theorists provided justification for subsequent architects to turn their backs on real world problems and find refuge in exotic formal exercises.

In both literary criticism and architecture, the "post" in "Postmodern" initially asserted a position after, and indeed beyond, Modernism. But in fact, the "post" in both cases referred to a series of practices still deeply indebted to Modernism. During the 1970s, Peter Eisenman, following the theories of Noam Chomsky, attempted to produce a design methodology in line with the Structuralist search for the universal and "structural," which for Eisenman meant a compositional strategy that was completely autonomous, that is, independent of the will of the specific producer, and universal. This demonstrated the anxiety of American architectural theorists who yearned for a more intellectually substantive basis for architecture. It seemed that if theories drawn from other fields could be found to work in architecture, the status of architecture as an academic discipline would be enhanced. It is worth repeating that the number of architects and educators who were interested in applying new theoretical structures to architecture was extremely limited and marginal. But their presence in the larger architectural discourse was not. Through such journals as *Perspecta*, *Oppositions*, and the *Harvard Architectural Review*, and through an exhausting round of conferences and exhibitions, those who were investigating linguistic theories acquired a significance altogether greater than the import of their architectural production.

Through them, the theories of Derrida and Foucault, but especially the former, began to penetrate the world of architecture. Derrida essentially agreed with the Structuralists about the sources of meaning, but his argument proceeded to address the Western tradition, which he held had always acted as if the structural bases for meaning could be elucidated. No such ground, be it God, nature, history or science, exists, Derrida asserted, but philosophical investigations have regularly been conducted with that underlying assumption. Therefore the meanings of texts are infinite and dependent upon other texts. His Deconstructionist criticism proposed a continual reenactment of this analytical strategy on the great works of the Western tradition. He insisted, for example, upon the fundamental incoherence of texts rather than on a basic, underlying order, and rejected the notion of a transparent relation between objects and the language we use to describe them. Meaning is also not generated from human intentionality, but rather from the very absence of stability in language itself. Therefore the simple notions of representation by which we normally operate are called into question for language, and, enthusiastic converts in architecture claimed, hence for the architectural objects.

Among its other great weaknesses, Derrida's philosophy assumed a unitary notion of "West" or "Western," which his own theories and arguments rendered problematical. In order to enact his critique, he had to assume this as a totalizing system which he could unravel again and again in his analyses. Derrida's reception was auspicious, for it opened the door to studies of feminism, imperialism, and racism, even though most of his followers emulated his example in choosing abstract reflection over political engagement. Nonetheless, the oppositional position that Deconstruction took toward a presumed "Western" tradition, and the way it helped structure feminist and post-colonial critiques, allowed it to acquire the appearance of being positioned within the domain of political engagement.

Certainly in its American form, the practice of Deconstruction in literary criticism, where it has been most prevalent, induced a political quietism at odds with Derrida's pretensions about the political impulse of his work. It tended to produce sterile, arcane, and distinctly unengaged work that did little more than ape an existing tradition of textual emendation and commentary. Deconstruction conveniently allowed its practitioners to avoid coming to terms with power and its exercise, or with social and political life, whether in the United States or Europe. It seemed sufficient to theorize problems of race, gender and identity in order to have confronted them, obviating the need for further action. No real consequences attached to the practice of Deconstruction, whether in literary theory or in architectural design, adding to the attractiveness of something that otherwise appeared to involve political positions.

This was precisely the appeal of Deconstruction in the world of architecture during the mid- to late 1980s. Coyly referring to themselves as the new avant-garde, and therefore affiliating with a militant and politically engaged Modernism of the early part of the century, "Deconstructivist" practioners variously identified their formal sources as Russian Constructivism, contemporary sculpture, and painting. By association, they laid claim to radicalism while maintaining an aloof detachment from real political struggles.

The architecture produced in the name of Deconstruction attempts to embrace notions of fragmentation, dispersion and discontinuity through formal means. Coop Himmelblau's Rooftop Remodeling in Vienna (1984–89) and Zaha Hadid's Fire Station at the Vitra Factory in Weil-am-Rhein (1994) testify to straining the architectural envelope beyond its customary limits, shifting and rotating surfaces and designs populated by clusters of various types of metal, announcing their difference from adjacent buildings—and little else. As with the work of Eisenman, Gehry and Koolhaas, the formal exercises offer little toward the construction of a theory different from that of Modernism, and even less to rethinking the

22 Coop Himmelblau, Rooftop Remodeling, Falkestrasse, Vienna, 1984–89.

role of the architect—and this despite dramatic social and economic changes since the late 1960s. Indeed, in their absolute indifference to issues of context, their exaltation of the role of the architect as form-giver and interpreter of society, it is difficult to discern significant departures from dogmatic Modernism except in the particularities of form.

During this period, a group of trends variously labeled "post-industrial," "post-Fordist," or "globalized" has taken shape in advanced Western economies. "Fordism" refers to the state-regulated system of mass production and mass consumption which, undergirded by welfare and social security, dominated advanced capitalist countries in the West roughly from the Depression to the crisis of the 1970s. Post-Fordism, on the other hand, is a system of flexible accumulation and niche market consumption that has been developing since the 1970s. With a shift away from Fordist economic organization, this new configuration is principally characterized by flexibility: flexible machinery and equipment that can be adapted to different tasks relatively quickly; smaller and more

23 Zaha Hadid, Fire Station, Vitra Factory, Weil-am-Rhein, Germany, 1994.

specialized firms; greater general skills on the part of workers, who need to adapt to constantly changing products; flexible accumulation of goods in order to respond quickly to demand; and more temporary and part-time labor. As I discuss in Chapter Three, this also entails greater geographical clustering of information in cities such as New York and London, high-technology districts concentrated in new areas throughout the United States and Western Europe, and the Fordist mode of production shifting to areas of the world with less advanced economies.

The post-industrial, post-Fordist, global economic world is imaged as one of transnational cultural and population flows and information superhighways. The steady movement of tourists, refugees, immigrants and business people is paralleled in architecture, where for example a French architect designs in Bangkok, an architect from New Jersey jets to Berlin to oversee construction of a building, and Italian architects have projects in Houston and Galveston, Texas.

All of these characteristics of Western economies led to sharply altered labor patterns, social patterns (including gender, racial and ethnic ones), and income distribution, among many other things, as well as the increased industrialization of the service sector. Overall, the pattern of increased income polarization leads to much greater social and economic marginalization. These trends also raise questions about their impact upon diversity and autonomy at the local level. Areas previously in tenuous contact are now linked in the most visible of ways, emblematized by the presence of Cable Network News (CNN) even in remote villages.

Although these changes impact the daily lives of everyone, and certainly also the built environment (as I discuss later), remarkably, they rarely figure in architectural discussions. From the sleek, taut buildings of the Modern Movement to the bristling bundles of metal in Deconstructivist buildings is a long voyage in terms of style, but in terms of the heroic architect formalizing personal interpretations of social crises there is no distance at all. However, as even professional societies have acknowledged in the United States and elsewhere, the architect's role has been steadily eroded and increasingly marginalized in a world dominated by developers, engineers and builders since the 19th century.

In the United States architects design only a fraction of all buildings, and the figure is lower elsewhere. This means that the suburbs, markets, warehouses, schools, apartments and most of the rest of the built environment are designed by builders or contractors. On the negative side, the very talents and training that might enhance the broad landscape are generally confined to public buildings, the houses of the wealthy, and corporate offices. On the positive side, given the general indifference of architects to the built environment, and particularly the environments of those with limited means, this leaves space for marginalized groups to shape their surroundings and to design the settings where they live, play, and even sometimes work.

One of the historic defects of the architectural profession in the United States is that its dominant economic model is that of professional services for hire; in an economy dominated by entrepreneurial capitalism, this rules out many building possibilities. As a result, architects as a rule focus on large, expensive projects, often megaprojects, rather than on the diversity and multiplicity of the experiences of individuals and groups in the social and public spaces of cities and even rural areas, ignoring the potential impact of even a very small intervention. Sam Mockbee's rural studio for Auburn University in Hale County, Alabama, teaches students how their skills can make a difference to families and individuals living on the margins of society. Hay Bale House was 24 designed and built for $6,000 by thirty-three students over three class terms in 1993–94. The little house does not proclaim grand social goals. Rather it insists on the dignity of the residents and their right to decent, inexpensive housing built according to their wishes, and even to skilled design. Self-help buildings in developing countries or economically

24 Sam Mockbee, supervisor, Hay Bale House, Auburn University, Hale County, Alabama, 1993–94.

depressed areas attempt to achieve the same goals. In urban areas, architectural firms such as Cavaedium in Los Angeles toiled through bureaucratic nightmares to produce modest single-room-occupancy hotels such as the Prentice Hotel (1990).

Some of these projects are included in this book. However, what I intend is a survey not of the built environment but rather of general trends in architecture over the last quarter-century. No survey of reasonable length could cover all of the interesting and important buildings over this period of time, so I have chosen to focus on a selected body of work. I also wanted to avoid the drawbacks of surveys by juxtaposing a broad range of buildings to a more focused analysis of specific projects defined as "megaprojects."

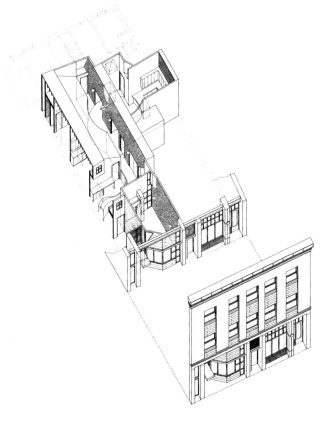

25 Cavaedium Architects, Prentice Hotel, Los Angeles, California, 1990: isometric view of facade and first-floor commons.

Movement, violent upheaval, and partisan clashes: the years after 1970 were marked by momentous changes, including the collapse of the Soviet bloc, the lightning-quick mobility of capital, and enormous migrations of people fleeing war and economic hardship. These forces powerfully reconfigured topographical as well as economic landscapes. Speculation on both global and local levels focused extensively on building, but the modalities, much less the consequences, of these transformations on the built environment rarely figure in architectural histories and criticism, even if they have a direct impact on architecture and on architects. Indeed, during the 1980s, architects and developers envisioned a landscape refashioned according to swollen notions of grandeur, shaped around megaprojects from which would flow an endless stream of wealth.

During the 1980s, Vittorio Gregotti theorized a mega-architecture in a series of articles in the magazine *Casabella*, and subsequently realized it in projects such as the Belém Cultural Center in Lisbon (with Manuel Salgado, 1992). Despite successfully negotiating the demands of a very difficult site—it is designed with careful attention to its relation to the massive 16th-century Jerónimos Monastery across the street—the Cultural Center vividly expresses Gregotti's idea of an architecture of massive dimensions that is imposed forcefully on the site and the city, a fortress in modern garb. Megaprojects came in many other forms: acres of leisure facilities and theme parks, huge regional shopping centers adrift in seas of asphalt parking lots, gigantic business parks well removed from urban centers, housing complexes inserted into dense city fabrics. Of all the buildings considered in this book, these megaprojects may be the most enduring emblems of a decade of greed and waste.

While large-scale building projects are no novelty—the 19th-century transformations of Vienna and Paris come to mind, not to mention decades of colonialist building in Latin America and Asia—the global scale of the financing, the involvement of international corporations, the participation of architects from throughout the Western world differentiate the megaprojects studied here from their predecessors. For the purposes of this study, I have divided architectural production into three categories: public space, domestic space, and urban restructuring for new living and working environments. Each topic is then subdivided, with an analysis of a wide range of projects in which a general set of issues is addressed, and the more detailed study of a specific megaproject allowing a close examination of the forces at work in the production of these architectural enterprises. The buildings can thus be comprehended both in formal terms and in connection with underlying social, economic, and political forces. For public space, I study Disney's theme parks; for domestic space, the IBA in Berlin; and for the restructuring of cities for new working patterns, London's Docklands. The choices of these particular enterprises are not fortuitous: the role of architecture was central to each, specifically to provide marketable images. So was the participation of major international firms, often so-called avant-garde ones, for a similar reason: to endow the enterprises with cultural legitimacy. All three, in their separate ways, epitomize the new, international character of architectural practice, and they are also emblematic of many other smaller projects that were completed during the 1980s. In fundamental ways, all came to be architectural exhibitions with more in common with Disney's worlds than might initially appear to be the case.

Disney theme parks seem to be important because they made explicit the kinds of social controls that have been enacted to define "public spaces" in cities and to reserve them for the middle classes. For the most part, the mechanisms for doing this have been masked from middle-class beneficiaries, who could claim spaces as public spaces without confronting the mechanics of exclusion. When Charles Moore and others examined Disneyland in an effort to understand its appeal, they recognized that its very restrictive attributes (admission fees, restricted access, defined boundaries, codes of conduct for employees and implicit codes for visitors, regimentation, efficient servicing) were the sources of comfort for middle-class visitors, enabling them to feel at ease and secure.

There is a direct link between the culture of the megaproject and the role of architecture at the end of the second millennium. Perhaps this was most tellingly expressed at a meeting in 1992 of the Architecture Faculty at the University of Southern California in Los Angeles, to consider the University's proposal to merge Architecture with another faculty. The Architecture Faculty resisted being brought into what would seem on the face of things the most likely partnerships, with either the School of Urban Planning or the School of Fine Arts. Instead, a former dean proposed that Architecture be united with Theater, on the grounds that their enterprises converge: both are chiefly concerned with the production of scenography. The flaccid architectural culture of the United States and Western Europe appears, in many cases, to be composed of little more than scenography, and no doubt the prominent twin elements of the megaproject and the Disney vision of systematic commercialized reality are major forces behind these developments.

CHAPTER ONE

Public Space

Public space in the 19th and 20th centuries has been optimistically defined as the space of the collective, understood not as belonging to an individual or a class or a corporation, but to the people as a whole. A discussion of public space can usefully be understood in relation to a contemporary debate on the public sphere, since public space constitutes the spatialized realization of the public sphere. The public sphere is how German philosopher Jürgen Habermas refers to the setting in which citizens engage specifically in political participation, and indeed he insists that this is essential for democratic political practices. Habermas was at pains to argue that the public sphere was traditionally distinct from those of the market and of government, but that in the late 20th century, with this traditional realm so necessary for democracy no longer possible, new models must be developed.

Among the chief assumptions of Habermas's theory was the notion that these public spheres and spaces were settings where free and equal citizens could deliberate on political issues. Scholars Nancy Fraser, Geoff Eley, Joan Landes and Mary Ryan countered Habermas's definitions by pointing out that the liberal bourgeois public realm he described as historical antecedent in fact existed only through the rigorous practice of exclusion, based on class, race and gender. It was only one of a number of possible public spheres, although those constituted by other groups were systematically ignored or disparaged both in practice and by later historians. These would include voluntary associations of women or workers that broke the rigid distinction between public and private, a "public realm" in which political discussion was not the *sine qua non*. Much the same is true of our concept of public space: optimistically celebrated as open to all, it often in reality masks a series of exclusionary practices, usually based on race, gender, or class, that limit the definition of "public" in important ways. What we often see as publicly accessible places—theme parks, shopping malls, festival marketplaces—are more appropriately described as social space.

Perhaps one of the most significant developments of the late 20th century has been the interpretation of public space in two related ways:

43

as spaces for consumption, and as spaces to be segregated in highly specific ways, to be monitored and controlled. The exclusionary practices that made earlier public spaces so much the realm of male elites and that allowed them to be defined as public, thereby denying legitimacy to competing definitions, were matched by the parallel practices of monarchs, oligarchies and dictators who also exercised control over the public sphere, in turn defining access for men and women of lower classes.

The aspiration for democratic public space, however occasionally realized, remains one of openness and accessibility. When white male elites in the United States during the 19th century defined squares and streets in cities as public, they conceptualized the only relevant "public" as consisting of men like themselves. In the 20th century, a rhetoric of inclusion of other races and women replaced that exclusionary rhetoric, and the public areas of cities did effectively become more accessible to most people. But there are ominous signs of a new set of exclusionary practices masked by inclusionary rhetoric today. Raids rousting homeless people from makeshift shelters on public property, the burgeoning of video-camera surveillance, and the enclosure of purportedly public space point toward a shift in which the traditional goal of achieving democratic cities and indeed the notion of the public itself are undergoing redefinition. Perhaps the most compelling recognition is that there is not "a" public, but competing publics, often in conflict with one another and with their own venues for action, indeed, their own definitions of action.

Too often, architects understand public space as negative or empty, useless for marketing purposes without some intervention on the part of civic authorities to control access, monitor behavior, and minimize distractions from the vastly more important activities of consumption. Almost completely ignored by this popular conception of public space is the wide range of temporary or provisional claims on urban areas for such things as teen-age cruising (in automobiles in American cities and small towns, on vespas or on foot in many European cities); garage sales and other temporary street vendors; demonstrations, marches and parades; block parties and other urban and suburban festivals. None of these depends upon massive mechanisms of control, and none depends for its success upon well designed public spaces. On the contrary, often the less hospitable and more bleak a setting, the more successful the ephemeral event. Because of this, these activities are typically ignored by architects and urban designers. They are not ignored by others, however. It is instructive to consider the many efforts in Los Angeles to restrict teen cruising on Sunset and Hollywood Boulevards and in Westwood. Under pressure from merchants who believed that it diminished business and from residents irritated by the difficulty of getting through, police effectively stopped the practice in the early 1990s. Cruisers moved elsewhere, and business declined further. Only residents were pleased with the return to normal traffic flows.

A similar battle for control of urban centers is underway in many European cities. In Rome, the expanded subway lines and the availability of other cheap forms of transportation have brought residents from outlying areas into the center during the evening and at night. During warm summer months, their numbers are augmented by tourists. The noise of restaurants, outdoor cafes, clubs, and thousands of people strolling and talking has led to protests from residents and consequent government action to curb the noise. The chief lament of many residents, however, is that lower class groups (such as southern immigrants) from city-edge housing projects now have easier access to an urban center they would like to preserve for elites.

Some of the sources for attitudes about public space that emphasize mass consumption and official and corporate control emerge in the discussion which follows. The chapter begins with a discussion of Disney theme parks as exemplars of this notion of public space, and then proceeds to discuss shopping malls and museums, two of the most common types of public buildings of the late 20th century, and in the cultural realm the related genres of libraries, theaters and concert halls.

DISNEY TAKES COMMAND

Beginning in the 1930s, Walt Disney constructed an empire based on his pioneering animated characters, moving from cartoon shorts to full-length movies in a few years. Mickey Mouse, Donald Duck, Goofy, and the other creations became internationally known and loved features of childhood. By the early 1950s the company had added daily and weekly television programs (the Mickey Mouse Club, the Walt Disney Show, and others) to its repertoire, and the planning for Disneyland in Anaheim, California, was underway. With its opening in 1955, Disney made a quantitative conceptual and spatial leap to a new zone, where time and space collapsed in a new organizational scheme for the consumption of leisure. Dismissed by other amusement park owners as destined for failure, Disneyland instead became an immediate and total success. The three subsequent additions to the empire—Disney World in Florida (1971), in particular the Magic Kingdom and Epcot Center (1982), Tokyo Disney (1984), and EuroDisney just outside Paris (1992)—elaborated and enormously enlarged on the ideas embodied in that first project.

As a result of its popular appeal, Disneyland drew praise from some quarters as a fine example of urban planning, but received less complimentary reviews from intellectuals and journalists, who consistently criticized it for superficiality, historicizing pastiche, escapism, and empty fantasy. When the Prime Minister of Italy, Giuliano Amato, warned the Italian Senate about serious problems in his country in 1992, he held out the gloomy prospect of Italy becoming the Disneyland of Europe, a playground not to be taken seriously politically, economically or socially. However valid the criticisms, they made no dent in the company's perennially favorable economic condition or popular image as one of the world's chief tourist meccas. Some measure of Disneyland's success is the proliferation of other theme parks in the ensuing forty years, not just in the United States but in Europe and Asia. In fact, the staggering success of Tokyo Disney—a near duplicate of Disney World—coupled with the strong yen led to the flowering of other amusement parks in Japan, all with American or European themes, such as Sesame Street Land, Canadian World, Festival Village and Holland World. More significantly, the approaches to public space, work space, and urbanism embodied in Disneyland and its successors came to appeal both to developers and to architects as a standard against which to assess buildings and public spaces.

Disneyland carried the amusement park and world's fair concepts to a new level. Within the confines of the sprawling complex, five separate amusement parks clustered around different themes: Adventureland, It's a Small World, Fantasyland, Frontierland, and Main Street, U.S.A. Together they collapsed the American urban and rural landscape into one manageable, idealized setting. What Disney disarmingly presented as theme park history did violence to the real events by simply writing out disparate points of view—for example, by presenting Frontierland as the tranquil movement of happy citizens into uninhabited lands rather than as also a government-approved campaign of conquest, land stealing, and genocide. Later, in Epcot Center at Florida's Disney World, idyllic visions of the blessings of American capitalism rise to a high point in the American Express/Coca Cola motion picture *The American Adventure*, an example of corporate propaganda disguised as education.

26, 27 Main Street, U.S.A., opening out from the entrance to the park, encapsulates the complicated reality of the entire Disney enterprise. It consists of a seven-eighths-scale representation of an idealized town center in the United States from the late 19th century, complete with colorful trolley cars, festive Queen Anne houses and blocks of Victorian-style buildings, sidewalks, Victorian lamp posts, and even characters dressed in period clothing. Clean and colorful, Main Street, U.S.A. preempts competing

26, 27 Imagineers, Main Street, U.S.A., Disneyland, Anaheim, California, 1955.

historical interpretations by offering an urban landscape that only generically resembles a 19th-century town; functionally and historically, things were quite different. Pure consumerism drives Main Street, for the only activities possible entail spending money on food or trinkets. Main Street lacks industry, poverty, and, most of all, political life. It does have private police and laws, however unobtrusively they are inserted. As private terrain, the Disney Corporation can and does forbid political activity, just as it enforces a dress and comportment code on its employees, for whom disobedience means dismissal.

Disneyland's appeal partially rests on the fiction that only visitors inhabit it, but in fact Walt Disney took up residence there. Most of the second stories of a Main Street block were designed as a rambling weekend apartment, where he could survey unseen the roving spectacle of the masses moving—and spending—through his empire. By contrast with the temporary, paying visitors outside, only Disney and his privileged guests could really inhabit his fantasy world. In certain respects, however, it was hauntingly real. By some reports, he outfitted the dining room with hidden microphones, so that he could strategically leave his guests to talk among themselves and secretly overhear their conversations. Since we know he was then an FBI informant, this setup no doubt often proved useful. By contrast with Jeremy Bentham's Panopticon, the control on Disney's Main Street is far more subtle, guided by sophisticated marketing and crowd control techniques, but the surveillance is just as pervasive—and just as particular.

The desire to inhabit fantasy worlds enacted as architectural theme parks did not begin with Disney. The Roman Emperor Hadrian erected the buildings of his villa near Tivoli in emulation of the most spectacular buildings he had found in his travels around the Mediterranean. Much later, in the 18th and early 19th centuries, European rulers and landowners decorated their parks with Classical temples, rustic dairies, Swiss chalets and Gothic houses. But the contrasts between Versailles or Wörlitz or English parks like Stowe or Stourhead and Disneyland are telling. These precedents were elite retreats, not open to the general public, and as a direction for architecture they were decisively rejected. By the mid-19th century, German architects and theorists largely turned away from the production of empty images to focus on tectonics. Disney's theme parks have instead supplied the template for altogether too much architectural production in the United States and Western Europe. Among the most recent examples of the idea of the architectural theme park is at the University of California, Irvine, where Charles Moore, Frank Gehry, Rebecca Binder and other architects were summoned to design campus buildings. To be sure, some of these are fine works of architecture, particularly Gehry's Engineering Building and Binder's Social Science Satellite Food Facility, but collectively they turn the University itself into a theme park, with prominent architects providing a variety of architectural themes.

28

Perhaps more telling are the resorts under construction in Japan, such as Nasu Highlands by the SWA Group, and Furano Northstar Resort in Hokkaido by Robert Mortensen. For Nasu, the SWA Group revised and expanded an existing theme park, and added resort hotels, villas, vacation houses, golf and other sports facilities. Remarkably, everything is unambiguously Western, from the theme park, Fantasy Pointe, with its 1950s Main Street, U.S.A., Rock and Roll Plaza and French parterre garden, to the Akebien Hotel in the style of a French Renaissance chateau. Despite the location of the resort in dense forests some 95 miles (150 kilometers) northeast of Tokyo, everything is themed and controlled, evidently because nature is not considered a sufficient draw and certainly not sufficiently lucrative for the developers.

Although Disneyland is large (76 acres/31 hectares), the epic scale of Walt Disney World in Orlando, Florida, dwarfs it. There the Magic Kingdom alone covers 100 acres (40 hectares), augmented by the Disney-MGM Studios theme park, Typhoon Lagoon, Pleasure Island and the Disney Village Marketplace, Discovery Island, and Epcot Center, as well as various resort facilities. At the Disney-MGM Studios, visitors tour re-creations of the sets of major motion pictures such as *Teenage Mutant*

28 Rebecca Binder in association with Widom, Wein, Cohen Architects, Social Science Satellite Food Facility, University of California, Irvine, California, 1989.

Ninja Turtles, an animation gallery, Catastrophe Canyon and other examples of special effects. One of the major events is the re-creation of Hollywood Boulevard, not as it is today but "in its heyday," complete with the famous corner of Hollywood Boulevard and Vine, Grauman's Chinese Theater (with new hand- and footprints in cement), and fabled but subsequently destroyed movie star haunts such as the Brown Derby. This Disney re-creation constitutes yet another emblematic demonstration of the blurring of reality and fantasy—Disney reality.

Hollywood Boulevard in Los Angeles today is a far more volatile, complicated mix than the Disney version, and for most visitors can only suffer by comparison. In Los Angeles, the street population includes teen runaways, prostitutes, drug dealers, and homeless people, as well as new and used book stores, electronics stores, record and souvenir shops, and other forms of new gentrification. In the Los Angeles rebellion of 29 April–1 May 1992, Hollywood Boulevard encountered a very different fate than the one envisioned in Orlando. Boisterous Friday and Saturday night teenage cruisers had been banned from the streets, and an urban redevelopment program was underway to eradicate the misfits and restore the Boulevard to an idealized Disneyesque version of its heyday, but now the street became one of the chief targets, with rioters breaking windows and looting and burning shops. The carnivalesque atmosphere that surrounded the violence almost appeared to fulfill Nathanael West's 1939 vision of the apocalyptic end of Hollywood in Tod Hackett's painting in *Day of the Locust*: "He wanted the city to have quite a gala air as it burned, to appear almost gay. And the people who set it on fire would be a holiday crowd." Disney's world leaves no place for the political and economic problems that exasperated masses of people enough to erupt into violent action: although Disneyland in Orange County is only a few miles from the center of the rebellion in South Central Los Angeles, it is light years away in everything but geography.

As Disney expanded, looking ever more like a cleverly masked developer, the Corporation revealed a canny grasp of economics and politics. After announcing plans for a major expansion, in 1990 it ingeniously pitted Anaheim (where Disneyland already stood) and Long Beach against one another as the site for this supposedly lucrative development, forcing the two cities to raise the ante again and again until Disney got the financial and urban package it was looking for—a strategy that the Corporation pursued effectively elsewhere. When the dust cleared, Anaheim stood alone. Its initial appeal in the 1950s derived in part from the fact that it consisted of agricultural land, largely unbuilt-on. Long Beach, by contrast, was a city with a real downtown. The planned expansion of Disneyland into the next millennium will drain millions of dollars of state and local funds for highway and infrastructure development to render the park more accessible to visitors—and hence more remunerative for Disney. In the wake of the 1992 rebellion, it is difficult to avoid asking what South Central Los Angeles would be like with a comparably lavish financial package from the state, city, and county.

Frontierland, Fantasyland, and the other theme units followed the model of Main Street in offering stage-set architecture designed for uninterrupted visual pleasure. To achieve the desired effect, as Disney remarked, they had to control the environment. This meant that nothing could be out of place, no wrong notes anywhere. Attendants unobtrusively pick up litter almost as soon as it is dropped, no Gilded Age music mars Frontierland or Western music Adventureland, there is no accretion of buildings to reflect historical change and development over time. Apart from the rides and other interactive attractions, shopping and eating are the two biggest activities in Disneyland. Public life is conceived as passive, guided movement through controlled spaces, where the only arenas of active choice are the selection of foods and shopping. Visitors are shuffled through exhibits and tours with brisk efficiency. By social organization and because of its operation, then, Disneyland is not a town in any sense of the term, as some hasty observers have remarked. It is a combination amusement park, world's fair, shopping center and movie set.

Perhaps because he realized that he had only partly achieved his idealized town, in early 1964 Walt Disney began to plan a real new town as part of Disney World in Florida, to be called Epcot Center—Experimental Prototype Community of Tomorrow. This showcase for a utopian society grew out of the utopian urban projects presented at world's fairs in the 19th century, where exotic environments could be shared through the purchase of souvenirs and food in the various pavilions. More recent precedents in the United States included the Chicago World's Fair of 1893 (with the White City project) and the 1939 New York World's Fair (the Town of Tomorrow), but the reality ultimately resembled the 1964 New York World's Fair, in which Disney himself participated.

For several years, Disney quietly bought up some 30,000 acres (12,000 hectares) of land outside Orlando, Florida (an area twice as large as Manhattan and comparable to San Francisco), well before announcing that he planned to build a larger, East Coast version of Disneyland. But as plans developed for the Magic Kingdom, Disney also imagined a community that would "take its cue from the new ideas and new technologies that are now emerging from the creative centers of American industry." In his

29 Imagineers, Pavilion of Italy, Epcot Center, Walt Disney World, Orlando, Florida, opened in 1982.

vision, it would never be completed, but rather would continue testing, introducing and demonstrating new materials and systems, a "showcase to the world for the ingenuity and imagination of American free enterprise." This patriotic impulse was to be expressed in a new town with 20,000 inhabitants in which new technologies would be used for everything from waste disposal to sewer and telephone systems. Although destined to be outfitted with schools and cultural facilities, it would differ from typical American communities in certain key respects. Residents would not own land and therefore would be unable to exercise control by voting; there would be no slums; and only working people would be eligible—therefore no elderly, either.

Walt Disney died in October 1966 before he could complete his vision. In no time at all the Corporation abandoned the residential community idea on the grounds that it entailed too many legal problems. Although the scale of the new Epcot Center remained large, residents would be temporary. In other words, it would merely be a resort with a futuristic theme park connected to it. Such American industries as Eastman Kodak, Bell Telephone, Exxon, General Motors, and Kraft Food Products sponsored exhibits at Epcot, which have included such features as the 3-D Michael Jackson video *Captain EO*, a surprisingly clunky "Journey through Imagination," and an optimistic view of the future enhanced by the benefits of American industry and technology in "Horizons." A 180-foot (155-meter) tall "geosphere" clad with aluminum panels, a descendant of French architect Etienne-Louis Boullée's late 18th-century Cenotaph to Sir Isaac Newton, dominates the whole complex.

In addition to the industrial exhibits and the geosphere, a third area, underwritten by other countries, consists of the World Showcase, a series of international pavilions which ring a lagoon on the southern part of Epcot. Here liberal interpretations of foreign monuments or environments, such as the Temple of Heaven in Beijing, parts of St. Mark's Square 29 in Venice, and a German village, are reduced in scale and inserted into visually complementary environments entirely unrelated to the settings of the real buildings. Once again, historical precedents for this approach abound, from Canaletto's paintings of a fantastic Venice with works by Palladio inserted into the cityscape, to the last panorama Karl Friedrich Schinkel was planning before he died, bringing all of the monuments of the world together in one 360-degree two-dimensional image. But as with the idea of architectural theme parks, there are glaring differences. The jump from two to three dimensions is an enormous one, and there is no question that the promotion of consumerism at a far larger scale drives Epcot Center. Each country hosts an exhibit as a sideshow to the principal activity, shopping for trinkets of the sort found in airport gift shops around the world. A degree of kitsch delirium overlays the pavilions, where visitors can buy "passports" to be stamped and autographed in the native language of each "country" visited. The space warp offered here in the illusory environments of distant places finds its complement in a materials warp in the buildings, where roof tiles and other decorative elements fabricated of painted glass fibers cast an unreal, brittle aura over the pavilions. Although only an amusement park, to be sure, it unfortunately often acts as a cleaner, unforeign version of the original for many visitors.

All of the exhibits, rides and landscapes were designed by Disney "Imagineers." Disappointed because a team of architects proved unable to transform his idea for a new kind of amusement park into the reality of Disneyland in the early 1950s, Disney turned to some of his own in-house architects and show designers. After he died, these Imagineers continued with Walt Disney World, Epcot Center, and Tokyo Disney. Nearly one-half century later, architectural professionals finally got the idea. Under a new chairman, Michael Eisner, the Disney Corporation began to consider the possibility that famous architects constitute a

30 Michael Graves, Dolphin Hotel, Walt Disney World, Lake BuenaVista, Florida, 1987.

powerful weapon in an already formidable arsenal with which to conquer the marketplace, and began to commission prominent architects to design its facilities. They were invited at first to design only hotels for Disney World in Florida, followed by corporate offices in California and Florida, and finally hotels and entertainment centers at EuroDisney. Another addition to Disney World currently under construction is a shadow of the old Disney dream of a planned community; this one to be called Celebration, a 20,000-inhabitant new town scheduled to contain an office park by Aldo Rossi, a shopping center by Helmut Jahn, and a Disney Institute by Charles Moore, in addition to 8,000 housing units.

While the architects selected to participate in informal limited competitions for each project represent widely diverse tendencies, from Michael Graves, Robert A. M. Stern, Arata Isozaki, Frank Gehry, and Gwathmey Siegel to Antoine Predock, they are all male and (with the exception of Isozaki) Western and white, and the buildings they are expected to produce must be "themed" with fancy and fantasy.

Architects whose works had long been dismissed as kitsch exercises in Disneyesque regalia finally found their patron at Disney World. The most 30, 31 surreal expressions of the Disney type are doubtlessly Graves's two hotels (actually for a joint venture group which included Metropolitan Life Insurance Company), the Swan and the Dolphin (1987). Although they fall into the second of the two categories of architecture identified by Venturi in the early 1970s, the duck and the decorated shed, they clearly yearn to be ducks. With gigantic eponymous figures of swans and dolphins nearly 50 feet (15 meters) high on the corners, huge shells spilling

54

31 Michael Graves, Swan Hotel, Walt Disney World, Lake BuenaVista, Florida, 1987.

water, and circus-striped awnings at every entrance, the exteriors fairly ooze decorative excess. The interiors jack the decorative impulse up a notch further, for hardly a surface is left untouched. In the pyramidal-shaped Dolphin, the tented interior bursts with plastic plants streaming down on latticed columns, bundled columns topped by cartoon fish frame doors, and ceilings rarely fail to have something draped or hanging from them. All mask a somewhat incoherent spatial organization. In the Swan, a tent festoons another lobby decorated with papyrus reed columns and palm frond capitals: Barnum and Bailey in wood and plastic. For the corporate headquarters in Burbank, California, Graves came up with an office building routine in most respects, except for arches along the attic and gigantic figures of the Seven Dwarfs as modern-day cary-atids appearing to support the pediment, showing once and for all that no cultural icon is too amusing—or embarrassing—to be incorporated *in toto* into his storehouse of forms.

By comparison, the remaining architect-designed buildings erected at Disney World are models of restraint. Stern produced two historically accurate hotels, the Yacht Club based on the late 19th-century East Coast Shingle Style resort, and its neighbor, the Beach Club, based on Stick Style resorts of the same period. Both face a man-made lake and share the same plan and materials: Werzalite (glued sawdust) for exterior fake wood cladding and fiberglass for cornices, columns, railings and trims. Impervious to the humidity of Florida, these materials require less maintenance than the locally dominant wood, cement block, and stucco (render). But above all, they resist the corrosive effects of time. No crumbling plaster,

55

chipped stone or weathered wood here—unless deliberately designed that way by the Imagineers. In Disney's fantasy world, nothing is permitted to mar the perfection of the image, whether the odd scrap of paper dropped by a negligent tourist, historical veracity, or the simple aging and weathering of materials. Another design by Stern, the Lake Buena Vista hiring facility, sports a vaguely neo-Venetian air, with orange and yellow diamonds on the facade and pointed windows of indeterminate stylistic origin. By contrast with the fawning air of Disney's amusement parks and hotels, this one aspires to austere, authoritarian grandeur within, particularly with the long, narrow, and deliberately intimidating ramp lined with murals depicting Walt Disney in pristine pastel environments up which prospective employees must ascend to the reception room.

Finally, Japanese architect Arata Isozaki designed the Team Disney Building nearby, a multicolored pastel confection with a giant silhouette of Mickey Mouse ears and framed by a gigantic parking lot at the entrance and Lake Buena Vista at the rear. In the center of two long grey-and-pink-paneled office wings stands a multicolored tower open to the sky. The interior functions as an enormous sundial. Like the other Disney buildings, its materials, fiberglass and Werzalite, endow it with a peculiar hollowness and the same air of unreal, pristine newness characteristic of the hotels. Carnivalesque exteriors conceal austere interiors, where offices surround long rectangular atrium spaces broken only by staircases. Balcony corridors flank endless rows of office cubbyholes, each a small rectangular module open on one side and at the top. Privacy is minimal in these huge, mostly open spaces. It is no surprise, then, that the employee newsletter at Disney World in Florida is called *Eyes and Ears*—a chilling reminder of the employer's watchful attentiveness, and a direct descendant of Walt Disney's own secret surveillance in his apartment on Main Street and elsewhere for the FBI during the 1950s.

Stripped of whimsical facades and comforting appearance, the Disney Corporation is a vast real estate venture, a fact finally acknowledged in 1985 with the creation of the Disney Development Corporation (DDC), a wholly owned subsidiary, to oversee its extensive land development enterprises. As we saw, it was the Corporation that shrewdly manipulated the two cities of Anaheim and Long Beach in their bidding war for the next expansion plan, and then sat around to see which would come up with the best package. The opening premise of the bidding war required special concessions in land, building codes, and infrastructure work, in particular freeway connections. The hook for the two recession-plagued communities was the promise of thousands of new jobs, local sales and hotel taxes, and the inevitable though elusive lure of prestige.

The state of Florida and the city of Orlando might have warned the two California cities that things are not as rosy as the Disney Corporation promises. Apart from the modest impact on its financial well-being, Orlando has found the Corporation a less than cooperative neighbor when it comes to anything that crosses its corporate borders, whether traffic, the environment, or regional planning issues. When Walt Disney decided to move to Orlando, he received the right to create a separate government, the Reedy Creek Improvement District, with its own police and fire departments, building codes, and taxation powers. Fewer than three dozen families live in the district, all selected by the Corporation. All of the members of its Board of Supervisors work for Disney. Needless to say, this body controls all development on the enormous parcel of land owned by Disney, and no other agency has any power to intervene. Only in 1989 did the Corporation grudgingly agree to pay the county $14 million for road work, necessitated by heavy usage by tourists. In return, the county agreed not to challenge Disney government powers for seven years. A few weeks later, the Corporation announced a fourth amusement park, seven more hotels, more than two dozen new attractions and 19,000 new, mostly low-income employees, all of whom will be looking for housing in an area already suffering a housing shortage. In 1990 the state of Florida had to concede an entire special, first-come first-served fund of $57 million to Disney, simply because the Corporation entered its request first. The city of Orlando had planned to request money for low-cost housing. But by the rules of the competition, Disney received all of the money, in addition to the corporate profits of over $700 million the same year. The Disney Corporation's cynical self-interest and greed came as a shock to Floridians who associated the name with its lovable cartoon characters.

Tokyo Disneyland may be the most successful of all the ventures, less because of entrance fees than because of the enormous amounts spent on souvenirs. The Japanese owners shrewdly resisted the Corporation's attempt to introduce Japanese elements such as a Samurai Land, and insisted that Tokyo Disneyland be a duplicate of the California original. But in fact, the Japanese version incorporates subtle, telling differences. Instead of Main Street, Tokyo has "World Bazaar," shifting the emphasis from layers of possible activities on Main Street to a more straight-forward acknowledgment of a setting programmed for consumption. Instead of being at a three-quarter-scale, Tokyo's Victorian street is full-size and topped by a glazed roof because of the climate, more like a giant shopping mall than the faintly nostalgic and exotic atmosphere would suggest. The narrative sequence of the original Disneyland in California carries the visitor through Main Street and westward to Adventureland, New Orleans Square, and the rigors of Frontierland as the promise of the American West, to arrive at a vision of fantasies in Fantasyland, followed by their potential actualization in Tomorrowland. The logic embraces various phases of American dreams, past and future. This sequence shifts in Japan, where even some names are changed. The notion of the frontier as the early focus of the American Dream is irrelevant in Tokyo, and indeed here the renamed Westernland and Adventureland are separated off by the railroad, whereas in the United States the railroad encircles the entire park. Disneyland and Disney World offer purified versions of American history and destiny cleansed of the genocide of the American Indian; so too does the Tokyo version boast an exhibit that cleanses its own history of any account of the complicated history of relations with Korea.

Following the success of the first three theme parks, under Michael Eisner the Disney Corporation rolled confidently into another continent, this time Europe, using the same technique of pre-selecting two sites (Spain and France), and then fomenting a bidding war between the two contenders. Everyone but the two target countries knew that location, wealth, prestige, and Eisner's own predilections made the choice of France a foregone conclusion, yet Disney nonetheless managed to wring hefty deals out of the French government, with a government entity, EPA France, providing the infrastructural work, both on the site and in transportation networks, as well as acquiring land on Disney's behalf and selling it to them at cost. The 5,000 acres (over 2,000 hectares) located 20 miles (32 kilometers) east of Paris, former beet fields and farm lands bulldozed and reconfigured to accommodate the mammoth contents of EuroDisneyland, are equivalent to one-fifth the land area of the city of Paris.

EuroDisneyland, EuroDisney, or as it is known on its promotional material, Disneyland Paris, consists of many features familiar from earlier Disney parks, including Sleeping Beauty's Castle, Thunder Mountain, Pirates of the Caribbean, and It's a Small World, all set within the five traditional Disney lands—Main Street, U.S.A., Adventureland, Fantasyland, Frontierland, and Discoveryland—although most have undergone design revisions for their European incarnations. To the old world, then, Disney brings a taste of Americana in its customary squeaky clean and untroubled guise, much as the World Showcase brought a whiff of faux internationalism to the Orlando park. As mammoth as the EuroDisney enterprise is, the plans for future development dwarf any of the other enterprises: the opening of a Disney-MGM Studios theme park will be followed by a giant convention center, more hotels and campsites, and a water park, with a planning schedule that extends into 2017.

As in Orlando, star architects for the most part received commissions to design hotels. Initially, Eisner invited such diverse architectural personalities as Rem Koolhaas, Robert Venturi, Hans Hollein, Bernard Tschumi, Peter Eisenman, Jean Nouvel and Christian de Portzamparc, but none proved able to realize the Disney vision as Eisner saw it. Ultimately the architects chosen were nearly all American. The virtually total and uncontested reign of white male architects, observable in all of the megaprojects examined here, is least justified in the case of Disney, precisely because the powers and responsibilities assigned to them were so slight, and so closely controlled by corporate bureaucrats, that in many cases just about anyone could have accomplished as much. Since the architectural assignment entails drawing up a scheme to represent a theme, and even then only in very broad strokes, it is clear that Disney is consuming reputations with presumed cultural cachet, which predetermines the selection of white male architects. Women and minority architects (of whom there are in fact large numbers) would appear to lack that cachet.

The Disneyland Hotel (1992), by the Imagineers and Wimberly, Allison, Tong and Goo, designated as the flagship hotel, forms the entrance to EuroDisney. Outfitted in Victorian architectural trappings with turrets and gables, the hotel offers panoramic vistas into the park itself, almost as if the Magic Kingdom were a real environment. French architect Antoine Grumbach interpreted a rustic Western resort for the Sequoia Lodge (1992), a series of rambling buildings outfitted with wood and stone facades. Although apparently diminutive in photographs, it is vastly overscaled and far removed from the smaller, environmentally appropriate character of such lodges as they were originally constructed in Yosemite, Glacier, and Yellowstone parks. The same scale problem afflicts Robert A. M. Stern's Newport Bay Club (1992), in the guise of a New England resort but likewise puffed up beyond recognition—another bit of evidence that bigger is not always better. The Newport Bay Club shares lakeside frontage with Michael Graves's New York Hotel (1992), supposedly outfitted with "typical" New York elevations, but the relationship eludes most observers. The five towers are intended to recall the towers of Manhattan, with wings extending out on either side, one supposedly recalling East Side brownstones, the other Gramercy Park. The pool in front of the hotel is destined to be turned into a winter skating rink, apparently in homage to Rockefeller Center.

The other two hotels, the Hotel Santa Fe by Antoine Predock (1992) and the Hotel Cheyenne by Stern (1992), have Western themes. Since

32, 33

Predock has long specialized in architecture of the Southwest, he was the perfect choice for the pale grey and pink pseudo-adobe buildings, but just as in Disney movies, Predock's complex aims to tell a story about the life and experience of the late 20th-century American West. The entrance is marked by neon lettering and a huge fake drive-in movie screen (with a painting of Clint Eastwood), a yellow painted strip disappearing into the distance in homage to the endless highways of the Southwest, and a series of abandoned pick-up trucks littered along the way. The stucco hotel units are in a style based on ancient Anasazi pueblos. Stern's Hotel Cheyenne re-creates a Western townscape not unlike Frontierland, but actually assembled so as to give the aura of movie sets for a Hollywood Western with its thin, precariously propped up wood elevations. As is by now customary for Disney, things are not as they appear, so most of the facades consist of synthetic materials. When it opened, the freshly planted landscaping left the entire complex exposed and uncomfortable, so the passage from the dense historical texture of Paris to the much-adorned fakery of EuroDisneyland was a particularly awkward displacement.

Given the scale of the parks and the hotels, Disney-cum-real-estate-developer is pushing a clever gimmick, and, unlike traditional real estate development, one destined to keep the money rolling in day after day.

Where a housing development or office park might encounter lengthy delays in the planning phase, not only from planning agencies but from banks and other financial groups, corporate hardheadedness seems to dissipate in the face of Disney's Magic Kingdom. Nonetheless, for a time at least the gravy train seemed to have reached its limits. Just as in the case of Docklands, where developers Olympia and York overextended their resources in the race for the biggest development of all time, so Disney appeared to have misjudged the prospects for EuroDisney. Although Paris boasts a long tradition of major commercial and leisure expositions which deposited structures on the urban fabric and conditioned future urban growth, from the Eiffel Tower to the now destroyed Trocadero, EuroDisney was not nearly as welcome. I no sooner wrote a paragraph comparing the financial success of Disney to the ever-worsening financial condition of Olympia and York and the bankruptcy of Nexus in Fukuoka, than newspapers announced that "Mickey Mouse fails to seduce the French—EuroDisney, on with the layoffs." In fact, within two months of opening in 1992, during the peak travel months of May and June visitor numbers were between 10,000 and 20,000 a day, far from the expected 65,000. With the parking lots and hotels virtually empty, Disney

32, 33 *opposite and below* Antoine Predock, Hotel Santa Fe, EuroDisney, near Paris, France, 1992: entrance, and hotel units.

promptly laid off hundreds of employees, reducing the work force from 16,000 to 13,000 or 14,000 (Disney's figures and those of the press disagreed). Only English and Italian tourists regularly visited Euro-Disneyland: the French snubbed it altogether. EuroDisneyland stocks on the New York and Paris Exchanges rapidly lost over one-third of their value, threatening the entertainment-development behemoth with a very public humiliation and potentially serious problems for its American enterprises. Even at the end of the first year, when Michael Eisner received a multi-million-dollar bonus timed to avoid tougher laws on executive compensation, EuroDisney was still floundering. Since then, the park's popularity has increased slowly.

A further setback marred Disney's previously unsullied record of success. In 1994, a bitter battle pitted the Corporation against a coalition of historians, preservationists, and others over the plan to open an American history theme park—to be called "Disney's America"—near the Civil War battlefield of Manassas, Virginia. In the face of genuine outrage that a fabricated and themed version of American history would be sited near one of the nation's genuine monuments, and after a protracted battle waged at community meetings and in the press, the project was abandoned. In early 1995, once again following record losses at EuroDisneyland and declining attendance at the two American theme parks, the Corporation scaled back expansion plans in Anaheim. With its image dented but not destroyed, stocks rose again, and executives still reaped windfall profits.

These blots on Disney's consistent record of success failed to dampen enthusiasm for the model; all of the enterprises have spawned progeny throughout the world, on different scales and for different types of activities. More depressingly, Disney's version of public space has seeped into diverse settings.

Whatever the appeal of Disney's lands, as a political ethic it represents the tyranny of engineered happiness and consensus. It is undergirded by the fundamental notion that conflict disrupts the satisfaction of consumption and hence the construction of identities through the purchase of yet more artifacts. Instead, conflict is essential to maintain a democratic society, which is why Disney's attempt to achieve cultural legitimacy through programmed versions of history and through architectural patronage is so troubling. By 1995, Disney controlled one of the biggest television networks in the United States, ABC, which would put major newscasts into its hands. Disney's linkage of freedom and free-market spreads into more realms while its architectural patronage reinforces its cultural image as benign and innocuous.

Just as the Disney notion of historical and contemporary architectural theme parks had historical precedents, so too has it participated in major changes in the character of public space developed and built in the last quarter-century. Although I mentioned the University of California at Irvine as an architectural theme park, other kinds of public spaces have been affected by those things that most characterize Disney's worlds: spectacle, surveillance, and control.

Charles Moore took his cues from Disney's Imagineers for a public space to represent Italian contributions to the culture of New Orleans, Piazza d'Italia (1979). Moore identified other sources for his design as   34 Nicola Salvi's Trevi Fountain in Rome (1732), Andrea Palladio's Basilica in Vicenza (1549), Karl Friedrich Schinkel's Neue Wache in Berlin (1818), and the broad tradition of classical architecture, brought together to produce an artifact of pure scenography. Despite the ingratiating populist aspirations of this scheme, with its high camp Delicatessen Order (based on hanging sausages), vivid colors, enormous Serlian motif gateway, fountain in the shape of Italy, temple-like structure and campanile shunted behind the Italian-American Federation Building high-rise, the Piazza d'Italia remains resolutely empty of all but the hardiest tourists, largely because the adjacent development that was to attract visitors never happened. Moreover, cheap construction meant that by 1994 the Piazza was in poor physical condition and needed a fresh infusion of cash

34 Charles Moore, Piazza d'Italia, New Orleans, Louisiana, 1979.

for a renovation despite having been renovated once already for the New Orleans World Fair in 1984. Nonetheless, the little scheme yielded an emblematic icon of Postmodernist design, so much so that it became a favored backdrop for movies set in New Orleans such as *The Big Easy*, which opened with a body dumped in the Piazza's fountain. With the abundance of architectural elements, Moore abandoned any pretense of architecture and urban design as anything other than playful fantasy.

Cities of consumption

Perhaps the most obvious instance of the conflation of the three essentials of Disney's worlds is the shopping mall, a mid-20th-century invention that reached its peak with the West Edmonton Mall in Canada (1986), designed by the developers, only to be exceeded in size in 1992 by the Mall of America in Minnesota. No better indicator of how the regional shopping center has supplanted traditional town centers can be found than the maps given out at Edmonton's Visitor Information Center. On one side is a general plan of the city, while on the other a detailed plan of the Mall supplants the traditional downtown map. With its amusement park, themed streets and fantasyland hotel (with themed rooms), not to mention a nearly full-scale replica of Columbus's ship, the *Santa Maria*, the West Edmonton Mall represented the culmination of nearly three decades of refinement in shopping center construction in North America. Under the auspices of shrewd developers, locations are chosen according to sophisticated demographic and economic analyses, as are the mixes of shops and other activities, in order to enhance sales and target specific populations with specific types of goods.

One of the earliest pioneers of the shopping center, the Viennese-born Los Angeles architect Victor Gruen, believed that the growth of suburbs and of automobile ownership in the United States presented an opportunity to redress the problems of city centers with healthy, happy environments that easily accommodated automobiles. This anti-urban project, which he realized with his first enclosed and air-conditioned regional shopping center, the Southdale Mall in Minnesota (1956), envisioned enhanced opportunities for a full range of cultural, civic and recreational activities, easily accessible and integrated into the larger suburban environment—all within the context of consumption. In the shopping mall, Gruen exulted in 1955, the individualistic expressions of different shops would be held in check by architectural controls, and as the first planning efforts by capitalists, malls would ideally join commerce and modernism. Gruen's Fox Hills Mall in Los Angeles (1975) exemplifies the classic type: department store anchors at either end and in the middle of one side, parking decks along the southern flank, and an attempt to create an urban interior, with what is designated a "public square" in the center, at the intersection of two lateral "streets."

The orgy of shopping mall construction spread over the next four decades from the United States to the rest of the world, from England to Australia, Singapore to Korea, Italy to Argentina, and involved both private and public developers. Initially one- to two-story structures set into an asphalt sea of parking, malls gradually took on different forms, with underground parking or separate multi-level parking. They also moved from suburban or even rural settings to town centers, airports, and other places. Unfortunately, when shopping centers have been developed in other countries, they have often adopted the worst features of the United States model. Such is the case with Joyland, in the Marche province of Italy, where the glazed and arcaded shopping center sits in rich agricultural land surrounded by a vast parking lot.

Architecturally, one of the most striking features of malls has been the contrast between a highly articulated interior and a relatively blank exterior. The earliest examples lacked a context to respond to because of their settings far from other buildings. Indeed, one of the specific functions of the mall was to enclose all the shops usually in air-conditioned comfort and under the control of management. Quite logically, design attention focused on enticing shoppers inside. However, once development spread to more urbanized areas, a few designers began to pay attention to the exterior as well. Jon Jerde's Westside Pavilion (1985) in Los Angeles, with its variegated facade, offered an unexpected gesture toward the street and the urbanity typically denied in other malls, however banal the interior. 35

35 Jon Jerde, Westside Pavilion, Los Angeles, California, 1985.

This was a relatively isolated case. More typical is the Arndale Centre at Manchester in England (1976), one of many malls to face the street with blank walls (another is Scotia Square, Halifax, Nova Scotia). Like the Westside Pavilion, it even provides a pedestrian overpass so that shoppers can avoid the city altogether. The quintessential example of the unfriendly street elevation is the Beverly Center in West Hollywood (1982), by Welton Becket Associates, where the lower floors of the expensive mall contain only parking. From the exterior the Center is an enormous blank if colorful whale much like its neighbor, Victor Gruen and Cesar Pelli's Pacific Design Center (1974 and 1990), an upscale mart for designer fabrics and furniture that consists of two massive monolithic structures, clad in blue and green glazed panels. The PDC rises from a small-scale residential neighborhood in open defiance of any remotely suburban values, its blank panels resolutely and forbiddingly closed off against the street.

Adorned with streets decked out in urban facades, and with trees, ice skating rinks, amusement parks, organized public activities, art shows and plays, West Edmonton and other regional malls drew shops and shoppers away from the hearts of cities in the United States, Canada, and the United Kingdom, leading to the pervasive decline of traditional retail districts in these countries. At the same time, the types of unorganized political and social activities associated with cities have often not been allowed in malls: in the United States, the Supreme Court has ruled that because they are private spaces, they may prohibit or control such activities. This ruling cast in sharp relief the function of the carefully controlled mall, reducing the notion of civic participation to that of consumption.

European shopping centers avoided some of these problems because they have often have been sponsored by the state—as in Marne-la-Vallée, outside of Paris, or in England at Cofferidge Close near Milton Keynes or Covent Garden in London. But the primacy of consumption as the only true public activity is no less prominent. In the United States, cities that found their tax bases severely eroded by suburban shopping centers granted tax breaks and other incentives to developers to invest in the city, often in rehabilitating historic buildings such as Faneuil Hall and Quincy Market, Boston (1976), or to include shopping malls in urban high-rise hotels, such as Water Tower Place in Chicago (1976). However economically successful they have been, little interesting architecture has resulted from four decades of mall design. Two Rodeo Drive in Beverly Hills, California (1990), the upscale mini-mall par excellence, is a rare instance of a cleverly designed mall with an urban and architectural presence, even if an extraordinarily pretentious one. For the site, amid the fabled wealth of

36 Cesar Pelli, Pacific Design Center, Los Angeles, California: the 1974 structure.

37 Welton Becket Associates, Beverly Center, Los Angeles, California, 1982.

the city's famous Golden Triangle, where property sells for $40 million per acre, developer Doug Stitzel had Kaplan McLaughlin Diaz produce three carefully crafted street frontages, a collage of diverse elevations representing different historical periods. With their porphyry cobblestone paving, they refer to a street typology of no particular period or country but rather generically "European" in appearance. The purpose was to create a congenial context for consumption, encouraging pedestrian activities in a setting other than an interior shopping mall, on a street famous as a site of conspicuous consumption.

Frank Gehry's Edgemar Center at Santa Monica, California (1988), represents the best of the small urban malls, with its parking discreetly concealed and the fanciful street facades scaled to harmonize with a one- to two-story streetscape of funky shop fronts and restaurants. Neatly penetrated by two meandering streets, the center of the 34,000-square-foot (3,000-square-meter) complex is a small open courtyard surrounded by restaurants, an odd mix of shops, and a small museum. Like much of Gehry's work, the strength of this project derives from the haphazard mix of quirky, irregularly shaped buildings and unexpected materials, such as his trademark chainlink fence, here used to drape the elevator tower. Gehry endowed each element with a distinct architectural character through manipulation of forms (the three towers and the ramps for handicapped patrons that become strong design elements themselves) and such materials as galvanized metal, chainlink, ceramic tile and grey stucco. Gehry demonstrated the potential of the small-scale urban complex in particular by the way he handled parking, which is both at

38 Kaplan McLaughlin Diaz, Two Rodeo Drive, Beverly Hills, California, 1990.

39 Frank Gehry, Edgemar Center, Santa Monica, California, 1988.

ground level and below ground, but tucked out of sight, leaving a lively and inviting frontage on the rare Los Angeles street with relatively heavy foot traffic.

In the public realm: carriers of culture

One of the most significant effects of shopping center development overall has been the conflation of the mall and the theme park in a wide range of other building types, most notably the museum but also the library and the concert hall and theater. If malls tend to lack architectural distinction, the opposite is true of the museum. Over the last twenty years, and particularly after 1980, the most prestigious and widely acclaimed commissions have been for some form of museum, art, or cultural center. This phenomenon is intriguing for at least two reasons. First, although the museum as cultural institution originated in Western Europe, the current phenomenon is global, extending, for example, from a small museum of local cultural history in Senegal by Pippo Ciorra (1990) to the vast Sainsbury Wing of the National Gallery in London by Venturi, Scott Brown and Associates (1991). Secondly, in an era of purportedly expanding democratization, why the vast renewal of interest in an institution whose origins are deeply aristocratic and private? No

41, 42

69

simple answers leap out, but clearly the underlying conditions vary from place to place, often having to do with issues as diverse as the changing activities and functions of the museum itself, the market value of art, types and sources of financing, tax laws, the ebb and flow of international mass tourism. In some cases, the state or the city commissions museums, sometimes to establish a first civic museum, or elsewhere to address specific or neglected areas of cultural studies, such as the Museum for Decorative Arts in Frankfurt by Richard Meier (1986). Germany conducted the most vigorous museum-building campaign during the 1980s. In at least two countries—the United States and Britain—the flowering of museums and museum additions in the 1980s coincided with two major developments: an economic boom that led to an increasing polarization of income (and hence a dramatic increase in poverty) and abundant supplies of cash available for investment in culture.

Other major factors in the diversity of museums include kinds of objects collected, location, local historical traditions, and relations to traditions in museum architecture, traditions which are of surprisingly recent origin. Although instances of art collecting can be found in antiquity, in baths and temples or, for example, in the Museion at Alexandria in Egypt, the practice began in earnest during the Renaissance. The nobility and high clergy of the Roman Catholic Church promoted art collecting and visiting collections as diversions available only to a select few. When clerics and aristocrats assembled Roman statues during the Renaissance, they exhibited them for personal pleasure and to impress visitors in their palaces or gardens, as Lorenzo de' Medici displayed his sculptures and paintings in the Medici Palace in Florence. Giorgio Vasari designed the Uffizi in Florence (1560) as administrative offices, but within a little over two decades it had been transformed into a private art gallery. At the same time, collecting shifted from antiquities into paintings, contemporary sculpture, and prints, as well as porcelain, jewelry, antique ceramics, armaments, scientific instruments, artifacts of natural history, and oddities assembled from voyages of exploration throughout the world. As their heterogeneity indicates, the items gathered were often chiefly distinguished by their rarity. These assemblages remained highly personal, within private palaces, and open to the public only at the discretion of the owner.

Beginning in the 18th century but more decisively in the 19th century and coinciding with the rise of the bourgeoisie and the nation-state, entire buildings began to be erected in which to house formerly private and often princely treasure troves in order to make them available to the public. As with the establishment of the Louvre Museum in Paris, diverse

40

40 Richard Meier, Museum for Decorative Arts, Frankfurt-am-Main, Germany, 1986.

impulses, ranging from the republican to the imperialist, combined to promote museum development. Karl Friedrich Schinkel designed the Altes Museum in Berlin (1824–30) as a shrine for great works of painting and sculpture, and as such it set a standard for many subsequent buildings. It was located on the Spree Island, a bastion of royal authority, but its position facing the royal palace signified the royal decision to adopt a more public presence. Such museums enshrined works of art designated as important and made them available for contemplation and education outside the framework of their sphere of traditional users. Subsequent museums in both the 19th and 20th centuries, such as the Metropolitan Museum of Art in New York, incorporated key elements of Schinkel's design and reflected a similar disposition toward art objects.

What had been an exclusive diversion of an idle aristocracy accessible only to a privileged few now could be appropriated by the bourgeoisie and disseminated on a mass basis. Part of the elite connotations and aristocratic status associated with the collection and appreciation of art was

71

the presupposition of a necessary economic surplus which left the individual free from the daily struggle to exist—initially a luxury only available to the nobility. And one of the most compelling emblems of high status connected with art was its position remote from the bourgeois world of production. As leisure time and excess funds became available to greater numbers of people than ever before during the 19th century, so were more art museums constructed. Their function was to educate the emerging bourgeois masses in the taste structure designated as appropriate by the upper classes, and to imbue them with an appropriate awe for works of art, reinforcing an imperialist historical narration in the language and rhetoric of classicism.

Until the 1970s, two main types of museums dominated: the shrine, which followed Schinkel's Altes Museum, exemplified in the 20th century by buildings such as John Russell Pope's National Gallery in Washington, D. C. (1941), and the storehouse or warehouse for diverse types of artifacts, from anthropological to scientific, such as the Smithsonian, also in Washington, by James Renwick, Jr. (1846). Both of these types continued to be built throughout the 20th century, although by the 1980s they tended to drift toward a third, more recent type, the cultural shopping mall, and on to the realm of spectacle.

Museum as shrine
The Sainsbury Wing of the National Gallery in London, by Venturi, Scott Brown and Associates (1991), exemplifies the shrine type in 1990s dress. The large addition to William Wilkins's 1838 building was commissioned specifically to house the gallery's collection of Renaissance paintings. The Thatcher government refused to pay for the addition on the grounds that institutions should be self-supporting (although this doctrine was noticeably not applied to the development of the Docklands). Initially a British firm, Ahrends Burton & Koralek, won an architectural competition that involved reconciling the needs of the art gallery with those of a speculative office building that presumably would pay for the addition over time. The bond between commerce and art, normally well concealed in the museum as shrine, was far too apparent in this scheme for purist tastes, and set off a raging debate. When the winning design appeared in 1984, Charles, Prince of Wales, blasted the result, with the gallery placed atop offices, as a "monstrous carbuncle" on the face of a "much loved friend."

After the Sainsbury grocery market family donated the necessary funds, Venturi, Scott Brown and Associates won a second, limited competition for a scheme without the speculative offices. Their classicizing

41 Venturi, Scott Brown and Associates, Sainsbury Wing, National Gallery,
London, England, 1991.

facade is loosely inspired by that of the adjacent gallery, and executed in   41
the same warm, pale stone. A narrow passageway separates the new wing
from the old one, but they are joined at the main level by a vaguely
rotonda-shaped pedestrian bridge—a reference to a well-established
typological element typical of post-Schinkel museums as well as to the
National Gallery's own rotunda. In the sections of the facade nearest to
the older building, the architects dutifully picked up the Corinthian
pilasters, first bundling and overlapping them near the corner and then
spacing them out at irregular intervals. In the intercolumniations blind
windows appear, framed by moldings that break off and disappear unex-
pectedly. Although classical elements dominate, they break rules of classical composition in overdetermined ways, with mannerist handling of the
pilasters, for example, or thoroughly unclassical garage-door-type openings hacked out of the elevation for the entries, windows and loading
docks, at once undermining the classical sensibility and contradicting the

73

tectonic logic otherwise so emphatically registered. The classical skin peels away ignominiously as soon as the building rounds the corner away from Trafalgar Square, marching along at an uninspired pace but with the name boldly emblazoned all the way round the dreary north elevation, text substituting for architecture. Here Portland stone revetment dissolves into a brick-faced, Modernist envelope, both materials neatly marking the structural system of reinforced, poured-in-place concrete. This too derives from a philosophy common among those Post-modernist architects who conceive of structure as pure representation.

Some historians defend this technique of grafting a classicizing skin onto a far more technologically sophisticated structure on the grounds that nothing could be more appropriate for a building dedicated to Italian Renaissance paintings than to duplicate precisely the same strategy adopted by Italian Renaissance architects. From Alberti to Michelangelo and beyond, architects responded to the pleas of private, public and ecclesiastical patrons to adorn and unify existing buildings with classical revetments: the Senate building in Rome, the town hall in Montepulciano, and the Palazzo Rucellai in Florence are three of the most widely known examples. But the tasks of these earlier architects were quite different from those confronted by Venturi, and Scott Brown. Chiefly

42 Venturi, Scott Brown and Associates, Sainsbury Wing, National Gallery, London, 1991: the main staircase.

for reasons of economy and time, Renaissance patrons chose to retain existing buildings, so that the new facades merely supplied the required decorum and unity. The Sainsbury Wing, on the other hand, is an entirely new construction attached to a different building, so no existing structure demanded regularization and updating by means of a similar skin graft. Though rhetoric motivated the revetments of both the Sainsbury Wing and its Renaissance precedents, clearly the former is considerably more shrill to far less discernible purpose.

Sleights-of-hand continue on the interior, where the architects distorted columns in the Tuscan order as frames for the arched openings between galleries. Venturi and Scott Brown invoked odd historical pedigrees here, conflating the noble and the mundane, the shrine and the shed: Wilkins on the facade, Sir John Soane's Dulwich Picture Gallery in the galleries, and Victorian railroad stations for the decorative, non- 42 structural aluminum arches surmounting the main staircase.

Each classical detail or abundantly redundant element stands in counterpoint to another that undermines or contradicts classical verities. For Venturi and Scott Brown, contemporary cultural and social diversity calls for an architecture of richness and ambiguity rather than clarity and purity. At the same time, they argue that architecture must above all communicate meaning. Like Eisenman and other Deconstructivist architects, then, they hold their task as architects to be that of giving expression to their interpretation of the *Zeitgeist* by means of specific formal strategies. *Zeitgeist*-defining presents something of a burden for any architect or building, but serves handsomely as a means of surrounding the building task with the aura of mystery and mastery eagerly asserted by architects. Necessarily then, the richness and ambiguity in design of which they speak direct communication not toward the masses but toward architects or architecture *aficionados*. The Sainsbury Wing highlights without resolving one of the problems faced by architects such as Venturi and Scott Brown: how to design a museum as a shrine able to satisfy both erudite fellow architects and critics, and as a cultural appendage for a general public less likely to be informed about witty mannerist references and inside jokes. Judging from the building rather than the rhetoric, their answer is that the masses will at best grasp the vaguely classical, so there is no point in designing for them.

Several other examples of the museum as shrine propose different strategies for serving essentially the same ends. A world away from the Sainsbury Wing, the Davis Museum and Cultural Center at Wellesley, Massachusetts (1993), by Rafael Moneo dispenses with classical crutches altogether in an austere brick building for the college's art collection and

43 Rafael Moneo, Davis Museum and Cultural Center, Wellesley, Massachusetts, 1993.

43   temporary exhibits. The simple boxy exterior responds with singular understatement to the campus context, then gives way inside to soaring spaces infused laterally by natural light, an essay in complexity that is achieved in the simplest materials—slate, hardwood, white walls. Split by a grand staircase lined with maple paneling and set between perforated walls, the building beautifully marries the shrine to the warehouse with a tectonic logic missing altogether from the Sainsbury Wing. Moneo's ear-

44, 45   lier museums, such as the National Museum of Roman Art in Mérida, Spain (1980-85), equally brilliantly brought together different traditions—in that case, the modern, the antique and the medieval. The modern concrete museum, revetted in brick deliberately proportioned like Roman brick, is suspended above excavated remnants of Roman Mérida, permitting the collection to be situated in a building at once of its own era and of the modern.

46   Equally dramatic in its own quiet fashion is Álvaro Siza's Center for Contemporary Galician Art in Santiago de Compostela, Spain (1993). The clean lines and crisp surfaces are emphatically inspired by the Modern Movement, but the siting, orientation, and relation to the pre-existing building, a rehabilitated monastic church and cloister, are not. Siza's career has been predicated on an architecture intimately responsive

76

44, 45 Rafael Moneo, National Museum of Roman Art, Mérida, Spain, 1980–85.

46 Álvaro Siza, Center for Contemporary Galician Art, Santiago de Compostela, Spain, 1993.

46 to its surroundings, but without succumbing to bouts of nostalgia or naive contextualism. The Center carries the city's complex of ramped and terraced passageways into the heart of the building, just as its massive granite volumes echo the traditional materials and morphology of the city's urban tissue. Likewise, the bright white marble and stucco interiors recall those of local houses, even though Siza deftly controls periodic infusions of natural, diffused and artificial light and vectors of mass and movement to an altogether different effect.

47 Ricardo Legorreta's Museo de Arte Contemporaneo ("MARCO") or Museum of Contemporary Art in Monterrey, Mexico (1992), also marries the museum-as-shrine with local design traditions, specifically in the organization of the building as an overscaled patio house—a central space surrounded by arcades opening out into the individual galleries, its exterior elevations massive and its dusky red wall planes turned decisively against the street. The connection to the courtyard house frankly disappears because of the enormous scale of the project. Legorreta enlivened the most visibly public spaces, such as the atrium, with bold splashes of warm colors and a shallow reflecting pool. On the other hand, highly traditional enfilades of white galleries form a virginal backdrop for uninterrupted aesthetic contemplation in the tradition of the exaltation of art and its separation from the problems of daily life. Among the things

47 Legorreta Arquitectos, Museum of Contemporary Art, Monterrey, Mexico, 1992.

the project is designed to forget are the museum's construction in a much contested urban renewal zone, the devastation of the historic core of Monterrey with the backing of local corporate interests, and the domination of the institution by one wealthy family set up as cultural arbiter.

Antoine Predock's Las Vegas Library and Discovery Museum in Nevada (1990) is of a different order. In a city known for its tacky buildings and its endless strip of fast food outlets and casinos (celebrated by Venturi, Scott Brown and Izenour in *Learning from Las Vegas* in 1972), Predock refused to accept the banalities of tarting up the local vernacular, as many Postmodernists would have been content to do—as indeed Venturi and Scott Brown did for their Children's Museum in Houston, Texas. The program did not call for a shrine, but an interactive setting for youthful explorations, so Predock opted for a structure of rich spatial expression and handsome materials, attractive and appealing to children, unpretentious by contrast with other celebrated Las Vegas institutions. The Las Vegas Library makes a handsome counterpoint to Predock's Nelson Fine Arts Center at Arizona State University (1989), a collection of buildings for study, performance and exhibition with a rich and diverse array of spaces, lighting and forms. Predock again found inspiration in local Spanish and Indian traditions of the Southwest, but his adaptations avoided banal reproductions, offering instead imaginative

50

48, 49

79

48, 49 *left and below* Antoine Predock, Nelson Fine Arts Center, Arizona State University, Tempe, Arizona, 1989: view toward museum and dance studio, and longitudinal section.

50 *opposite* Antoine Predock, Las Vegas Library and Discovery Museum, Las Vegas, Nevada, 1990.

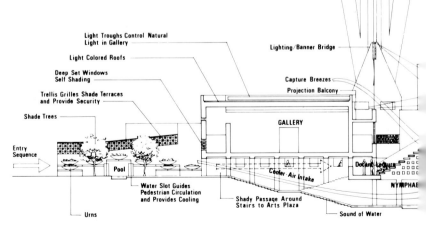

Light Troughs Control Natural Light in Gallery

Light Colored Roofs

Deep Set Windows Self Shading

Trellis Grilles Shade Terraces and Provide Security

Shade Trees

Entry Sequence

Pool

Urns

Water Slot Guides Pedestrian Circulation and Provides Cooling

Lighting/Banner Bridge

Capture Breezes

Projection Balcony

GALLERY

Cooler Air Intake

Shady Passage Around Stairs to Arts Plaza

Docent

NYMPHAE

Sound of Water

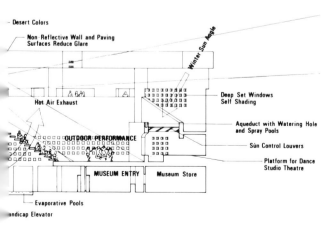

Desert Colors

Non-Reflective Wall and Paving
Surfaces Reduce Glare

Winter Sun Angle

Hot Air Exhaust

Deep Set Windows
Self Shading

OUTDOOR PERFORMANCE

Aqueduct with Watering Hole
and Spray Pools

Sun Control Louvers

Platform for Dance
Studio Theatre

MUSEUM ENTRY   Museum Store

Evaporative Pools

Handicap Elevator

and highly individual variations on traditional themes. The longitudinal
49 section through the Fine Arts Center begins to convey some of the
spatial complexity that Predock achieves with effortless elegance.

Museum as warehouse
The second type of museum is the warehouse. One of the most recent
examples initiated the wave of museum construction in the late 1970s
51, 52 and 1980s in Europe, the Pompidou Center, also known as the
Beaubourg, in Paris (1972–77), by Richard Rogers and Renzo Piano—a
structure as indifferent to its surroundings and as driven by the image of
technology as the Sainsbury Wing was obsequious to its context and
infatuated with classicism. In the tradition of the great exhibitions of the
19th century, this vast steel cage celebrated universal spaces capable of
infinite modulations and able to accommodate the most diverse types of
exhibitions and activities. The Pompidou Center is a gigantic, open-plan
shed containing a modern art museum, cinema, library, industrial design,
music and acoustical research center, offices, and parking facilities. The
architects expressed their two fundamental aspirations—technological
sophistication and flexible space—on the exterior without the standard
51 Modernist or classical features. With the exceptionally busy facade, Piano
and Rogers emphasized the warehouse type as an artifact of high technology but especially as a historically neutral container for culture of
various levels. Unfortunately, they did not consider the consequences
on such mundane matters as maintenance, and visitors have watched
bemused over the years as dirt accumulated in unreachable corners,
corroding the exuberant technological display.

Uninterrupted floor space was possible because, as in any commercial
warehouse for the storage of goods, services and structural elements
never intrude on floor space. In this case, the architects moved everything, from structural elements to circulation, onto the exterior. The large
steel tube truss beams form thirteen bays, each beam attached to ger-
berettes of steel, which in turn connect with the vertical bracing. But the
52 exterior exposes much more than the structural system, for color-coded
elements boldly thrust onto the elevations contain escalators, elevators,
and stairs (red), air conditioning and heating (blue), water (green), and
electrical systems (yellow). Rarely has so much uninteresting information
been communicated on a facade with such chromatic aggressiveness.

Although only a little higher than its neighbors, the gigantic, garishly
colored box sprouting curved duct pipes and glazed escalator arcades
snaking along its flanks snubs the surrounding 17th- to 19th-century
urban fabric. The architects deliberately elected to ignore the context,

making no attempt to fit the design into its surroundings or to diminish its intrusiveness, except for stepped terraces on the southern end. In fact, they even aspired to extend the museum's territory and to convert adjacent housing into associated studios and dwellings. The dream never faded for Piano, whose subsequent museum-warehouse for the Menil Collection in Houston, Texas (1987), casts its grey mantle over the surrounding suburban streets, where the bungalows purchased by Dominique De Menil and made available to artists and museum staff had already been tinted the same hue in 1974. Here, however, he underplayed the technological sophistication in deference to the decidedly suburban setting, handling the issue of context far more sympathetically.

In their brief for the Pompidou, the architects insistently reiterated their goal of achieving maximum flexibility, to the extent that even the floors could be moved, because the building was destined to contain the most diverse kinds of exhibits, from modern art through architecture, furniture, and decorative arts to other kinds of explorations of contemporary culture. Although the flexible structure allowed for manipulable

51 Richard Rogers and Renzo Piano, Centre Georges Pompidou, Paris, France, 1972–77: facade to the piazza.

53 Patkau Associates, Canadian Clay and Glass Gallery, Waterloo, Ontario, 1988.

52 *opposite* Richard Rogers and Renzo Piano, Centre Georges Pompidou, Paris, 1972–77: elevation to Rue Beaubourg.

spaces that accommodate specific events, superabundance rendered the scheme troublesome. In practice, the endless, indeterminate space and the highly visible and colorful exterior elements made exhibitions of art—its chief mission—difficult, so that a second interior box had to be erected to screen out the exterior and provide sufficient wall space.

A quite unusual example of the warehouse type of museum points in an altogether different direction. Patkau Associates' Canadian Clay and Glass Gallery at Waterloo, Ontario (1988), was intended to exhibit glass and ceramics as products of a process that was to be expressed in the building, moving from glass blowing and throwing pots to the selection of special objects and their display as objects of art. Delays and cost cutting unrelated to the architects led to the erosion of the program and hence the design, so that the critique of this process needed to be conveyed in the remainder of the design. Foregoing the crisp white cube of the shrine type, the architects exposed and celebrated the construction and its materials and opened enormous windows to flood the spaces with natural light and to afford views out to the city—as with the portico of Schinkel's Altes Museum, reinforcing the relationship of the art objects to everyday life without.

The search for infinitely flexible space as well as fondness for the visible exaltation of technology meant that the appeal of the warehouse museum type extended widely: in England for example we have the Sainsbury Centre of the University of East Anglia at Norwich (1978) by Norman Foster, and in the United States Frank Gehry's Temporary Museum of Contemporary Art in Los Angeles (1984), and in the smaller cinema archives for Paramount Pictures by Holt Hinshaw Pfau Jones in the same city (1990). Glenn Murcutt also adapted a warehouse scheme realized in steel and corrugated iron for a far more modest and unpretentious mining museum in Broken Hill (1988) in the Australian outback. In fact, the chief feature that distinguishes the warehouses by Gehry and Murcutt from most of the others is their lack of pretension within and without, almost defiantly artless and emphasizing the precariousness of the institution.

The paradigmatic warehouse museum came not at the end of a historical trajectory of progress, but rather at the outset of the period under discussion. Even as the Pompidou Center lumbered into its garish existence, Louis Kahn's Yale Center for British Art at New Haven, Connecticut (1969-77), commandingly expressed a different version of the warehouse, based on a concrete structural frame both inside and out, with metal, glass, and wood infill panels. Only the volume of the cylindrical staircase soaring up through the vast skylit atrium interrupts the

54, 55 Louis Kahn, Yale Center for British Art, New Haven, Connecticut, 1969–77.

otherwise steady and regular rhythm of the modular units. For Kahn, the museum-warehouse called not for a glorification of high technology but rather for the craftlike refinement of all construction materials; not for universal, infinitely malleable space, but for regular units that could be reduced or expanded within certain limits. Kahn resolutely rejected the conceits of most of the museums discussed above: at Yale service and mechanical systems are tucked conveniently out of sight, not expressed on the facade, and classicism is relegated to the art on exhibit. A building revealing its tectonic quality with disarming, deceptive simplicity therefore provides noble settings rather than classical details, and the pomposity of expressing the spirit of the times simply does not figure.

Museum as cultural shopping mall
Museum marketing strategies blurred the distinctions between commerce and art through the introduction of increasingly elaborate and prominent museum stores, new exhibition strategies that tie art on display to the sale of a wide range of items no longer limited to posters, postcards or catalogues, and art rental enterprises, just as shopping malls have widened their range of facilities to include cinemas, concerts, and art exhibitions. This newer type of museum, as cultural shopping mall, includes facilities from restaurants to extensive shops to auditoriums and theaters. For both museum and mall, the primary activity is generating income by stimulating consumption. The mall may have become the paradigmatic building type of the late 20th century, where the distinctions between cultural and economic institutions have faded beyond recognition. Everything from museums to universities to city streets and even amusement parks replicates the organization of the shopping mall.

29　Such is the case with Epcot Center, in Disney World, where international monuments are reproduced—even the Sistine Chapel ceiling—as decorative backgrounds for a thinly disguised mall.

56　　The Neue Staatsgalerie or New State Gallery at Stuttgart in Germany (1984) by James Stirling and Michael Wilford, which may well be the most significant museum of the 1980s, confronted issues not unlike those faced slightly later by Venturi and Scott Brown. As in the case of the Sainsbury Wing, the Staatsgalerie competition called for an addition to an existing, classical building dating from the early 19th century. Stirling's response could not have differed more from the labored allusions of the Sainsbury Wing, for a simple reason: although the museum housed a permanent collection, it was also planned to accommodate traveling exhibitions. When Stirling's building opened, cognoscenti claimed to locate clever references to Le Corbusier, Soane, Schinkel, Lutyens, even

88

Frank Lloyd Wright. A raging debate broke out between Modernist purists on the one hand, who lamented Stirling's supposed capitulation to Postmodernism because of his bold use of color and classical elements such as voussoirs, pediments and architraves, and on the other, adherents of Postmodernism, who believed that Stirling helped open up architecture to its own rich historical traditions.

The debates obscured the most important features of the museum, particularly its ingenious response to an unpromising location and the way it is embedded in the city's local building traditions. On a site fronted by an eight-lane expressway and by the almost endless and dreary back elevation of the Staatstheater, and hemmed in by a variety of new and older buildings, Stirling countered with a complex sculptural mass of two-toned bands of golden-hued sandstone, undulating glass walls with bright green mullions, and broad ramps lined by oversized dusky pink and blue handrails. Inspired by a landscape of hillsides laced with vineyards framed by stone retaining walls, stone ramps punctuated by layers of foliage and vegetation lead into the museum. Instead of offering a

56 James Stirling, Michael Wilford and Associates, Neue Staatsgalerie, Stuttgart, Germany, 1984.

diminished version of Schinkel's rotunda, as Michael Graves had with his competition entry for the Wexner Center in Columbus, Ohio (1983), Stirling opened his rotunda to the sky, with a public passageway winding around the atrium overlooking the sculpture garden.

Despite the reference to local agrarian traditions, the Staatsgalerie, its entrance revetted with grids and polychrome infill panels, was conceived as a thoroughly urban artifact. Unlike most of the museums of the last two decades, here in most cases admission is free, with the art, café, and open spaces public in every respect. Intended to be not a shrine (if it were, children would not be allowed to roller skate on its splendid ramps) but a cultural and leisure center for the city, in important respects the Staatsgalerie most resembles a cultural shopping mall.

The lifeblood of the modern museum is the itinerant exhibition, the blockbuster shows that regularly feature long lines and complicated advance ticket purchases akin to those of rock concerts. Usually defined as representing the treasures or golden age of some culture or country, these tend to reinforce stereotypes about the superiority of certain cultures or artifacts over others. In this respect, shrine and cultural mall converge, much as designer boutique and shopping center do. Elaborating a fictional narrative of cultural homogeneity and historical continuity —perhaps most compellingly presented in the West Edmonton Mall, with its juxtapositions of themed streets such as Bourbon Street (New Orleans) with a generic "European" street—the cultural shopping mall pretends to offer democratic access to a symbolically charged, elite preserve. The quintessential feature of the mall, however, is that it is a contained precinct, with controlled access both for retailers and for consumers. These features are indeed a metaphor for the undemocratic, non-heterogeneous, racist and exclusionary public spaces of the late 20th century, all of which, to be sure, have precedents in the past. That women and senior citizens feel safer in shopping centers than on city streets only underscores this.

Museum as spectacle
Kurt Forster identified a more recent though uncommon museum type, where the visitor is expected to enjoy an aesthetic experience because of the architecture itself—examples being Richard Meier's Decorative Arts Museum in Frankfurt (1986), Arata Isozaki's Museum of Contemporary Art in Los Angeles (1986), and Peter Eisenman's Wexner Center in Columbus, Ohio (1990). It is difficult to see this type as other than a conflation of shrine and mall, but a combination that is intended at the outset rather than achieved through the transformation of an older

40

57

57 Peter Eisenman, Wexner Center, Columbus, Ohio, 1990.

building. Ostensibly configured according to Eisenman's interpretation of Deconstructivist architecture, every space, every element, including the landscape, of the Wexner Center is subject to the tyranny of arbitrary grids. Although Eisenman designated the source of the grids as everything from Federal Aviation Authority flightpaths to the location of the university football stadium, they are simply devices that he has consistently used to control his designs. Instead of infinitely rich and varied theatrical, spatial, or aesthetic experiences, the Wexner offers a sequence of architectural one-liners that is predictable from Eisenman's previous work. More than anything else, what is celebrated here is the new architectural style. The building's opening, with no art to distract attention from the architecture, demonstrated this convincingly.

Despite the emphasis on the theatrical, the architecture of this newer museum type is organized to accomplish the same reverence and appreciation of art found in the more restrained shrine type, where the aesthetic experience was expected only of the most cultivated viewers and the object was to cultivate the uncultivated, but it also typically includes the characteristics of the cultural shopping mall. These museums as spectacles expect an artistically, not to mention architecturally, literate

58 Tadao Ando, Children's Museum, Himeji, Hyogo, Japan, 1988–89.

audience, so that definitions of the aesthetic may be broader than the older ones, but still demand the same reverence from the viewer.

Museums: some alternative solutions
Overwhelming as the brash cultural shopping mall-cum-aesthetic shrine has been since 1970, it is important to acknowledge that other approaches to the design of museums have also occasionally appeared. Determined clients and thoughtful architects willing to forego the allure of fashion and the readily marketable image are the two necessary

59, 60 Charles Correa,
Jawahar Kala Kendra,
Jaipur, India, 1990:
entrance, and view into
the interior courtyard.

ingredients of more enduring results. As I noted earlier with Predock's museum in Las Vegas, museums for children are less constrained by a tradition of canonical building types, therefore they are susceptible to great inventiveness. Tadao Ando aspires to create buildings with a clear logic, responses to the everyday needs of their occupants that engage in a dialogue with nature—wind, water, light, sky, plants—distilled from complexity into what he characterizes as a greater purity. The Children's Museum in Hyogo (1988–89), with a library, playroom, children's theater, and workshop, sits on a spectacular wooded hillside site overlooking a beautiful lake. After dividing the project into three separate units, Ando set the complex into a shallow pool with a series of small waterfalls—not an untouchable piece of landscape architecture but an inviting site for children's play. The design depends upon the deep interpenetration of built form and nature, spaces designed with geometric rigor, but articulated above all by the sensuous treatment of the poured-in-place concrete and dramatic transformations in different kinds of light. Ando fashioned this museum free of the need to venerate icons of culture, free of the demands of giftshops, lecture halls, and the other features of the contemporary museum: the result is a delightful, austerely simple but magical setting for children's imaginative play.

Two museums, one in India and one in Texas, stand apart from the typologies of shrine, warehouse and mall. Charles Correa's Jawahar Kala

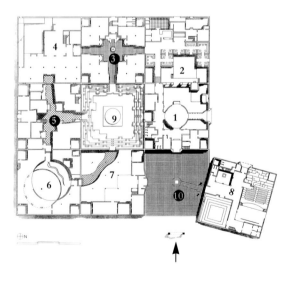

61 Charles Correa, Jawahar Kala Kendra, Jaipur, 1990: plan. The entrance is marked by the arrow bottom right.

1. MANGAL	Administration
2. CHANDRA	Cafeteria, Guest rooms
3. BUDH	Jewelry, Manuscripts Miniatures, etc.
4. KETU	Textiles and Costumes
5. SHANI	Craft Workshops
6. RAHU	Weaponry
7. GURU	Library & Documentation
8. SHUKRA	Theatres
9. SURYA	Kund
10. Entrance	

Kendra museum in Jaipur (1990) is not a repository for expensive master- 59–61
pieces of high art: instead, it is dedicated to the memory of Jawaharlal
Nehru, India's first prime minister. Correa took his cues from the rich
traditions of the city of Jaipur, founded as a new town in the 18th century by Maharajah Jai Singh and laid out with reference to a pattern
of nine squares within a larger square. This pattern, the Vastupurusha
mandala according to the ancient Vedic Shastras, was the model for the
cosmos, as was architecture itself. Correa divided his museum into nine
squares within a square, with one of the squares pulled out of alignment 61
to set off the entrance and the theater, just as one of Jai Singh's squares
was pulled out of the larger one. Correa's choice was not capricious, for
apart from the link with the city's history, his building had to be divided
to accommodate specific functions as well as to contend with the traditional, piecemeal financing of public projects in India. The pavilions contain traditional houses to be used by local artisans for displays of jewelry,
textiles, arms, costumes and manuscripts, and also a library, a cafeteria,
administration offices, and space for performances of local music and
dance. Clad in local reddish sandstone, the concrete frame walls of each
square are eroded at the corners and inscribed with an identifying symbol corresponding to the sections of the mandala. Within each of the
compressed units, Correa worked out a remarkable variety of spaces,
each with its own distinct atmosphere. The contemplative stillness in the
library, for example, with its reflecting pool, stands in contrast to the
grandeur of the administration pavilion, with its brightly hued dome and
enfilade of carved out passageways.

The diminutive Lynn Goode Gallery in Houston (1991), by Carlos 62
Jiménez, embodies an entirely different type of sensibility from the massive public projects discussed above. Here the architect adapted the features of the suburban house to the needs of a gallery. He first layered the
elevation's stucco plane over a recessed, four-bay steel-paneled entrance,
at once summoning the neighborhood typology of porch/garage/living
room picture window and abstracting it to its tectonic essence. In the
delicate geometric ordering of the facade, with one window on the second floor pulled down into the high portico over the entrance, the Lynn
Goode Gallery recalls both the controlled playfulness of an elevation by
Adolf Loos and the calculated syncopation of one by Irving Gill. One
enters through the recessed portico into a double-height entrance, square
in plan and opening out on all four sides—on the right to offices and
storage space, on the left to the exhibition spaces. The broken fenestration rhythm on the front elevation also hints at varied interior levels and
qualities of light, and in fact the irregularly placed window illuminates

62 Carlos Jiménez,
Lynn Goode Gallery,
Houston, Texas, 1991

the double-height entrance volume. From here one passes through a series of spaces orchestrated to expand and contract, enlivening the passage which offers different possibilities for displaying art.

Libraries, concert halls, and theaters

Libraries, if anything, remain variations on an earlier urban warehouse type. Until the 18th century, they traditionally consisted of private collections belonging to wealthy individuals or scholars, of the holdings of universities and colleges, or of manuscripts preserved by ecclesiastical authorities. Michelangelo's spectacular staircase in the vestibule of the Laurentian Library in Florence (begun 1524), paid for by the Medici family, is famous; less well known is the reading room itself, with its sequence of amply lit bays defined by flat pilasters in a long rectangular space appropriate for reading and storage of folios. Two other important early libraries were those by Jacopo Sansovino in Venice, the Library of St. Mark's (1536), and by Christopher Wren for Trinity College, Cambridge (1676).

At the same time that private art collections began to be made public and new buildings were erected in which to store and display them during the 19th century, libraries also began to be opened to the public and housed in new building types. Among the great exemplars, two of the most significant were those of Henri Labrouste in Paris, the Bibliothèque Ste.-Geneviève (1842-50) and the Bibliothèque Nationale (1858-68), both of which celebrated the use of the new high-technology material, iron. In the United States, the library tradition developed first along the lines of H. H. Richardson's neo-Romanesque designs, followed by neo-classical facades and grand, freestanding columns, even under the impetus of the Carnegie reform program, which built philanthropic libraries in the late 19th and early 20th centuries.

Within the basic typology of the urban warehouse, Beth Galí, Marius Quintana and Antoní Solanas's Municipal Library in Barcelona 63 (1988–90), located next to the Joan Miró Park at the edge of the old Cerdá grid, deploys tactics similar to those of Ando to achieve an oasis of stillness in harmony with nature. In this case, however, only part of the

63 Beth Galí, Marius Quintana and Antoní Solanas, Municipal Library, Barcelona, Spain, 1988–90.

64 Hodgetts and Fung, Towell Library, University of California, Los Angeles, 1992.

building opens to a verdant landscape. The other side confronts the city itself. Blank Spanish travertine revetment encloses the urban facade, while the reading rooms open to the park with floor-to-ceiling windows, and the complex is set into a reflecting pool so that, as in Ando's museum, cascades introduce sounds and sparkling reflections. But in this urban setting they emphasize the detachment of the library from the rush of the city without.

At the end of the 20th century, libraries demand rethinking: they are burdened by books that are deteriorating because of the acid-based wood pulp used since the 19th century, and they must confront new technologies and new needs. Two designs for contemporary libraries that addressed these changes stand out. The first is by Hodgetts and Fung, the

64 Towell Library at the University of California, Los Angeles (1992). The name "Towell" is a combination of Temporary and Powell, since the new library is to be a temporary replacement for the Powell Library while that undergoes seismic restructuring. Set in the middle of a neo-Romanesque brick and stone campus, the Towell appears to be a partially masonry Quonset or Nissen hut opened up and split apart, bristling with steel columns, aluminum ribs and brightly colored polyester fabrics. It fulfills the need to store books and provide space for studying, and it also accommodates all of the new electronic devices common to the late 20th-century library. Handsomely detailed and full of kinetic and playful energy, brashly but efficiently staking out a site on the staid

campus grounds, the Towell probably garnered more attention than any other temporary structure in Los Angeles, including Gehry's Temporary Contemporary.

The second important design is the 1989 competition entry for the Bibliothèque de France in Paris by Rem Koolhaas's Office for Metropolitan Architecture or OMA. Although it did not win, it proposed the most daring response of all the entries to the challenge of contemporary technological developments in electronic communications. Koolhaas's project envisioned stacking books within a translucent glass cube, by day a solid, milky white mass sheathed in a variety of transparent and translucent surfaces, by night a glowing symphony of stacks, floors, lecture halls, constantly changing as the activities within change, just as the information flow moves in diverse and unexpected ways, ready to burst from the confines of the old containers, the old warehouses for books.

Along with museums and libraries, two other types of building have developed for an expanding bourgeoisie from the 19th century forward. Over the last two decades architects have enjoyed wide success with designs for concert halls and theaters. Aldo Rossi's Carlo Felice Theater 65 at Genoa in Italy (1987–90) and Frank Gehry's Disney Concert Hall in 66 Los Angeles perhaps best express two broad strategies in Western Europe and the United States during the 1980s. As a result of Allied bombing raids during World War II, all that remained of the Carlo Felice Theater

65 Aldo Rossi, Carlo Felice Theater, Genoa, Italy, 1987–90.

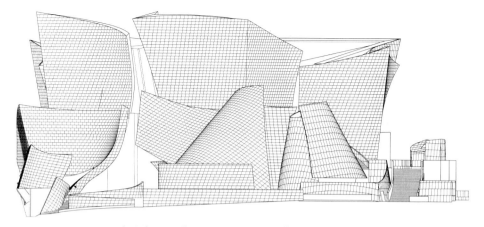

66 Frank Gehry, Walt Disney Concert Hall, Los Angeles, California, begun 1989: elevation plot.

(originally built in 1828) was some Doric columns and the side portico. After winning a limited competition in 1983, Rossi took the damaged remnants as the basis for his design, restoring them to their original appearance and function within the urban setting. Instead of a simple reconstruction, however, Rossi's design aimed to reveal the complex interplay of city and theater, reality and representation, in both the interior and the exterior. To the two main entrances facing on two piazzas, Rossi added a third leading to the 19th-century shopping arcade, the Galleria Mazzini, thus fixing the theater as the center of public and commercial activity in the heart of Genoa. Once in the theater, Rossi turned the tables and replaced what had been a sumptuous retreat from the city with a re-created cityscape, proscenium and lateral walls repeating typical Genoese elevations with marble revetments, shuttered windows, and marble and pearwood balconies, reminding the audience of the link between city and theater, civic activity and spectacle.

66   Gehry's Disney Concert Hall (begun 1989) eschews any references to classicism, or for that matter to anything but Gehry's other designs. It is to perch atop windswept Bunker Hill, an area razed of its Victorian housing by zealous urban renewal advocates during the 1950s. Alone of the invited competitors, Gehry proposed a complex without aspirations to monumentality, diagonally sited with a generous public plaza bridging the gap that separates adjacent buildings, the Chandler Pavilion, the Department of Justice, and the Department of Water and Power. Gehry's trademark sculptural forms, ranging from ziggurat to ramp, crisply

molded in limestone through precise computer calculations, were intended to distinguish the structure from its 1960s era neighbors, perhaps most effectively in the vast glazed foyer and reception hall, with the roof soaring like a bird on the wing from the plaza. In this way, Gehry sought to make the Disney Hall, in his words, "the city's living room." The complex array of forms, held tightly together by adroitly placed ramps and platforms, also testify to Gehry's rejection of traditional architectural forms in favor of something more personal and poetic. Unfortunately, the precision cutting of the stone turned out to be impossible to achieve with Gehry's curved forms, or only at more than double the original cost estimate. As of this writing, construction has been halted and no firm plans to continue have been announced.

After the urban uprisings of 1992, Los Angeles' living room acquired a different configuration when sponsors decided to make the concert hall an enclosed precinct with extensive surveillance like so many other purportedly public spaces in the city. Gehry had already designed one of these public fortresses in Hollywood, the Samuel Goldwyn Library 67 (1986), a forbiddingly closed building with spacious and inviting interiors, that foregrounds such low-technology security measures as high walls, enormous gates and graffiti-proof finishes instead of adopting discreet, high-technology security, as the critic Mike Davis has trenchantly observed. The Disney Hall will have few of the forbidding accoutrements 66

67 Frank Gehry, Samuel Goldwyn Library, Hollywood, California, 1986.

of the library, but it will be barricaded against possible urban unrest in deference to middle-class paranoia. Whatever its other merits—such as the sculpted mass of its sensuously curved limestone surfaces in striking contrast to the skyscraper boxes of Los Angeles, and the addition of an altogether unexpected richness to this otherwise desolate site in a sea of concrete, asphalt, and depressingly mediocre buildings—its defensive character seriously qualifies its success as an urban public building.

PUBLIC SPACE: AN EPILOGUE

Perhaps the issues concerning public space coalesce most neatly in Aldo Rossi's monument to former President Sandro Pertini, erected on the Via Croce Rossa in Milan in 1990. It immediately drew attention to a series of questions regarding who owns the city, who defines its public realms, and how different groups define the notion of the public. In its own modest fashion, the monument crystallized the issues in the battle being waged among conflicting interests for control of cities, and the even more ominous drive to turn cities into centers of undiluted consumption. During the 1960s, the Metropolitana Milanese (MM), the subway system, commissioned a series of interventions in the heart of Milan as part of a program to reconfigure and restore urban spaces that for years had been appropriated as subway construction sites. Twin imperatives of the program included embellishing degraded urban sites and taking advantage of the subway by discouraging automobiles in the center.

Via Croce Rossa sits at the intersection of four major thoroughfares near the antique perimeter of the city. One of the streets, Via Borgonuovo, began as the site of aristocratic palaces during the Baroque period, and with Via Montenapoleone provided grand classical panoramas during the 19th century. They remained upper-class strongholds in the 20th century, with Via Montenapoleone internationally known as the most exclusive, chic and expensive shopping street in Italy.

In designing the monument, Rossi made two fundamental choices: to treat it as a small urban theater, a theater for everyday life but also for concerts and live productions; and to summon historical memory not by means of artificial re-creation or representation of styles, but with the intelligent use of natural and man-made materials. He designed a simple cubic block 8 meters high and 6 meters square (26/20 feet) set deep in the site near Via Borgonuovo. The grey and pink marble-revetted block is closed on three sides, and the fourth is opened by a broad and steep flight of stairs leading to a viewing platform. Rossi specified a pavement

68

68 Aldo Rossi, monument to Sandro Pertini, Via Croce Rossa, Milan, Italy, 1990.

fabricated of the rose granite squares that had earlier been pulled from Milan's streets for subway construction. The lateral approaches to the monument are marked by rows of six graceful mulberry trees alternating with 6-meter (20-foot) tall light standards, and granite benches in the intercolumniations. At the top, through a bronze-framed rectangular opening, one can peer out at the city and even catch a glimpse of the Duomo a few blocks away.

Milanese traditions pervade each element. The paving, as we saw, was reused. The marble revetment is drawn from the same quarry as that of the Duomo. The mulberry trees, now small but destined to reach 40 or 50 feet (12–15 meters), are a typical, if by now rare, thick-foliaged Lombard tree. The deep green lamp poles, pale rose pavement, green and brown trees, bronze framing, and the grey and pink marble panels set to achieve maximum visual texture together endow the complex with a subtle and rich polychromy. With the benches and stairs, the piazza ideally accommodates activities ranging from casual appointments with friends to reading the newspaper or soaking up sun in the hot summer months. Cars speed by on either side, but in the hectic center city the piazza is an oasis of calm and a perfect termination for Via Montenapoleone, where public seating is non-existent yet is sorely needed in a district now largely occupied by shops and offices.

The objections to the monument included disagreement with the proportions (from architects), grumbles that it was non-representational (politicians), and assertions that it was ugly (local merchants)—even though in preceding years the merchants never complained about the increasingly polluted, congested, noisy traffic interchange at Via Croce Rossa, certainly ugly by anyone's definition. Nor had they complained during the five years when the site was an even noisier, dirtier construction yard. In fact, only when a solution which could be described as aesthetic was proposed did opinions emerge from all quarters. Aesthetic objects invite aesthetic judgments, judgments which in the end are based on taste patterns formed by a wide range of cultural and social forces. These judgments of taste, or personal preference, often oppose that which differs from the familiar, and are rarely rendered against things classified as purely situational, such as the chaos of the old Via Croce Rossa. If one followed the merchants' logic, one could even argue that worse aesthetic damage inflicted on Milan and this area in particular derives precisely from the signs and storefronts of these and other commercial establishments.

But the merchants also based their opposition on a second point: the stairs and benches, otherwise quite rare in this part of the city. In order to pause and linger in Milan's upscale Manzoni zone, one must spend money in a bar, restaurant, or shop. Such a view implicitly contracts the field of legitimate users of the city to a very few with fat bank accounts. Rossi's stairs and benches are free and open to all, regardless of economic standing. The merchants feared this would invite people to loiter without spending money. Free seating might also encourage another unwelcome group—drug users, a highly visible subculture in Italy, particularly at night in public spaces with seating. The merchants did not propose confronting the structural or social causes of drug use, but rather acted to neutralize it, preferably by banishment, thereby neutralizing its impact on the privileged few who stay in hotels or shop there.

The implicit assumption in the merchants' arguments was that urban public spaces are either simply utilitarian or neutral "green spaces." Not surprisingly, they proposed three trees, a fountain, but no seating. Such a proposal embodies a political view of the city in which social space is totally dedicated to specific, limited functions, a view at variance with what Rossi's monument so clearly offers. United by materials (Candoglia marble), by inviting public stairs and colonnades (though Rossi's are exterior and alternate nature and artifice), and by elevated viewing platforms for panoramic vistas of the city, the Duomo and the monument are most deeply, most fundamentally bound by their generous political views of the uses of urban spaces.

The attitudes about public space voiced in relation to the monument spring in part from changes Italy has undergone over the past two decades, especially as Asian, Polish and North African immigrants have entered the country despite high rates of under- and unemployment. Newspapers regularly report on roving gangs of youths severely beating Africans, and groups of Africans are routinely rousted from abandoned factories or provisional encampments. When cities attempt to set aside housing for immigrants, angry residents often quell the efforts through violent protest. The same desire for spatial segregation resonates within Italian society, where bourgeois urbanites and the remnants of Italy's aristocracy lament the public transportation systems that have brought Italians living on the periphery of major cities, generally lower income groups, into the centers.

Immigrants receive similar treatment in the United States, Britain, Germany, and most other so-called First World countries. But the sharp differentiation that marks the late capitalist city is as characteristic of cities in Brazil as in Britain, India as in Italy. Massive influxes of international capital in countries where major industries have recently been privatized, such as Argentina, Mexico, and Brazil, have helped to erode rural economies further and to push larger numbers of people into cities, where the battle for control of public space is being ferociously waged.

The public buildings designed by architects and described here tend to be connected to elite institutions, to which the social groups with the most money restrict access in one way or another, as perhaps most unreservedly conveyed in the Goldwyn Library. Architects certainly are not the cause of this situation, but they are ensnared in it.

Urban space as it has been conceptualized in the post-Enlightenment West, that is, places where diverse classes and individuals freely mingle, without overt restraint or control, and where political discussions could take place, depended on the strategic exclusion of women, workers, the poor or the non-citizen. The spatial expressions of the public sphere, such as the Italian piazza and the Greek agora, represent the standard architectural conception of public space. However remote this vision actually is, it is at risk of becoming an aspiration which has been abandoned, even if the ideal still characterizes many architectural projects. What we might call public spaces are increasingly left to the poor and the marginalized, conceptualized as uncontrolled and potentially dangerous areas, while an elite and segregated type of public space has taken shape for other, more privileged classes.

CHAPTER TWO

Domestic Space

The staple projects of small architectural firms in most Western countries are for housing of some type. Even when an office expands to larger, more prestigious assignments, housing often remains the mainstay of the practice. Such was the case for Robert Venturi, who initiated his career with the Vanna Venturi House (with John Short, 1962). Even though he graduated nearly thirty years later to the Sainsbury Wing of the National Gallery in London (with Denise Scott Brown), his office continued to work in residential design. Bound up as it is with the dominance of fashion, status, and image of wealthy patrons, the architect-designed single-family house also provides a ready index of developments in styles since 1970. At the same time, few of the single family houses examined in this chapter deliberately reflect changes in demographic patterns—the growing number of nontraditional families, single individuals, single-parent homes, the elderly living alone or in groups, older children living with parents or the reverse—not to mention pressing issues such as energy costs, toxic materials, and the depletion of natural resources.

Discussions about housing that flourished in architectural circles in the United States and Western Europe through the 1980s addressed almost exclusively formal matters, accurately reflecting the chief concerns of designers, and they largely ignored issues in other countries. Although many architects insist that they are "working on the language of architecture" in their residential projects, the significance of such narrow concerns pales beside the surfeit of problems involved in housing when it is understood as something more than the design of singular objects. In this chapter I have divided housing into three categories. The first section addresses one of the mega-residential projects of the 1980s, the IBA in Berlin. This is followed by a discussion of the single-family house designed largely by prestigious Western firms. Finally I will consider multi-family and alternative housing.

Most of the fresh, thoughtful, and provocative designs I will discuss entail some reconceptualization of the role of the architect from the solitary artist to one member of a large team involved in housing as part of a larger attack on poor living conditions. Perhaps the contrast between the two strategies became most apparent in the two-pronged large-scale enterprise in West Berlin, the IBA.

IBA (INTERNATIONALE BAUAUSTELLUNG), BERLIN

With the goals of refurbishing old and providing new housing, as well as improving depressed areas of Berlin, the IBA or International Building Exhibition initiated in 1977 set out to weave together public funds, public interest, private development, and some of the most prominent architects in the world in order to realize an ambitious, city-wide building and rehabilitation program, announced at its inception as a permanent exhibition as well as a patrimony of new housing. The IBA was but the most recent of multi-purpose building exhibitions in Germany spanning nearly a century, from the Darmstadt artists' colony (1899) to the Berlin Interbau (1957), of which the best-known was surely the Weissenhofsiedlung in Stuttgart (1927), organized by Mies van der Rohe as a display of the best housing designs offered by international modern architects. In both the Stuttgart and Berlin exhibitions, well-known young architects with similar aesthetic preferences designed apartments destined to remain permanent additions to the city's architectural and housing patrimony.

The initial program for the IBA envisioned carrying on in much the same vein, but in 1977 Josef Paul Kleihues and Wolf Jobst Siedler successfully intervened to redirect the proposed exhibition to different objectives. First, they argued that the buildings should be integrated into the existing city rather than set apart in a suburban park as those in the earlier exhibitions had been: the IBA should engage Berlin's historic fabric, its social problems, and the economic exigencies of depressed areas through a combination of *Neubau* (new building) and *Altbau* (rehabilitation). In addition to the individual buildings, then, the IBA from the outset was envisioned as a complex urban project. Although international architectural magazines published the new buildings, they largely ignored such Altbau projects as garages, nursery schools, and the reconfiguration of unused factories into youth centers, sports facilities, trade school, recreation and education facilities for the deaf and speech-impaired, cultural centers, and old age homes, as well as the restructuring of streets, blocks, and parks. These were not just additions to the IBA, but essential elements of the whole program without which the individual buildings and projects would be meaningless. In short, IBA organizers envisioned not a series of spectacular monuments which also happened to be social housing, but a fabric of new and old buildings, functional transformations, and reconceptualized, redefined and reorganized street networks.

Politicians and designers did not develop the IBA in a vacuum: the impulse came from the residents of Berlin. Tired of living in the shadow of hulks and vacant lots left behind from World War II bombings (which obliterated 50 per cent of the housing stock) and the even more disruptive Wall, not to mention suffering severe housing shortages, residents began to demand in the early 1970s that politicians do something about their devastated city. With slogans such as "rescue the ruined city," "the inner city as a dwelling place," and "democracy as construction manager," they urged that the urban fabric become a political priority and that new housing be erected without tearing down what remained of the old. They also decisively rejected the skyscraper as a housing solution.

These positions only partly concerned issues of architectural design. A severe housing shortage had prompted the 1957 Interbau exhibition, in which Modernist towers and slabs set apart in green areas on the urban periphery were to rehouse residents from the inner city. In turn, older dwellings in the central area were to be torn down to make land available for office development and green spaces. But before city officials could complete their plans, residents took matters into their own hands and occupied old buildings, even in the absence of such basic amenities as toilets. Several things made these structures desirable to students and Turkish immigrants: low rents, locations in proximity to low-wage employment opportunities, and centrality, which meant cultural, transportation and social facilities within easy walking distance. By the same token, several things made the squatters undesirable to city officials. They were either poor, students, or foreign minorities, hardly the ideal residents for a new urban center in the eyes of bourgeois politicians, and hence politically expendable. The battles between squatters and Berlin police made international news during the 1970s, and without the intervention of a second, more "respectable" social group—preservationists bent on rescuing what little remained of traditional Berlin housing stock and buildings—the outcome of the battle could well have been different.

After passing the bill authorizing the IBA, the Berlin Senate appointed Kleihues director of the Neubau section, and Hardt Waltherr Hamer director of the Altbau, each supplemented by a board composed of architects, politicians and planners serving as advisors on the development of designated sites but without development powers of its own. Along with the broad ambitions for the IBA went the involvement of a significantly larger part of the city. The scope as originally outlined was breathtaking. Initially they planned for 9,000 new or restored living units to be completed by 1987 (to coincide with the city's 750th anniversary). Within a few years the number was revised downward to 6,000, but even that

Tegeler Hafen

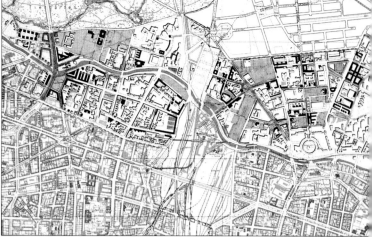

Prager Platz   South Tiergarten   Potdamer Platz   South Friedrichstadt

optimistic figure remained a distant goal in 1987, the official conclusion of the IBA. Four different parts of the city were singled out as sites for Neubau development, from suburban Tegel to the bombed-out districts of South Tiergarten, each with its own set of problems. Two more areas, Luisenstadt and Kreuzberg SO 36, were selected to undergo rehabilitation under the Altbau program.

From the beginning, as Kleihues later observed, the organizers conceived of Berlin as a crippled city in need of repair, just as they believed their task included rejecting the insensitive architecture of apartment buildings erected during the 1960s and 1970s. The need to replace lost housing stock rapidly and retain existing infrastructures drove much of the building in Cold War Berlin. But after the Interbau exhibition of 1957 and with the rising economic fortunes of West Germany, more and more housing clustered on the urban periphery. The oil crisis of 1973 and the subsequent economic downturn led Berliners to rethink their dependence on the automobile and the standard scheme of zoning residences on the outskirts of the city and workplaces in the center. For Kleihues, the apolitical blandness of building in postwar Berlin and the emphasis on the automobile for urban transportation were two of the chief causes of the city's degradation. Hence the IBA needed to confront and, he hoped, resolve both. Kleihues also recognized that the principles of modern architecture had come under attack since the mid-1960s. Adopting a different perspective on the city and on the architecture being elaborated by a new generation of architects, the IBA promised to be an ideal laboratory in which to confront Berlin's all too real urban problems with new ideas.

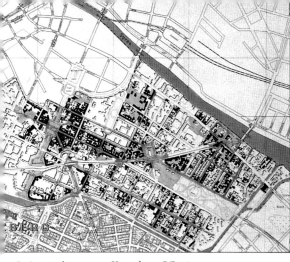

69 Plan showing
IBA sites, Berlin,
Germany, 1977–87
and after.

Luisenstadt   Kreuzberg SO 36

In the early 1970s, Kleihues found provocative insights in the urban and architectural theories of Robert Venturi and Aldo Rossi, both of whom repudiated key tenets of the Modern Movement regarding cities and their architecture. Rossi in particular urged that the traditional city not be destroyed in order to make way for office towers in the park, nor should residents be transferred from urban areas to suburban towers. Rather, new buildings which reflected an understanding of the city's history and of how people live today should be stitched thoughtfully into the existing fabric, with positive architectural and urbanistic results. In the early planning phase, Kleihues summoned a diverse group of architects and historians to confer on the specific character of Berlin's urban problems: Rossi, Carlo Aymonino, James Stirling, Kurt Forster and Wolfgang Pehnt, among others. From these consultations and those with the Berlin Senate came the idea of a series of competitions, some invited, some limited, and some open, for different sites in the Neubau areas, to open up the IBA not just to one design philosophy but to the full range of ideas and approaches current in architecture in the late 1970s and the 1980s.

The challenge to the designers was daunting. The Wall cut off the western suburbs from much of the traditional center, leaving West Berlin with fragments of the old imperial urban core but without a full-scale center of its own. Rather than seeking an artificial new one, key provisions of the IBA mandated that design solutions emphasize the polycentric character of West Berlin and the distinctive nature of its different sections. Tegel's densely wooded suburban atmosphere, with its lake and old harbor, demanded entirely different solutions from those called for by South Tiergarten, the former diplomatic quarter, with chunks of vacant land

111

left behind after bombing and subsequent unrealized transportation schemes. Two Neubau zones—South Tiergarten and South Friedrich-stadt—and two Altbau zones—Luisenstadt and SO 36 in Krenzberg—abutted the Wall. That such a wide strip of land was available for rehabilitation and repair is a telling index of the character of some of the oldest parts of the city following World War II bombings, and the effect of the erection of the Wall in 1961.

Neubau

Since social housing was the chief imperative in the Neubau districts, the IBA's guidelines called for architects to design buildings in sympathy with the area's history and tradition, specifically to make historical conti-nuity a factor. Certain models were not desirable: the anonymous towers of Modernist inspiration and the notorious *Mietskasernen* (tenement blocks, literally rental barracks) of the late 19th century were both rejected, even though the decision to retain the existing street pattern heavily conditioned the possible options for new solutions. Inviting architects to be sympathetic to Berlin's traditions also opened problems, for Berlin's planning history combined two traditions. One was based on artistic principles, with picturesque curving streets, important buildings as focal points, emphasis on a small scale, mixture of uses, clear distinc-tions between public, semi-public and private spheres, and irregularity in buildings without undue discontinuity in scale or design. A second model was developed later in the 19th century, based upon notions of rationality and efficiency and characterized by separation of land uses, maximization of built areas, higher densities, and vast scales in buildings. By the mid-20th century, this rational model included an aesthetic based upon industrialization which incorporated concrete, steel, and extensive use of glass in free-standing high-rise structures set in green spaces rather than the continuous street frontage of the earlier model.

For architects who won competitions for IBA sites, confronting these traditions was only one of the problems. A more serious one came from the IBA's lack of power. The transfer of power from the liberal SPD-dominated Senate to a conservative majority midway through the IBA's lifespan aggravated already nearly insurmountable difficulties. As an advi-sory body, the IBA lacked control over finances, which remained in the hands of developers, bankers, and contractors. Additionally, as Kleihues later remarked, the IBA had far fewer conflicts with clients than with local administrations and the Senate building department over zoning and building codes. Because providing housing was the primary goal, facilities for other uses were often eliminated during the construction

70 Gustav Peichl, phosphate elimination plant, Tegeler Hafen, Berlin, 1980–84.

phase in order to save money or to make more dwelling units available. This often meant that the mixed use community remained a dream, apartment blocks went up without some of the desired ancillary services, and the initial demand for a return to an urban core hospitable to residential use did not come to fruition.

As of now, none of the Neubau areas has been fully realized as originally planned. This is also true of the two zones remote from the areas adjacent to the Wall, Tegel and Prager Platz, although some components of the Tegel scheme have been completed or are under construction. Tegel should remain rural, IBA organizers maintained. Even though it is largely a wealthy residential area, its woods and lakes provide recreation for the entire city. The IBA planned two ventures, the transformation of the harbor on the lake (Tegeler Hafen) into a residential, cultural and leisure complex designed by Charles Moore of Moore, Ruble, Yudell, and a phosphate elimination plant on the north canal to purify the unhealthy 70 waters of the lake, designed by the Austrian architect Gustav Peichl.

The second area scheduled for revision distinct from the main areas along the borders of the Wall is at Prager Platz in Schöneberg, a 19th-century square virtually leveled first by bombs and then by traffic planners in the 1950s. A circle of green grass set in an oval space with five streets radiating out, Prager Platz was once surrounded by the decorative facades of apartment buildings, with colorful shops and ample public life on the streets below. The IBA proposed to regenerate the area by rebuilding the wall of buildings, and three architects—Rob Krier, Carlo Aymonino and Gottfried Böhm—won competitions. Their specific charge was to create a continuous wall of differentiated facades and a mix of commercial and residential areas, although this has yet to be completed.

Known as the Diplomats' Quarter before World War II and the most devastated of all the IBA areas, the Southern Tiergarten was originally scheduled to be the site of an Interbau-type exhibition before the IBA was established. In the 1960s the city decided to make the northern section of the city a cultural forum for residents of both East and West Berlin, a replica of the Museum Island in the East, with Hans Scharoun's Philharmonie the first of the facilities to be built. But the intrusion of the Wall left the area a no-man's-land on the city's edge. In 1984 Austrian architect Hans Hollein proposed to link the isolated monuments of the Philharmonie, the New National Gallery by Mies van der Rohe, the National Library and the Museum of Music, both by Scharoun, the Arts and Crafts Museum by Rolf Gutbrod, and the new, IBA-sponsored Wissenschaftscentrum (academic center) by James Stirling, Michael Wilford and Associates in a giant "Kulturforum," an enormous piazza terminated at one end by the New National Gallery and flanked by a 19th-century church, St. Matthew's, and a branch of the Landwehrkanal. Hollein's proposal remains on the drawing board, but one large, four-wing apartment building with three courts opening to the west was completed by Kurt Ackermann & Partners to the west of the gallery.

Wedged between this complex, the Landwehrkanal and the gallery, the Wissenschaftscentrum (1979-87) was finally completed, drawing together three institutes (Management, Comparative Social Studies, and Ecology), plus an additional two added during the construction phase, on the same site in order to facilitate interaction among them. Stirling and Wilford won this competition (on the heels of the widely praised Staatsgalerie extension in Stuttgart) with a design incorporating the late 19th-century facade of August Busse's Reichsversicherungsamt. In keeping with their historicist leanings and deploying a design strategy of decomposition and collage, they developed a ground plan with a distinctly antique character, comprising elements based on simple geometric configurations that recall an ancient theater, a basilica, a campanile, and a stoa. These distinct units enclose a green interior courtyard shaped to follow the orientation of the institutes. Such a plan allowed the architects to differentiate functional areas such as laboratories, conference rooms, and office space, and

71 James Stirling, Michael Wilford and Associates, Wissenschaftscentrum, South Tiergarten, Berlin, 1979–87.

to signal differentiation in the forms themselves, thereby avoiding the potential monotony of the standard office building with a uniform skin and modular spaces within. Given this strategy, it is no surprise that the elevations, with alternate banding of blue and pink stone revetments, excited polemics. The long, four-story north elevation is the most controversial, for despite rejecting the monotony of the standard office block, Stirling and Wilford simply proposed another kind of monotony, that of rows of windows framed by inverted, U-shaped sandstone casements 40 centimeters (about 16 inches) deep. Although tying together otherwise disparate structures, the primary reason for the repetition of the frames was to avoid complications during construction. The heaviness of the elevations is quite in keeping with neighboring buildings, and the frames at times provide a strong articulation, a handsome chiaroscuro, on this long facade. From inside, the deep casements give a remarkably satisfying illusion of the thick walls typical of masonry structures, making the interiors altogether consistent with the ponderous exterior.

72, 73 Aldo Rossi,
apartment building,
Rauchstrasse, South
Tiergarten, Berlin,
1983–84: view and plan.

The dozens of projects elsewhere in South Tiergarten include apartments by Vittorio Gregotti, O. M. Ungers, Antoine Grumbach, Heinz Hilmer and Christoph Sattler, Heinrich and Inken Baller and others; the reconstruction of the Graf-Spee Bridge by Klaus Theo Brenner and Benedict Tonon; landscape architecture at Magdeburger Platz, Tiergartenstrasse, Reichpietschufer and elsewhere by Cornelia Müller, Elmar Knippschild, and Jan Wehberg; and proposals for nursery schools by

Jasper Halfmann and Klaus Zillich, and by Reinhard Schmock and Gunther Schöneweiss.

Another section of the IBA program is the Rauchstrasse development, a series of housing enterprises for rental and owner-occupied units. Master-planned by Rob Krier, the project is anchored by Aldo Rossi's apartment complex on the western end which faces an existing building (the former Norwegian Embassy) from which Rossi picked up the L-configuration of his building's footprint. Other than parts of Rob Krier's complex on the eastern edge of the site, the formal entrance to the entire project, only Rossi's building has brick revetment. For Rossi, Berlin's traditional architecture was characterized by its stone and unplastered brick elevations and simple, block-like shapes, and his response to the city through the careful adaptation of its traditional building materials marked a new high in the IBA projects, setting an example picked up by Vittorio Gregotti, among others. 72, 73

Rossi's building consists of thirty flats distributed on five floors. From inside and outside, the staircase tower, topped by an octagonal cupola, forms the visual and functional center. Red brick and stringcourses of yellow ceramic tile provide unifying elements. The apartments themselves range from two to six rooms, deftly planned to allow maximum privacy, something often missing in social housing. Two-thirds of the units have only one adjacent neighbor, the terraces do not abut, and most units have a large central space giving access to the rest of the rooms and serving as a buffer zone. Rossi conceived this space as an enlargement of the kitchen, reflecting his own belief that the kitchen is the center of the house.

Although neither the materials nor the aesthetic were typical of his designs, Rossi adapted his ideals to the demands of the IBA, incorporating features familiar from his projects in Italy but reassembled with new elements and building traditions redolent of the architectural landscape of Berlin. One of the chief worries of German architects at the launching of the IBA was that foreign architects would simply reproduce their own work with only marginal sensitivity to Berlin—and in fact, many did. But in some cases, such as Rossi's apartment blocks, non-German architects reinterpreted and successfully merged local traditions with those from elsewhere, a historically potent means of enriching architectural languages and urban environments.

In any case, the IBA project proved to be remarkably open to divergent styles. Organizers extended equal hospitality to Peter Eisenman's snazzily gridded apartment house and the far more sedate designs of Rob Krier. 76

Another group of apartments lies next to the Landwehrkanal to the southwest of the Stirling and Wilford Wissenschaftscentrum. The IBA collaborated on a competition for the five structures with the Ministry of Urban Planning in order to explore energy-saving design possibilities. Each of the Lutzowufer buildings offers a different approach to energy conservation, relying in various degrees on passive approaches achieved through selection of materials, construction technology and disposition of plans, and on active systems, including such technologies for exploiting energy as solar collectors. With the canal on one side and a common garden on the other, the buildings enjoy an extremely favorable location. Common height, square bases and axial entrances unite them with a series of two-story units on the ground level, linking all into one differentiated but harmonious group. The energy concerns were met throughout despite the variety in treatment of elevations. The unit by Bernd Faskel and Vladimir Nikolic provides fenestrated winter gardens on all four corners the full height of the building, so that each unit enjoys two large enclosed terraces, with living zones facing the canal (south) and sleeping areas toward the garden (north). Such devices as the brick revetment on the canal elevation and the paneled extrusions on the lateral elevations with fenestration slits along the sides further enhance the thermal effectiveness of the design.

The commercial heart of prewar Berlin, South Friedrichstadt, laid out with Baroque urban spaces in the early 18th century, was a center of National Socialist activity during the 1930s. Perhaps the most thoroughly devastated of all of the designated IBA areas, it also suffered a series of incoherent and confusing reconstruction attempts in the early Cold War period. Nonetheless, much of the former street network remained, and an early decision was taken to retain it (perhaps in the prescient hope of the eventual reunification of the two cities) instead of redirecting the streets toward the new center of Berlin around the Kurfürstendamm. The IBA chose to restore the street dimensions and even to retain the prewar scale of traditional blocks of housing along the major boulevards—that is, no high-rise construction, with the exception of Pietro Derossi's flats on Wilhelmstrasse.

With the appropriate blend of commercial, residential and manufacturing, IBA planners hoped to have South Friedrichstadt become a working-class district. Much of the Neubau construction was concentrated here, with nearly one hundred different architects or teams of architects presenting proposals. The firms eventually selected to build included some of the most internationally recognized names of the 1980s: Herman Hertzberger, Aldo Rossi, Stirling and Wilford, Eisenman/Robertson, Raimund Abraham, John Hejduk, Zaha Hadid, and Gino Valle. Not surprisingly, this area received the most press. Here too some of the directions in architectural languages—at least as far as exterior elevations are concerned—can be traced. In his apartment house on Friedrichstrasse, for example, Abraham prominently displayed both tectonic structure and circulation devices on the street elevation, and as a consequence the facade is alive with deep shadows and bold reliefs. Hejduk's contribution consists of two wings surrounding a court, into which he inserted a fourteen-story tower for artists' ateliers. Here the apartment plans differ from those commonly found in many of the IBA projects. With artists' needs in mind, Hejduk devised a large open central space and pushed kitchens, bathrooms, and stairs to the exterior. Tenants had some opportunity to partition off these central spaces as needed. Herman Hertzberger ensured that residents would have even greater opportunities to shape their apartments in his Lindenstrasse 74 housing by turning the project over to them well before completion. He also reworked many of the ideas from his earlier buildings about common staircases and sitting areas, and gradations of public and private spaces to permit maximum security and maximum privacy, in a handsome complex that rounds the corner behind a church on Lindenstrasse and Markgrafenstrasse.

Between two historic buildings near Checkpoint Charlie on Fried- 75 richstrasse, Elia Zenghelis and Matthias Sauerbruch of OMA (Office for Metropolitan Architecture) inserted an aggressively Modernist apartment house with vaguely Constructivist overtones. OMA flatly refused to restore the site to its earlier condition. While respecting the scale and the line of the street, they ruptured the line of stringcourses and the pattern of 19th-century detailing on the neighboring buildings with strips of ribbon windows on the residential floors and a series of diverse

74 Herman Hertzberger, apartment building, Lindenstrasse, South Friedrichstadt, Berlin, 1984-86.

75 Elia Zenghelis and
Matthias Sauerbruch (OMA),
Block 4, Friedrichstrasse,
South Friedrichstadt, Berlin,
1985–89.

76 Eisenman/Robertson,
Block 5, Friedrichstrasse/
Kochstrasse, South
Friedrichstadt, Berlin, 1981–86.

volumes—round, square, parallelogram—on the ground level as pavilions for didactic material on the East-West frontier (now obsolete) and a bus station waiting room. Topping it all on the attic level, an asymmetrical cornice projects out over the street far more boldly than the heavy cornices of the adjoining buildings.

Peter Eisenman's building at the corner of Friedrichstrasse and Kochstrasse reveals his approach to interpreting the history of the site in order to advance personal design strategies. Eisenman decided to undertake a conceptual "excavation," superimposing maps of varying degrees of abstraction in order to develop a sequence of layers for the design. Two grids—the contemporary street and the Mercator Grid—collide on the elevation in an attempt to link the building both to the specific site and to its global position. (The fenestration pattern of one of the adjacent buildings offers a faint link to Eisenman's bustling chromatic conjunction of grids.) Whether the residents or neighbors found much significance in this gesture is open to question. In any case, the scheme left behind some

76

77, 78 Zaha Hadid, with Michael Wolfson, David Gommersall, Piers Smerin, David Winslow and Paivi Jaaskelainen, apartment and commercial building, Stresemannstrasse, Kreuzberg, Berlin, 1987–94: second-floor plan and view.

oddly shaped rooms, no doubt inconvenient for anything but a ready source of conversation. Animated neither by the energy efficiency of the Lutzowufer projects nor the imaginativeness of Rossi's Tiergarten apartments, the plans of individual units here are surprisingly conventional. With this project, Eisenman made his earliest, hesitant sally—a little tinkering with the facade and the awkward plans of the apartments—into what became the architectural fashion of the 1980s, Deconstruction.

77, 78 Zaha Hadid's Kreuzberg apartment and commercial block (1994), one of the few Deconstructivist designs to be erected, confirmed the IBA's willingness to experiment with form. Apart from the corner tower, Hadid's project remained within the broad scale and height guidelines for low-cost housing, but rejected any accommodation to existing typologies, building traditions and materials. Most of the structure simply repeats the standard single-loaded exterior corridor apartment block, with the addition of yellow and red elements on the interior of the site that demark the end of one group of apartment units and the staircase. At the end of the three-story block, Hadid appended an eight-story wedge that juts out like the prow of a ship—its sheet metal cladding only heightening the parallel. Nothing else in the design matches the bold, metallic thrust of the tower. Within the dwelling units, an occasional slanted wall refers to this massive aggressive form and feebly modifies the otherwise routine apartments.

Altbau

In many respects, the rehabilitation and selective additions in the Altbau were the most successful, because when the projects were completed, damaged and decaying areas had gained renewed vitality without massive displacement of people or demolition of buildings. In a century where the most violent peacetime destruction of living and working environments has gone hand in hand with ambitious megaprojects indifferent to the needs of those with modest incomes, this is no small accomplishment. Workplaces, childcare centers and housing for the elderly were stitched into existing buildings, and tenants often helped design and build their own housing. Architects played a different role in these projects from the one they played in the Neubau, a role which demanded different attitudes about the client as well as the construction itself. It is no accident that few firms crossed over from Neubau to Altbau, where clients became collaborators and designers, architects became partners. Few of the international stars here or elsewhere demonstrate much interest in reconceptualizing the role of the architect. (Among notable earlier exceptions to this rule are Renzo Piano, with his scheme for partial self-design and build projects for the Corciano suburb of Perugia, of 1983.) In one of several infill projects on Admiralstrasse, the Wohnregal, architects Nylund/Puttfarken/Stürzebecher developed a basic reinforced concrete frame and floor slabs, and then devised a timber construction system so that untrained residents could erect their own facades, elevations, partitions and balconies according to personal needs and preferences. Clearly such a system did not yield the symmetrical or balanced elevations standard in most architect-designed buildings, so they overlaid the elevation with a metal grid, both as an organizing device and as an armature for flower boxes. Compared to Eisenman/Robertson's over-lapping grids a few blocks away, this one appears to be a scaffolding, lending the building an arrestingly provisional aura, as if construction were ongoing rather than already terminated.

Several more self-built cooperative projects were completed on Admiralstrasse, with architects including Berg/Christian, Dorr/Jendrzey and

79 Nylund/Puttfarken/
Stürzebecher, Wohnregal
infill project, Admiralstrasse,
Luisenstadt, Berlin, 1986.

Kaufmann + Partner assisting individuals and families with rehabilitations or infill units. In other projects involving rehabilitation, restructuring and revision, architects in the Altbau program worked with tenants and representatives of tenant groups in order to insure that urban and design planning went hand in hand with social planning. Wilhelm Holzbauer's handsome infill project in Luisenstadt in Block 88 on Mariannenstrasse was accomplished with regular tenant participation, as was the restructuring of the neighboring Block 79. The urban fabrics in Kreuzberg and Luisenstadt date mostly from the late 19th century, and consisted originally of perimeter blocks in whose large internal courtyards factories and other buildings were gradually added. This dense urban tissue offended not only Modernist architects but politicians in the Cold War period, and so even though many blocks such as Block 88 survived World War II, when the IBA began only parts of the old perimeter building had eluded the zealous slum clearance programs of the 1960s. The corner section added by Holzbauer conserved the variety of Kreuzberg courts as well as some of the traditional brickwork, and offered a wide variety of dwelling types and sizes, each with a private garden, terrace or balcony, facing into the interior green courtyard.

80 Axel Volkmann/IBA Berlin, Block 79, Mariannenstrasse, Luisenstadt, Berlin, 1986.

81 Wilhelm Holzbauer, Block 88, Mariannenstrasse, Luisenstadt, Berlin, 1985.

The badly decayed Block 79 (dating from 1884) contained many flats 80
and even a former bronze factory squeezed between a rabbit warren of
courts in the interior. Unusually, the entire perimeter block of four- to
six-story units remained intact, although many of the apartments had
been sliced up and converted to smaller flats during the 1930s. IBA
plans called for modernizing and enlarging the flats, adding two day care
centers and a women's center, providing gardens and green spaces, and

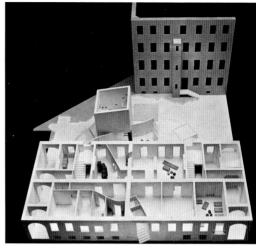

83 Werkfabrik, day care center, Oppelner Strasse, Kreuzberg SO 36, Berlin, 1983–86.

82 *left* Otto Steidle with Siegward Geiger, home for the elderly, Köpenicker Strasse, Kreuzberg SO 36, Berlin, 1985: glazed area between old and new buildings.

80   converting a former garage into studios and workshops. Over 600 flats were rehabilitated, and more than a dozen architectural firms worked on various parts of the block. In such a setting and with the strict set of demands negotiated by the residents of Kreuzberg, architects could not yield to aesthetic games. Rather they had to respect the concerns of residents as primary. Indeed, the second and third points on the residents' list of "Twelve Rules of Cautious Urban Renewal" require that designers, residents and storekeepers come to agreement on the scope and character of the renovations, and specifically, that the architectural character of Kreuzberg not be damaged by the interventions.

    Similar deliberations preceded the addition of new buildings or the conversion of others to homes for the elderly, cultural centers or day care

83   facilities. In Werkfabrik's day care center on Oppelner Strasse, the diagonal axis cut through the existing perimeter buildings to a cubical playroom in the courtyard not to fashion an arbitrary Deconstructivist composition but rather to connect the three parts efficiently, as resident consultation mandated, while providing a series of small, child-sized

82   spaces. A home for the elderly by Otto Steidle with Siegward Geiger near the Schlesisches Tor underground station was developed after the

126

future inhabitants rejected an earlier proposal by a developer on the grounds that it was too institutional. Steidle and Geiger combined new buildings, rehabilitation of existing structures, gardens and a glazed common area in layers moving from the older building out to the street line, from private to semi-private to public spaces.

The IBA and Berlin's future

Of the megaprojects examined in this book, the Berlin IBA is undoubtedly the most successful, not least because government sponsorship, resident participation, and the sound German economy helped avoid the economic disasters of Docklands, Fukuoka, and perhaps even Disney. Despite the many successful Altbau and Neubau projects, only a few of which are considered here, the IBA suffered from some glaring shortcomings. Some architects seriously attempted to engage the urban, social and architectural problems of Berlin in their designs, but others produced buildings of indeterminate site and sublime indifference to the city, whatever their compositional merits, more academic exercises than serious urban interventions, such as housing by Vittorio Gregotti in Lutzowstrasse, Oswald Mathias Ungers on Lutzowplatz, and Raimund Abraham on Friedrichstrasse, and some that fortunately remain unbuilt, particularly the singularly unengaged projects by Daniel Libeskind. In these cases, the insistence on choosing only prominent architects for the Neubau vitiated the most compelling principles of the original IBA program.

The greatest weakness of the IBA derived from the structural weakness of the program, which did not permit planners to generate mixed uses. Unfortunately, many of the Neubau buildings remain residential islands in an urban center. Only Kreuzberg, with its combination of light industry, dense housing, nursery schools, shops, restaurants, and commercial structures, enjoys the rich and lively urban texture Kleihues sought for the Neubau sections but ultimately lacked the power to produce.

At least two questions remain open. First, the IBA, with its many types of buildings and widely varying tasks, could have been an ideal opportunity to engage women and other minority architects. Instead, the architects called to participate were overwhelmingly white, European, male, and often international stars. Women typically constitute 50 per cent or more of the residents of most cities, and yet they are rarely called upon to participate in the design and building of their city. Likewise, Berlin's vast minority population participated in Altbau designs only in the roles of residents or consultants. How the IBA enterprise might have been resolved with the full participation of these other groups remains an open question, as in most other megaprojects.

127

The second question concerns the impact of the IBA on future urban development. After the destruction of the Wall and the reunification of the country, the issue of the future of Berlin as an undivided city was opened again. Many Altbau and Neubau enterprises successfully met the challenge of restitching a damaged urban fabric with sensitivity and community participation, sometimes achieving singular urban and architectural results. Will these or even stronger, more considered principles drive future urban projects? Potsdamer Platz offers a case in point. Some of the most important institutions of Nazi Germany were headquartered in this zone—the Air Ministry, the Chancellery, the SS and the Gestapo, and even Hitler's Bunker. Leveled during the war, it was further devastated by the Wall and the adjacent no-man's land. The first major invited competition after reunification, in 1991–94, intended to reconstruct the land around Potsdamer Platz and Leipziger Platz, bridging the area formerly occupied by the Wall. Most of the selected firms were German, but a few others also participated, including Foster Associates, Gregotti Associates, and Daniel Libeskind. The selection of the project occurred after city forums, hearings and congresses sponsored by the Berlin Senate, and when the jury awarded the commission to Munich architects Heinz Hilmer and Christoph Sattler, an uproar ensued, with developers and one jury member arguing for the project by Ungers.

84 The lines of the dispute were clear, and related directly to the lessons of the IBA. The Hilmer and Sattler design envisioned restoring the earlier street lines, limiting building heights to ten to twelve stories, structuring a series of public squares, adding green strips and a rectangular lake leading to the Landwehrkanal, and retaining the Berlin perimeter block building type. The design also regulated the relationship between building volumes and open spaces to ensure good ventilation and ample natural light, and placed shops on the street level, offices above, and apartments at the upper levels. With the experience of successful designs for housing and parks for the IBA in areas near Potsdamer Platz, Hilmer and Sattler understood and absorbed the IBA urban design program, and their project reflected an adherence to IBA principles.

85 Ungers's project, the one supported both by developers and by jury member Rem Koolhaas (who criticized the jury's decision as a "massacre of architectonic imagination" because all "progressive" designs were rejected) embodied an entirely different view of the city. Ungers proposed overlaying the current street system on the vanished Friedrichstadt one in order to generate a system of street junctions and blocks of different sizes. A third overlay, a grid, would indicate points where skyscrapers could be erected. Ungers proposed a dozen massive glazed (preferably

with reflective glass) skyscrapers, more than four times higher than the tallest buildings in the Hilmer and Sattler project, and exactly the kind of solution rejected by the IBA and Berlin's residents in the previous decade. Clearly the developers preferred this scheme not for aesthetic reasons but because it gave them more "bang for the bucks"—more leasable floor space on individual plots of land. Many other designers also proposed skyscrapers, including Laurids Ortner and Manfred Ortner, Hans Kollhoff, and Josef Paul Kleihues. What most of their designs project is a vision of Berlin as the new capital of Germany, center of Europe, and an international metropolis. Evidently, for many, this new stature could only be represented by skyscrapers, so that downtown Berlin would come to look more like downtown Hong Kong, Singapore, or

84 Heinz Hilmer and Christoph Sattler, project for Potsdamer Platz, Berlin, 1991–94.

85 O. M. Ungers, project for Potsdamer Platz, Berlin, 1991–94.

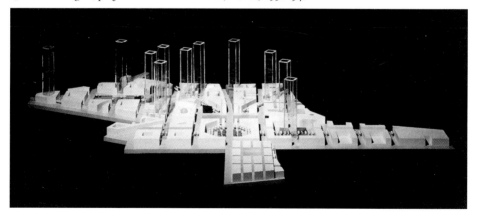

even Orange County in Southern California. Instead, Hilmer and Sattler's proposal insisted on Berlin's own physiognomy and history as the starting point for a successful new urban center. The conflict in values here is profound and apparently irreconcilable: the architect's will to produce a radical urban intervention versus the community's desire to retain some link to the city's history and, especially in this case, not to disfigure the skyline and the streetscape with skyscrapers. For architects schooled as potential stars, autonomous and prone to making bold gestures indifferent to all but the developer's bank balance and publication possibilities, the image to be configured takes precedence over all.

HOUSES FOR THE TRADITIONAL FAMILY

7 Venturi's Vanna Venturi House and his subsequent book, *Complexity and Contradiction in Architecture* (1966), constituted polemical responses to the rejection of historical references common in American architectural culture in the 1960s. Venturi insisted that the adaptation of historical models, appropriately modified to serve contemporary needs, allowed the architect to develop designs richer in experiences, meaning, and moods. That these references were iconographic rather than tectonic became apparent in the thin, flat facade and steeply gabled roof of the house, which Venturi described as an enlarged broken pediment with applied ornament. Classical architecture, including Michelangelo's Porta Pia, inspired him as he worked out the wood molding of the stringcourse and the shallow arch above the concrete lintel of the entrance on an otherwise planar facade. Within, historical allusions abounded as he blended traditional domestic elements into the highly functional program of the late 20th-century house.

Postmodern openness to historical styles also found a receptive audience outside of the United States, particularly in Japan. Among the many architects who seized upon the new Postmodern style, one of the earliest

86, 87 was Takefumi Aida, who produced the Toy Block House (1979). As the name suggests, the house was built up in the manner of children's blocks, with simple elemental forms used both as infill and as structural elements, post and lintel. Although governed by an overall symmetry, the Toy Block House included specific instances of asymmetries at various points to provide variety and visual interest. Like Venturi, Aida drew upon references to traditional exemplars, in this case Japanese houses, in small but precise ways, such as the addition of a ridge-post. Aida's efforts to produce an architecture at once modern and Japanese, that is, neither European nor North American, mirror the conundrums faced by

86, 87 Takefumi Aida, Toy Block House I, Hofu, Yamaguchi Prefecture, Japan, 1979: facade and interior.

architects in other countries. Luis Barragán incorporated Mexican vernacular with Modernist minimalism and a more remote Islamic-Iberian tradition in a body of work that extended over sixty years, most notably in the Egerstrom House at San Cristóbal (1967–68), but also in the Meyer House in Bosque de Las Lomas, Mexico City (1978–81), and his own house in Tacubaya, Mexico City (1947). The theme of seeking housing design at once modern and regional, or local, remained a constant from the late 1970s forward, in the United States and Europe and beyond.Venturi rejected what he saw as a sterile Modernism by promoting mannerism, but architects outside of the United States and Western Europe engaged in local resistance as part of an attempt to valorize their cultural traditions in the face of the onslaught of Western Modernism.

The architectural community hotly debated Postmodernism, with many individuals scorning historicist and eclectic designs. But impassioned debate took place largely in academic meetings, schools, and professional journals. Charles Moore's Burns House in Santa Monica, California (1974), exploited the gradual changes in stylistic preferences with a pastiche of historical styles, including a brightly hued approximation of Spanish rancho. By the mid-1980s, the Postmodern style had caught on with developers and contractors, who popularized it and included it in the portfolio of architectural styles available for everything from speculator-built homes to high-priced architect-designed mansions. In such cities as Los Angeles, houses based on a wide variety of historical models had long been standard, from pseudo-English Tudor mansions to faux French chateaux, but the new Postmodern off-the-peg models were at once more colorful, usually in soft pastel hues, and less literal, with only vaguely classicizing, generic historical references. To be sure, the phenomenon of Postmodernism in most of these houses almost exclusively concerned the simpler problems of facade treatments.

If Postmodernists such as Moore most compellingly appealed to history as a source for their designs, another small group in the United States claimed that the house could or should be an expression of broader cultural issues. Throughout the 1970s, their work received the lion's share of press attention, and they also found favor with fashion-conscious clients eager to build houses on the cutting edge of design that would convey elitist status. The paradigmatic exemplar of this position was Peter Eisenman, who designed "cardboard houses" during the 1970s that purported to supersede the relation between subject and object implied by the humanist tradition of architecture. With the cardboard houses, Eisenman claimed to question the reality of the physical environment. Identified by numbers and mostly unbuilt, these houses, he believed, gave evidence of an architecture that revealed its reality as a cultural system of meaning, but a meaning which could only be unlocked through the systematic generation of forms according to logical systems. Where Venturi inscribed putatively meaningful symbols on a facade, Eisenman manipulated every aspect of a house as if it were an autonomous, abstract system, unsettling conventional placements of windows, doors and other elements. He doggedly pursued an increasingly complex manipulation of forms according to abstract systems, linking his approaches to those Noam Chomsky was then articulating in linguistics. This led to such designs as a master bedroom in House VI (1978) where the marital bed was split in half, ruptured by a void that Eisenman believed symbolized the void that lies at the heart of contemporary culture. Maybe the void lay only at the heart of this house. According to the client, it had to be comprehensively renovated ten years after its construction.

By the late 1980s, these early strategies had been transformed into a general theory of Deconstructivist architecture, but had led to few buildings. Frank Gehry fabricated what is often described as the canonical Deconstructivist house out of an existing three-bedroom cottage in Santa Monica in 1978. Stripping a modest house to its bare essentials, he then draped a new outer shell of corrugated metal, chain-link fencing, wood and glass around it. These materials, a mix of traditional, unfashionable and cheap, menacing and comforting, were employed as expressive sculptural elements in an often transparent display of structure and artless

88 Peter Eisenman, House VI, Washington, Connecticut, 1978.

construction. The fruit of his fascination with the contemporary art scene in Los Angeles, this and other buildings designed by Gehry also testify to the expressive possibilities and limitations of the tradition of stucco and wood constructions common to earthquake-prone California. Gehry himself denied any connection to Deconstruction, or to being driven by theoretical concerns. Instead, he emphasized his role as an artist defined as an apolitical being positioned above partisan political disputes.

Neo-Modernism

Throughout the 1970s and 1980s, single-family homes designed by architects fell largely within the category of Postmodernism. In many places, however, variations on Modernism persisted, usually modified and adapted to local needs. Such was the case in housing designed by Peter DeBretteville and Ray Kappe in California, and by Richard Meier on the East Coast of the United States. If anything, the Modernist language persisted even longer in Europe. In the sleek, white Aznar House, Victoria Casasco offered an updating of the streamlined, sinuous curves of Modernism for a hillside site in Barcelona (1990). Karen Bausman and Leslie Gill adopted a crisp, austere Modernist aesthetic in the Huxford House in Larchmont, New York (1988). This two-story cubic structure is bound

89 below left Ray Kappe, Kappe House, Pacific Palisades, California, 1968.

90 below right Victoria Casasco, Aznar House, Barcelona, Spain, 1990.

91 Karen Bausman and Leslie Gill, Huxford House, Larchmont, New York, 1987.

to the patio and the adjacent cottage by means of a stucco wall that traverses the middle of the cottage and extends into the new house. Bausman and Gill treat the wall as the most dynamic feature of the design, at points opening, carving, slicing or hollowing it, or setting windows into it. Even Rem Koolhaas, erstwhile leader of the Deconstructivist movement in the late 1980s, designed the Patio Villa in Rotterdam (1985) in an austere Modernist language reminiscent of Mies van der Rohe's country villas of the 1920s. On a hillside lot in Saint-Cloud overlooking Paris, for the Dall'Ava House (1990) he adapted the Corbusian 92 elements of pilotis, free plan, ribbon windows and free facade to the constraints of an awkward site, and combined them with diverse materials—stone socle, windows of both frosted and transparent glass, slate floors, wood paneling and aluminum siding—and a bold chromatic scheme, to produce an inventive Postmodern recombination of familiar Modernist components.

In settings long ignored by critics and historians, designs animated by Modernist imagery still flourished. Ada Karmi-Melamede's Kauffman 93, 94 House in Tel Aviv, Israel (1994), followed in a tradition inherited from

92 Rem Koolhaas, Dall'Ava House, Saint-Cloud, Paris, France, 1990.

the Expressionist architecture of Erich Mendelsohn. Climatically sensitive and layered in both plan and elevation so as to modulate light in multiple ways, the elevations of the Kauffman House vary from planar, with strip windows on the entrance elevation, to plastic, in the expressive treatment of the rear elevation and curved walls framing the living room, library level and interior staircase. Within a tight cube, she investigated ways of distinguishing public and private zones in homage to Le Corbusier. The architectural promenade, a double-level L-shaped corridor leading from the ground floor front entrance to the corner living room on the first story, channels visitors past the private family bedrooms to the more public kitchen and living room on the second level.

In the commune of Sutri, an ancient town north of Rome surrounded by Etruscan tombs and ruins, Luigi Franciosini and Antonino Saggio designed a combination single-family house, guest apartment and doctor's office (1989). Diverse spaces are carved out of a long two-story rectangular block set into the verdant foliage, moving from the public (office) to semi-public (living rooms and kitchen) to circulation (staircases) to private (bedrooms and baths). The simple concrete block and reinforced concrete structure recalls the tufa blocks of local structural traditions without imitating them, and the living, dining and kitchen spaces surround a courtyard reminiscent of the typical disposition of rooms in ancient Roman villas.

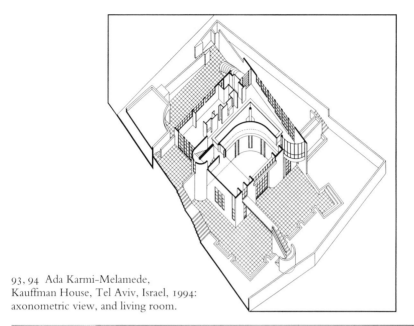

93, 94 Ada Karmi-Melamede,
Kauffman House, Tel Aviv, Israel, 1994:
axonometric view, and living room.

95 Luigi Franciosini and Antonino Saggio, house, Sutri, Italy, 1989.

96 *opposite, left* Carlos Jiménez, Jiménez House, Houston, Texas, begun 1982.

97 *opposite, right* Carlos Jiménez, Chadwick House, Houston, Texas, 1991.

Through materials, disposition or language, other houses are inflected with local traditions while retaining a strongly Modernist orientation. In Houston, Texas, Costa Rican-born architect Carlos Jiménez began his 96 architectural career with the design of his own house/studio (begun 1982), subsequently followed by two separate additions for his studio. Jiménez identified the spare, whitewashed walls of Costa Rican houses and churches, and their colorful window frames and doors, as parts of his personal heritage, which also cohered with some of Houston's architectural traditions. To these, he added a taut and austere version of Modernism, with lofty interiors and subtle variations of mass, volume and geometry that transformed small spaces into grand ones, ordinary vistas into spectacular panoramas. Even a shoestring budget did not hamper Jiménez, who perhaps most powerfully demonstrated that quality need 97 not mean high cost in the Chadwick House in Houston (1991), a bright, three-story structure with a generous range of spaces deployed within a tight frame.

138

As these designs demonstrate, rigid insistence on either Modernism or Postmodernism increasingly gave way in the 1980s to a new tolerance for different approaches, despite the insistence of hardliners that architects should concede the supremacy of one particular style conceived as embodying the spirit of the times. For all the diversity of architectural languages in the 1970s and 1980s, the belief that designs ought to conform to one or another formal language was remarkably persistent. An insistence on achieving conformity also infused debates during the 1920s and 1930s with a polemical charge against and for Modernist design. But then as now they ultimately remained sterile disputes over formal preferences that masked an underlying consensus on the role of architecture throughout the 20th century. These arguments also tended to obscure the fundamental vitality of design in an era when dogmas and rules had relaxed, excellence could be recognized in many different approaches, and architects could find inspiration in both common and uncommon sources, in local traditions as well as in broad, international trends.

Critical Regionalism

Of the design strategies consistently disparaged since the advent of Modernism, a favorite target of abuse has been regionalism, a studied response to local climatic, structural, and formal traditions that was itself one enduring theme of Modernism. This approach Kenneth Frampton characterized as Critical Regionalism. While hindsight suggests that adherents of the Modern Movement were no less provincial themselves, burdened by a singular incomprehension of architectural traditions outside of their own narrow Western European backgrounds, in the postwar years they dismissed as marginal architects whose designs were imbued with the texture of a specific geographical area, rather than recognizing that such a strategy necessitated an unusual sensitivity to everything from energy conservation to the use of local materials. Likewise, because of the insistence on the adherence to a dominant style, architects in non-Western countries who were disposed to design in different languages in response to client preferences found themselves derided as backward and incoherent.

Postmodern winds of change offered little to architects elsewhere in the world already struggling to combine modern housing needs with traditional architecture. Hassan Fathy fought for decades to reintroduce

98 Abdul El-Wakil, Halawa House, Agami, Egypt, 1975.

and ennoble traditional mud-brick building techniques for rural and even urban housing. His ambitious goal of providing better, cheaper shelter for Egypt's poor was sidelined by the resistance of government bureaucracies and vested building interests, neither of which had anything to gain from making cheap housing available to the masses, but he was also stalled by his own overt paternalism. Fathy often ended up with wealthy clients who chose to reject Western models and adopt traditional motifs for their houses for nationalistic purposes.

One of Fathy's most successful students, Abdul El-Wakil, built a practice on such a clientele by instructing them in the cultural significance and ecological good sense of traditional building types and materials. In works such as the Halawa House (1975) at Agami in Egypt, El-Wakil 98 adopted indigenous Islamic forms—loggia, windcatch, first-floor balcony, mastabas, oblique entrances, mushrabiyas—and at once also rejected the universalizing pretensions of Western housing models as the most appropriate designs for any location. By deploying these elements on a palatial scale, he effectively liberated local Islamic building traditions from their associations with poverty and the lower classes, a strategy not so different from that of Andrea Palladio with vernacular architecture for his designs of villas in the Veneto.

In the United States, a resilient minority pursued similar traditions. Mark Mack explored the conjunction of European Modernism, regional vernacular and classical austerity in country houses north of San Francisco such as the diminutive, rustic Goldman House (1979) and the stately Kirlin House (1980). In different settings further south in California, he abandoned these strategies in favor of a more complex interlocking of volumes, as in the Whitney House (1989) in Rustic Canyon, Santa 99, 100 Monica, a remodeling of an earlier house by Frank Gehry. Called upon to make a group of three independent pavilions cohere as a unified house, Mack opened and linked the discrete blocks with deftly juxtaposed and varied materials, luminous colors, and a complicated set of interior walkways, stairs and lofty passageways. Instead of leaving the separate fragments dispersed as random artifacts in the landscape, he deployed these architectural elements so as to highlight the tensions among the units, ultimately binding them as a single entity without imposing a monotonous homogeneity on them.

Antoine Predock spent the early years of his career learning about the materials and climate of the American Southwest, designing adobe housing complexes and single-family dwellings evocative of the desert landscapes of New Mexico and Arizona. In a rough and barren environment, Predock produced a tough, defensive architecture. The Winandy House 101

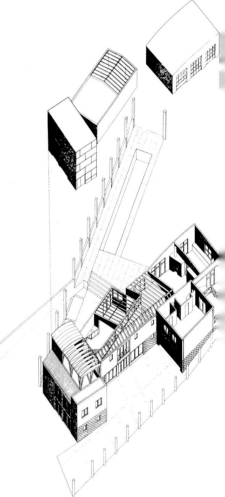

99, 100 Mark Mack, Whitney House, Santa Monica, California, 1989: two-story master bedroom suite with study over (*above*), and axonometric showing Mack's transformation of the Gehry house.

outside Scottsdale, Arizona (1991), exemplified his approach to living in harmony with the desert. From the sandy, golden-yellow soil came the aggregate for the sandblasted concrete blocks, so the house emerges as gracefully from the earth as Anasazi pueblos did over a millennium ago. After the searing heat of the desert, the house becomes an austere sanctuary of water and shade, its courtyard cooled by still pools of water and opening on four sides to rooms of the crisp simplicity typical of antique Pompeian villas. Steel-trussed roofs hover above thin clerestory strips running around the perimeter of the house and the courtyard, filtering light and affording fragmented views of surrounding hills and sky. Subtle manipulation of light individually defines each room. Predock's architectural tools are simple but strikingly effective: pierced masonry walls, sandblasted glass doors, black stucco inside the peristyle to absorb heat and light, shallow pools of water that dapple the courtyard with reflected light, and raking strips of light filtered down from the clerestory windows.

101 Antoine Predock, Winandy House, Scottsdale, Arizona, 1991.

102 Judith Scheine,
Sali House, Juniper
Hills, California, 1994.

Also taking her cues from a stark landscape, Judith Scheine opted for
a different approach for the Sali House near the Mojave Desert in California (1994), juxtaposing two competing interpretations of the desert:
outside, tough corrugated steel roof panels curve away from one another
atop a rough cement-block base and meet the harshness of the desert
head on, while inside pale yellow birch walls and the red steel cables and
frames of the two lofts, or open studio-like spaces, pick up the sunwashed
colors of hardy desert flora. Instead of Predock's expansive openness,
Scheine's design re-examines the 4-foot (1.22-meter) module favored by
Rudolph Schindler, an Austrian architect transplanted to California early
in the century. Enrique Norten of TEN Arquitectos responded to a
densely wooded site in Valle de Bravo, Mexico, for two holiday houses
(1991). With simple tile roofs and bright white exteriors, these fall nicely
into local traditions, but the trusses, fully glazed front wall, and I-beams
frankly acknowledge altogether different roots in Mexican Modernism.
Like many non-First-World architects, Peruvian designer Juvenal
Baracco received his training when Euro-American Modernism was the
standard against which all contemporary design was measured. Despite

the persuasive power of the architecture of Louis Kahn and Alvar Aalto, Baracco found special inspiration in Peru's own pre-Hispanic and colonial traditions. Like Fathy, he advocated low-cost housing in traditional and inexpensive materials (in this case for Peruvian laborers), and like Fathy, he also found his plans continually frustrated by bureaucratic interference and indifference. Although his practice also includes single-family houses for wealthy clients, he remains committed to the cause of low-cost housing. In the meantime, such projects as the Hastings House in Lima (1976) have permitted him to explore themes he believes could easily be adapted for mass housing. Set in a walled precinct like most of its neighbors, it unfolds as a series of individual episodes from the street into the working rooms of the owners, a dance studio and an artist's studio. The house is developed on several levels and linked by spiral staircases, with staggered roofs doubling as vegetation-filled terraces. The modulation of light through the strategic deployment of skylights and windows is his proudest accomplishment, for unlike Venturi and most American Postmodernists, Baracco is concerned chiefly with quality of light, tectonic and spatial elaboration rather than decoration.

In the domestic designs considered above, volumes were explored, exploded, or crafted, built up with an attention to tectonics rather than an abstract scheme of design or treated as if they were two-dimensional drawings on flat paper enlarged to life-size. Gehry's tormented, sculptured forms stand at one end of this extreme, and those of Venturi and Scott Brown and of Stern, with their flat, painterly designs, at the other. These two positions customarily mark the limits of residential design, and indeed of architectural design itself. But beyond the feats accomplished with form, a host of other factors can unleash architectural creativity. Although often disparaged by those who consider themselves among the avant-garde, architects less interested in fashion tend to restore a craft basis to architectural practice. I have chosen to illustrate the work of individuals and firms who are unusual because they treat building as the combination of the skills of an architect and a master mason, attentive to detail, intimately knowledgeable about the site (Casasco, Karmi-Melamede, Jiménez, El-Wakil, Mack, Baracco). Thoughtful in the placement of every aperture, sensitive in locating stairs, landings, balconies and other apparently functional units, they demonstrate that in the right hands these become essential and evocative points of linkage or division, of reflection, of spatial transition and transformation.

Despite the accomplishments of these and other architects, housing design has suffered a serious setback since 1970, when the house became the privileged site for designers to make a statement about the condition

103 Enrique Norten, TEN Arquitectos, House "N," Valle de Bravo, Mexico, 1991.

of contemporary culture in addition to advertising the status aspirations of their clients. Historians and archaeologists regularly uncover the intricacies of cultural values in the housing and urban fabrics of ancient cities. Even in more recent times, architects of the Renaissance sought to fit their buildings into a contemporary understanding of the cosmos, and to signify the status of the occupant through attention to architectural decorum. Only recently did it become incumbent on the architect to burden even the most modest house with the task of articulating its creator's interpretation of the philosophical, cultural, even scientific character of the era. On these grounds, some time in the 1970s Peter Eisenman, Michael Graves and Robert Venturi, from apparently different perspectives, led an assault on the poverty of meaning in the Modernist house. For Venturi and Graves, the problem could be resolved with the incorporation of historical detailing, while for Eisenman the solution lay elsewhere, in the manipulation of forms that were themselves carriers of what he believed to be true of contemporary culture. Their concerns had little in common with the vast majority of housing built in the world— residential suburbs in the United States, towers in Europe and major cities of the Third World, mud houses in Africa or India—nor did they propose strategies for addressing the severe housing problems in cities in Western Europe and the United States, let alone elsewhere in the world.

Low-cost and alternative housing

For most people living in metropolitan areas, single-family houses are luxuries unavailable to all but a fraction of the population. Nonetheless, after the production of a remarkable body of multi-family complexes in the 1960s, many prominent architectural firms disdained such commissions during the 1970s and 1980s in favor of far more lucrative commercial and cultural buildings. Ralph Erskine's justly famous Byker Wall 105 (1968–74), a low-rent public housing complex in Newcastle-upon-Tyne, England, and Lucien Kroll's Medical Faculty housing for the University of 104 Louvain, Belgium (1970–71), stood as singular examples of an approach radically different from that expressed in much housing, which dictates a vision to which future tenants are forced to submit. Both Erskine and Kroll abandoned preconceptions about architectural order, insisting that the architect engage in a dialogue with the client and that the building reflect the needs of its inhabitants rather than the fancy of the architect, banker or builder. In Louvain, the medical students sought a design not beholden to the dictates of the architectural profession, that was not elitist, and that would allow them to participate both in the decision-making

104 Lucien Kroll, Medical Faculty housing, University of Louvain, Woluwé-Saint-Lambert, Brussels, Belgium, 1970–71. In the foreground is the roof of the Alma metro station, developed in 1979–82.

105 Ralph Erskine, the Byker Wall, Newcastle-upon-Tyne, England, 1968–74.

process and in the construction of the building. The facades of many colors, materials, and proportions that they produced were dismissed as bricolage by some critics, but Kroll and the residents defended them as embodying freedom, equality, and independence from the typical master-slave relationship of architect and client. It is no small irony that by the 1990s bricolage had become a supposedly avant-garde aesthetic. Erskine's challenge, on the other hand, was to design low-cost worker housing in an overcrowded area without breaking up the vigorous community. The Byker Wall involved not only close collaboration with the tenants over several years, but the spatial reorganization of the community itself.

Although participatory housing design lost favor in the United States during the 1970s, it retained strong advocates elsewhere. Throughout the 1980s, Erskine and Kroll persisted in their attempts to address ecological issues as well as to involve future inhabitants in the design process, Kroll in Alphen-aan-den-Rijn near Utrecht, an urban scheme for 300 houses (100 to be built initially, 200 later). The plan centers on a lake, and privileges the pedestrian, the garden, and the relationship between houses, while including spaces for automobiles. Kroll selected nine different architects to design the first 100 units, with the goal of achieving the kind of variety found in a town built over time rather than all at once.

One fine example of participatory housing emerged as a result of the combined efforts of the architect Ivo Waldhör, the city of Malmø in

Sweden, a developer, the Swedish housing institute, and the residents of the housing project. From the first discussions to clarify needs and ideas to the final assembly, Waldhör worked in close collaboration with future tenants over a period of four years to produce a five-story apartment 106 block of individual units, each tailored to the preferences of specific families. The tenants had no previous experience with housing design, and all took advantage of the principle that they could make changes until construction had been completed. This flexibility led to delays so that the occupants could achieve the housing they desired. By contrast with Lucien Kroll's project for Louvain University, here choices are revealed inside as well as outside. Because tenants designed their units for their own needs, some things turned out to be uneconomical—party walls, kitchens, and bathrooms not aligned vertically, in particular—but the architect's intervention helped keep windows and other features to a limited number of types. On the exterior, the interior diversity is signalled by the windows and doors, each painted in colors selected by individual families. Waldhör's not inconsiderable achievement was to mold the diverse apartments into a variegated but harmonious building mass, binding the units together with such features as the green socle and roof treatments.

Such examples of architect–client collaboration in multi-family housing are rare. Far more common are adventures in Postmodernist languages imposed willy-nilly on an unknown group of future tenants, one of the boldest being the public housing by Ricardo Bofill and his Taller de Arquitectura known as the Espaces d'Abraxas or Spaces of Abraxas (1978–82, chief conceptual designer Peter Hodgkinson). This project was built in Marne-la-Vallée, one of a series of new towns planned by the French government in the countryside surrounding Paris, still undergirded by the discredited ideologies of the interwar period of decongesting urban centers and planning tightly controlled communities on the urban periphery. In a country where one-quarter of the population lives in government-sponsored housing, Bofill was the architect of choice for new towns such as Saint-Quentin-en-Yvelines (1974–82) and Cergy-Pontoise (1981–85). Although the center of the Espaces d'Abraxas on a ridge overlooking the Marne Valley includes a few shops and offices, it primarily consists of five dormitory suburbs for people who work elsewhere. Bofill and Hodgkinson echoed the Postmodernists in the United States by arguing that previous public housing lacked meaning and importance, to which they opposed an architecture in which daily life could be "exalted to become rich and meaningful." Bofill defined exaltation in three buildings: the nine-story Theater formed of a tiered cavea 107 based on the form of an ancient Roman theater, the nine-story Arch recalling a proscenium arch, and the eighteen-story Palace outfitted with the formal elements of 18th-century aristocratic palaces, but realized in polychrome precast concrete. Between the housing and the town a banal parking garage flanks an unceremonious entrance, for within the complex itself Bofill provided only 156 parking spaces.

107 Although the scheme was apparently straightforward, if pretentious, Bofill then bulked it up to a colossal scale so overpowering that it dwarfs even its classical predecessors. The Arch consists of 17 apartments, relatively modest by comparison to the others, and mediates the view from the gigantic Theater to the Palace, containing 126 and 441 apartments. Conceived as a gigantic work of art and organized as urban-scale stage sets, the Espaces d'Abraxas actually was intended to be occupied by low- and middle-income owners and renters. But the needs of residents and the interior organization of the units were appendages to the more important work of art, as if the basic premise were that architecture could exalt status and hence eliminate social problems in living conditions. In other words, the development seemed to suggest that a powerful image alone could wipe away centuries of class divisions, underemployment, lack of freedom, and poverty, to name but a few problems. Simply placing people in buildings redolent of aristocratic architecture, Bofill seemed to believe, would transform them into modern-day versions of earlier elites.

Not only Bofill, but the Communist and Socialist political groups who commissioned the project espoused the efficacy of formal devices for achieving social goals. Unfortunately, the apartment plans had to be contorted to accommodate quixotic aesthetic schemes, frequently resulting in awkward spaces, with no intermediate zones between the micro-scale of the units and the epic urban scale of the complex. However grand the Espaces d'Abraxas is as an object in the landscape visible from afar, it exacts a high price from the inhabitants who live in a monumental art object. For reasons that have never become clear, the French government persisted in awarding other massive projects to Bofill, such as the Antigone Quarter in Montpellier (begun 1981), an intervention a kilometer (more than half a mile) long directing the city's growth toward the east. In an arresting display of indifference to setting, Bofill designed similar enormous, classically-inspired urban schemes, most of which remained unbuilt, from Baghdad to Bordeaux, Moscow to Montreal, New Jersey to Casablanca.

A quite different view animated the housing complexes in Argentina of José Ignacio Díaz, whose work nonetheless responds to the imperatives of the real estate market. At the periphery of the city of Córdoba, Díaz

106 Ivo Waldhör, apartment building, Malmö, Sweden, 1991.

107 Ricardo Bofill Taller de Arquitectura, the Theater, Espaces d'Abraxas, Marne-la-Vallée, France, 1978–82.

designed and built well over one hundred apartment buildings within the city's height limit of thirteen stories. His brick-clad essays in expressionism, with their sinuous, varied surfaces and generous allowances for public spaces of many types, also challenge the monotonous towers common to much high-density residential development. Smaller-scale communities designed by Fernando Castillo in Chile depend instead on clusters of low-density housing, often with their own patios, interspersed with common public spaces and generous open spaces.

Except for the decorative scheme and for the specific footprints of the different buildings, little of significance distinguishes Bofill's complex from the much disparaged public housing schemes of the 1950s and 1960s, which were commissioned by government agencies and designed by architects according to criteria established by the client, but which failed to engage future residents and which ignored patterns of day-to-day living. One of the least successful developments of this type was George Hellmuth and Minoru Yamasaki's Pruitt Homes and Igoe Apartments in Saint Louis, Missouri (1954), famed for its levels of crime and subsequent demolition. Like many similar projects, Pruitt-Igoe suffered less from poor architectural design than from poor urban design strategies: land uses were zoned and rigorously separated, ensuring, for example, that residents lacked easy access to retail, commercial, recreation and leisure facilities; streets were rejected as public spaces; and the housing itself was isolated from the rest of the city.

108, 109 The case of the ZUP (*zone à urbaniser en priorité*) Perseigne in Alençon, France, is significant. Like many other such ambitious and inhumane government housing schemes designed between 1958 and 1969, this huge complex of austere long blocks set in vast expanses of green parkland suffered from construction flaws. But the most worrisome problem was the alienation people experienced because of the configuration of the project. Instead of blasting it into oblivion as has been done elsewhere, the municipality called on Lucien Kroll to stitch it together again. Kroll worked with the community to understand the precise nature of the problems, and ended up inserting new two-story units, outdoor furniture and lighting, balconies and roofs, and even joining some of the earlier units to make larger apartments. He attached his new houses to the older buildings as if they were barnacles on a ship, instantly violating the impersonal volumes and transforming arbitrarily reductive surfaces into an explosively lively and decisively personal cityscape.

In less industrialized societies, forces eager to establish Western housing models for the poor battle others equally insistent on developing updated versions of traditional housing and urban design patterns. Hassan Fathy was one of the earliest to argue that foreign technology and materials not only cost far more and decayed more rapidly than local building materials and techniques, but also failed to provide residents with communities responsive to their cultural traditions. In many so-called Third World countries, the overwhelming majority of housing has been constructed not by architects but by residents in desperate need of shelter. The UN estimates that some 90 per cent of the buildings erected annually in Latin America are built without professional advice, and since the recent growth in these countries depends upon the supply of desirable raw materials and cheap labor, a way out of the current poverty is not within sight.

B.V. Doshi's plan for Aranya Township outside of Indore in India (1982) 110 fell between typical non-participatory public housing and completely self-help housing. Like many such projects and, in particular, those proposed by Fathy at Gourna, the Aranya Township includes streets, housing, shops and a materials bank for owners' supplies, all supplemented by

108, 109 Lucien Kroll, ZUP Perseigne remodelling, Alençon, France, 1980: plan of the site, and detail showing a modified block with new small units attached.

110 B. V. Doshi, Aranya low-cost housing, Indore, India, 1982.

planning for the economic self-sufficiency of the inhabitants through the inclusion of training facilities for industrial and technical skills and light 110 industrial plants. The plan included 7,000 housing units, 65 per cent for low-income families, with an initial population of 40,000 expected to grow to 65,000. Lot sizes ranged from 35 square meters (377 square feet) to over 400 square meters (4,300 square feet) for the wealthy, plus plots for multi-story housing. As is characteristic of the "site and service" type project, each lot received a service core (washroom, bathroom) plus one room, a basic core to which residents could add as finances and time permitted. With the profits from the sale of upper-income lots, a materials bank was set up and the prices of the low-income units were reduced to an affordable range for prospective buyers. Although the scheme also provided for training in building, owners were free to modify and add to their small units as their particular family needs demanded, offering a degree of flexibility unheard of in typical public housing projects. Many architects resist leaving so much of the design process in the hands of untutored residents, but throughout history people have been responsible for building their own dwellings consistent with their own needs and aesthetic preferences. This type of scheme limits the role of architects to that of overall planners and urban designers, working more in an advisory capacity than anything else.

111, 112   In his housing in Belapur, Bombay (1984), Charles Correa argued that it was impossible to produce public or mass housing without taking into

154

111, 112 Charles Correa, housing, Belapur, Bombay, India, 1984: view of simple units, and drawings showing the development of a typical family unit over time.

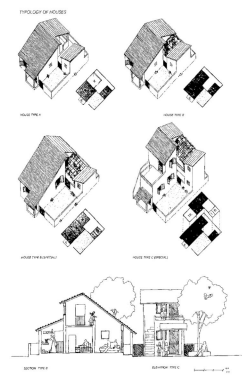

TYPOLOGY OF HOUSES

HOUSE TYPE A

HOUSE TYPE B

HOUSE TYPE B (SPECIAL)

HOUSE TYPE C (SPECIAL)

SECTION TYPE B

ELEVATION TYPE C

account the economic future of the inhabitants, and the building traditions in this part of India. The community was developed by following a spatial hierarchy extending from the private domestic world to the communal court and out into the public space of the city, the *maidan*, where shops and other enterprises would be built. Correa designed the basic housing units, each on a separate lot and without party walls. As in Aranya Township, residents had the opportunity to extend in any direction they chose according to their preferences, needs, and available income. Although the architect in this case established more of the early design decisions, it was with the full expectation that residents would supplement and overlay his ideas with theirs. The economic program involved dividing lots into equity plots, where the largest was only 30 square meters (323 square feet) larger than the smallest. In this way the architect attempted to minimize potentially corrosive conflicts between rich and poor. Correa intended the program as a model for housing for India's extremely poor, but Belapur in fact became a largely a middle-income suburb. Like many other architects, Correa found himself working within a circumscribed sphere in which intelligent designs increase values which in turn leads to gentrification—precisely the opposite of what was intended.

Broad demographic changes in the last two decades led some architects, politicians, and developers to rethink traditional housing concepts. The nuclear family, with the father as the breadwinner and the mother at home taking care of the children—the cliché of the 1950s—no longer represents the most common living group. Instead, in the West family units increasingly consist of single-parent families, most often headed by a woman; childless couples; families in which both parents work; families in which older children still live at home because of the high cost or scarcity of housing; families where grandparents live with the nuclear family. Additionally, temporary non-traditional living arrangements need to be made for abused women, homeless families and young single mothers, and rehabilitation communities must be founded for substance abusers, among others.

In countries such as France, Italy, Sweden and the Netherlands, where the government already recognizes a responsibility to provide housing for its most disadvantaged members, meeting many of these particular needs is less pressing because adequate accommodation is often available. But in the United States, where virtually all residential construction is controlled by private industry for the purpose of making money, people with unusual needs and few resources rarely have access to emergency or non-traditional housing. Major architectural firms rarely seek such commissions, discouraged equally by bureaucratic delays, low economic returns, and lesser professional status. Among the exceptions is the New York office of Cooper, Robertson & Partners, which designed West H.E.L.P. (Housing Enterprises for the Less Privileged) in Greenburgh, 113 New York (1991), for homeless single parents with young children. The wood-frame, cedar-shake-shingled buildings contain over one hundred housing units, where families live from six to nine months until permanent jobs and housing can be located. As in several of the low-income communities discussed above, this development included specific features aimed at ensuring the future wellbeing of the residents, in this case job training, drug rehabilitation and health care programs.

In the early 1970s, the concept of co-housing took shape in Denmark through the efforts of groups of middle-class families who developed residences with a mix of private and communal spaces quite different from those typical of most apartment buildings or suburban developments. Each family had a separate living unit, but kitchens, sitting rooms, play areas and meeting rooms were communal, with residents sharing cooking, cleaning, gardening, and child care tasks. Over two hundred such co-housing enterprises appeared in Denmark, the Netherlands, and Sweden. In Denmark, among the best-known early co-housing projects are Tinggården (1979) and Tinggården 2 (1984) in Herfolge, over 150 rental units designed by Tegnestuevo Vandkunsten and Karsten Vibild. The same firm designed Savvaerket in Jystrup (1984), with communal dining room, kitchen, laundry, wood shop, sewing and crafts room. Leo

113 Cooper, Robertson & Partners, West H.E.L.P. Project, Greenburgh, New York, 1991.

114 Edward Weinstein Associates, Winslow Co-housing, Bainbridge Island, Washington, 1992.

de Longe and Pieter Weeda designed Hilversumse Meent in Hilversum, Holland (1977), consisting of cluster housing for rent and common facilities. Other important co-housing projects include Trädet and Stacken in Gothenburg, Sweden (1980), and Purmerend at Purmerend in the Netherlands (1985). The first community in the United States was Muir Commons, which was established as part of a speculative suburb of Davis, California, in 1991. It was followed by a second, Winslow Co-housing, in Bainbridge Island, Washington (1992), designed by Edward Weinstein Associates. With co-housing groups, the entire planning and development of the settlement is initiated and carried through by the future residents, who also commit themselves to participate in community life once construction terminates. The architects called in confront residents who have already developed an idea of their community. Once again, their role is that of facilitator, rather than provider of philosophies about the notion of community. This does not mean that architects lack ideas; rather that these are always developed in concert with those of clients.

Other notable enterprises include cooperative housing for low-income families. Ocean Park Housing Cooperative in Santa Monica, California (1985–89), designed by Appleton, Mechur & Associates, provided 43 housing units dispersed on five building sites for low- and moderate-income families and senior citizens which will eventually become occupant-run, limited equity cooperatives. Peter Calthorpe's design for Laguna West consisted of a "pedestrian pocket," a different approach to suburban housing development in California. Calthorpe integrated housing, offices, retail, recreation, parks, and day care into the community serviced by a light rail system. In this mix of low- and moderate-density housing (begun in 1991), community facilities are all within walking distance, greatly reducing the need for automobiles. Based on early 20th-century settlement plans such as the Garden City (e.g. Letchworth and Welwyn in England) or even earlier suburban developments in the United States, Calthorpe's programs offer an alternative for middle-class housing to the endless suburban sprawl that now consumes ever greater tracts of farmland and pollutes ever greater quantities of air because of the enforced dependence on the automobile.

Of the firms that practice in the field of multi-family housing, few attempt to address the larger problem of the shape of cities designed chiefly to accommodate the automobile. Only a handful of architects and planners have tried to reconfigure the 20th-century automobile suburb in order to make it less wasteful of virtually every type of natural resource and more responsive to the goal of the formation of small, self-sufficient communities instead of dormitories for metropolitan areas.

Other than Peter Calthorpe, the Miami-based architectural firm of Andres Duany and Elizabeth Plater-Zyberk has been the most persistent critic of the traditional suburb and at the same time the designer of suburban villages attractive to developers and homebuyers of all races and income levels. Using the very tools that architects typically define as oppressive and confining—zoning and building codes and ordinances—Duany and Plater-Zyberk devise systems appropriate for different locations that result in developments congenial to pedestrians as well as automobiles, where activities are brought together rather than separated as in traditional zoning schemes, and services and parks are situated so as to minimize the need for the automobile. Their first project in Florida, Seaside (1978), was a small resort community, and as such was particularly 115–118 vulnerable to charges that it glorified nostalgia. Duany and Plater-Zyberk acknowledge that parts of the town did precisely that. More important, Seaside offered a pedestrian-scale, close-grained spatial organization remote both from contemporary residential enclaves and from typical suburbanized resort communities, a model that could be adapted to new developments elsewhere in Florida (Avalon Park near Orlando) as easily as to the center of Trenton, New Jersey. Their completed projects to date have been for upper-middle-class residential compounds, but

they have proposed schemes for low-income and minority clients that remain to be funded. Although their effort is to change the system of development from within, they are locked into addressing only as much of the problem as the market system allows them. Their vision of a small-scale neighborhood and town organization model, pursued by a group of urban designers known as Neo-Traditionalist town planners, responds to desires that cut across ethnic and class lines in rejecting typical late

115 *opposite, above* Andres Duany & Elizabeth Plater-Zyberk Architects, Seaside, Florida, planned in 1978.

116 *opposite, below* Steven Holl, Hybrid Building, Seaside, Florida, 1989.

117, 118 *above and right* Victoria Casasco, Appell Residence, Seaside, Florida, 1988–90: the Caribbean-style shutter room, and the rear elevation of the house with rooftop sun deck.

20th-century suburbanized patterns of real estate and transportation planning. In many respects, regardless of the income or ethnic origins of the groups that commission them, the new towns are most closely related to the gated communities that have taken shape throughout the United States since the 1980s, with entrances manned by private guards.

For architects, one of the most positive features of Seaside was that the building codes established by Duany and Plater-Zyberk allowed an enormous variety of expression: architects as diverse as Leon Krier, Victoria Casasco and Steven Holl built projects for Seaside, but they all worked effectively within the codes. The Appell House by Casasco (1989) is a brilliant example of deftly turning Seaside's building codes into an advantage for expressing the tectonic system within the constraints of the type and materials.

The chief argument against what its practitioners call the New Urbanism is that to many Seaside and its codes seemed to be just another exclusionary device, another way to design communities to keep out the undesirable, comparable to Las Colinas at Dallas, Texas (begun 1980). As we have seen, however, this is no fault of these particular architects, for in the United States low-income housing is particularly difficult to build. Ena Dubnoff struggled for seven years to complete the 48-unit low-income Willowbrook Glen Housing in Watts, Los Angeles (1991). Like all such projects, it suffered delays due to a devastating combination of financing difficulties and bureaucracy. Even more taxing was the single-room-occupancy Simone Hotel (1993) in downtown Los Angeles by Koning Eizenberg Architects. Future clients of this hotel are at the very bottom of the social ladder, but the architects shrewdly combined inexpensive materials with elegant design, ample lighting, and generous public spaces to provide dignified accommodation. Koning Eizenberg is one of the rare firms that insists on doing a certain amount of non-profit work, their many high-quality, low-cost projects carried by expensive single-family houses.

The Netherlands has been a longstanding leader in providing alternative social housing. Duinker and van der Torre's Battered Women's Shelter in Amsterdam (1994) follows elegantly in this tradition. They rehabilitated and adapted an old Roman Catholic church, carving mini-apartments with sleeping lofts out of the side aisles, and providing indoor and outdoor play areas for children. Both interiors and exteriors are enlivened by the richly textured brickwork of the original church, to which the architects added splashes of color. The shelter is an exemplary instance of fulfilling architectural, urban and social purposes in one sweep.

116
117, 118

119

120

121

119 *above, left* Ena Dubnoff, Willowbrook Glen Housing, Watts, Los Angeles, California, 1991.

120 *above, right* Koning Eizenberg Architects, Simone Hotel, Los Angeles, California, 1993.

121 *right* Duinker, van der Torre, samenwerkende architekten te Amsterdam, Battered Women's Shelter, Amsterdam, 1994.

Multi-family housing developments in Japan

If American and European town centers have undergone enormous transformations in the decades after World War II, the same is true more emphatically in Japan, where apocalyptic changes have caused block after block to be replaced by brand new buildings, often not once but twice in this century. The country's two eras of soaring good fortune, before and after the war, lie behind this situation. Additionally, it has a small land mass, limited space for building, and proportionately high land cost. Underlying the whole process is a different cultural attitude in earthquake-prone Japan, where land is important but buildings less so. There are relatively few old buildings: given the traditional construction material, wood, even the historic temples are for the most part relatively recent replicas.

By the end of the 1980s, the market value of land in Japan exceeded that of the entire United States by 500 per cent. At the same time, technology and society were undergoing transformations, which engendered a search for economical constructions to respond to changing needs. The buildings regularly erected anew are often considered provisional, even though they are constructed with care, precision, and handsome materials, particularly such buildings as office parks or those dedicated to commerce and leisure. For designers and developers, this presents a singular challenge: how temporary is temporary? Additionally, residential construction on expensive land, particularly in Tokyo, has suffered, with the result that the average family living space is 650 square feet (60 square meters). Demographic pressure remains strong. Japan in the late 1980s and early 1990s suffered a severe housing shortage at the same time that the yen rode stronger than ever and disposable family incomes remained among the highest in the world.

In the mid- to late 1980s, as the country rode the wave of a building boom similar to those in the United States and Western Europe, hundreds of foreign architects profited. Japanese developers turned to them not just to take advantage of lower fees but because the visions of architecture they brought with them often differed fundamentally from those of local architects. Foreigners were often more willing to experiment with new solutions rather than adapt to the norms, and developers banked on marketing the novelty appeal as well as soundness of design combined with high construction standards common to Japanese buildings. This led to commissions for architects as diverse as Michael Graves and Zaha Hadid—both of whom produced projects they might equally well have designed for sites in Berlin, London or Hong Kong.

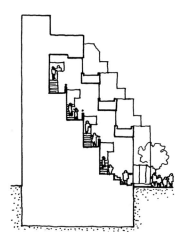

122, 123 Adèle Naudé
Santos, SDC Corporate
Headquarters "Kachofugetsu-
kan," Ichiban-cho, Tokyo,
Japan, 1988: view and
section.

Among the Westerners called to work in Japan was South African-
born and trained Adèle Naudé Santos, who received much more significant commissions in Tokyo than in the United States where she now
lives. Santos designed two office buildings with residential units, including one two-family house, to respond to the specific codes and demands
of building in Tokyo without sacrificing the principles that animate her
work in the United States. Constrained by tight sites, Santos worked all
of her schemes through the development of the section, to insure that
interiors received ample light by means of orientation and deftly configured corridors, staircases, and garden spaces. She handled light as an
essential element for molding spaces with equal ease in the single-floor
rooms of the Harajuku Illuminacion and in the complex layers of spaces
in its adjacent house. Only the SDC Corporate Headquarters have been   122, 123
completed to date.

The city of Fukuoka, to the south of Tokyo, received international
attention for a sequence of commissions awarded to foreign architects.
One of the earliest, and one highly satisfying for the developers, was
Aldo Rossi's Hotel Il Palazzo (1987). Part of the success of this building,   124
a beacon on a waterfront just beginning to undergo change and commercial success, was due to the developer's willingness to construct the
hotel as Rossi designed it, without cutting corners on materials or

workmanship—elevated on a high plinth, with solid travertine columns on the facade and no windows on the waterfront elevation. Michael Graves and Stanley Tigerman both designed apartment buildings, and in 1992 Emilio Ambasz completed a design for the Prefecture International Hall, a public–private enterprise involving a bold complex of green space and architecture for commercial and office use mixed with public and municipal activities.

Again in Fukuoka, a new settlement was conceived under the name of Nexus World Kashii, "Nexus" being a combination of "next" and "us," signifying "us in the near future." The developers wanted to reject the temporary status of much Japanese building and offer occupants more attractive and spacious housing. In other words, they wanted to provide a wide variety of multi-family dwellings on an unusual site, not surrounded by the typically dense Japanese urban tissue but in a carefully planned new town on land reclaimed from Hakata Bay. In an earlier project, Nexus Momochi, the developer Fukuoka Jisho hired Michael Graves and Stanley Tigerman to design condominiums along the lines of those they would insert in Chicago or Maryland: it was clear that these were successful precisely because the exotic is marketable in Japan, even if not necessarily suited to the many different kinds of family arrangements likely to be found there. For Nexus Kashii, the developer wanted to try something different, by making a range of options available to prospective buyers.

Fukuoka Jisho turned planning over to Arata Isozaki, who worked out a scheme with perimeter housing on the L-shaped site and two large high-rises in the interior. He specifically rejected a Modernist tradition of long blocks of relatively uniform buildings, opting instead to follow the example of the IBA in Berlin and summon an international group of architects to design the perimeter housing, assigning lots to each one and reserving the two high-rise towers for himself. The IBA model, however, in Isozaki's view, called for a fairly rigid framework set up in the planning phase to which the designers adhered, whereas a looser format was called for in Japan: each architect was to be confined only by site and by building volume to housing block ratio, leaving him or her free to elaborate the design in a personal way.

Like the developer, Isozaki apparently believed that most Japanese architects would be unable to undertake the dramatic revisions in housing the Nexus project proposed, so he selected an international team. But instead of choosing the biggest star names, such as Norman Foster, James Stirling or Richard Meier, Isozaki opted for a group with vaguely avant-garde reputations based on solid bodies of work: one Japanese (Osamu

124 Aldo Rossi, Hotel
Il Palazzo, Fukuoka,
Japan, 1987.

125 Mark Mack,
apartment complex,
Nexus World Kashii,
Fukuoka, 1991.

Ishiyama), one American (Steven Holl), and four European (Rem Koolhaas, Mark Mack, Christian de Portzamparc, and Oscar Tusquets), as well as an American landscape architect (Martha Schwartz). (Except for Schwartz, all were males of a certain prominence in Western architectural circles; whatever else can be said about these and other international schemes, they make little attempt to rupture any of the rules of the male-controlled architectural system.)

In a matter as delicate as the design of housing, where cultural traditions and social patterns are often most rooted and least susceptible to change, the choice of architects was provocative, since with the exception of Ishiyama they possessed little understanding of Japanese culture. As in most megaprojects, developers sought the image provided by name architects because they were convinced that their designs would garner publicity and sell more rapidly. All of the ingredients for success were present: an avant-garde sensibility, a rapidly expanding city, and an exotic, Western aura in dwelling units sharply different in fundamental ways from those on the market. The scheme repays study because some of the projects offer engaging suggestions for multi-family housing beyond the confines of Japan. The elements of Nexus World Kashii ran from the most subtle and sophisticated to the most ordinary, and each eventually found a niche in the market. It came as a surprise to non-Japanese architects that a developer would refuse to cut corners in construction, let alone be willing to tolerate such diversity, even going so far as to permit Koolhaas to ignore the iron-clad rule of southern exposure.

The most provocative and accomplished projects are those of Steven Holl, Rem Koolhaas and Mark Mack. Each seized the opportunity to explore multi-family housing from a fresh perspective, without relying on a bag of standard tricks, and, notably, each oversaw the various phases of construction. Their solutions offer diverse spatial organizations, usually on more than one floor, and afford greater privacy and openness than is typical of most apartment developments. Holl began his designs with perspective views, which he then rendered in plan fragments, rather than beginning with plans to be transformed later into perspective drawings. He responded to the curved street with a similarly curved spine broken by the alternate opening of four pairs of voids—half of them north-facing active spaces and half south-facing quiet spaces, still pools of water.

For the most part, the Western architects sought in some fashion to reconcile their buildings with Japanese traditions. Rem Koolhaas of OMA, with the help of Furinori Hoshino and Ron Steiner, placed private gardens based on traditional Japanese rock gardens on the first floor of his two blocks of twenty-four townhouses. Like the courtyard pools in

126 Steven Holl,
Void Space/Hinged
Space Housing,
Nexus World Kashii,
Fukuoka, 1991.

Holl's project, they are tranquil oases and rhythmic inflections that artic-
ulate the relationships among diverse spaces. More pragmatically, they
also provide secluded wells of light and space within each unit. This quiet
core stands in counterpoint to the sinuously curved girdle of faux
masonry rustication that sheathes the upper floors. For Koolhaas, the
bands of rough black concrete, loosely based on the features of the forti-
fied Japanese castle, serve as a visual basis for the as yet unbuilt towers by
Isozaki. The banded sections are cantilevered out over the retail spaces
and the white wall of the entrance, while the three wavy metal roofs soar
above the living rooms.

For residents of multi-family dwellings, one of the biggest problems
revolves around the competing demands for privacy and openness, but
Koolhaas deftly reconciled them here in Fukuoka. Using vast expanses of
glazed surfaces within each unit, he relied strictly on light, tectonics, and
spatial organization to achieve a sense of quiet and privacy, even as he
introduced elements of drama. On the debit side, while he sensitively
translated traditional notions about privacy in a language that conflates
Japanese and Western features, he utterly ignored the inevitable demand
for southern exposure as well as typical Japanese standards of size. Unit

169

areas were more than three times the average, and the high cost as well as the disposition on three floors restricted the potential clientele to a very small share of the market. Moreover, in a scheme whose chief goal was to introduce a new urbanism, Koolhaas's project failed miserably: the brilliant architectural design is still utterly closed off and unfriendly to the street and turns its back on the public realm.

125   Mark Mack's ingenious apartment complex occupies the corner site, and incorporates several different kinds of housing in two simple building blocks: one L-shaped and low-rise, coloured red, and the other a slightly taller grey and yellow slab. Mack's concerns in his earlier rural and suburban California houses centered around delimiting degrees of public and private space in relation to interior and exterior. Here, because of the urban setting and the shops on the ground floor, he chose to knit together the public realm of the street and the semi-public realm of the interior courtyard by penetrating the southern corner of the slab structure, making the garden (designed by Martha Schwartz) an urban asset as well. While Mack's building settles nicely into Fukuoka, the brilliant resolution of the urban frontage makes it a model suitable for virtually any urban location.

The most ingenious aspect of Mack's project, like that of Holl, is the crafting of a wide variety of plans and unit types within what appear from the street to be straightforward building envelopes. No two of the twenty-nine units are alike. Particularly in the slab structure, Mack devised complex sequences of levels which flow effortlessly inside but are difficult to grasp from outside. The only indication of the diversity of condominiums is the apparently abstract treatment of the street elevations, a masterful orchestration of asymmetrical solids and voids within the confines of a concrete frame, with no repetition of the panel–window–balcony schemes. The harmonious confrontation of diverse materials, forms and colors on the exterior echoes a similar strategy on the interior, where a sunbathed red wall, pale green or yellow doors, stepped cabinets, and a boldly curved tile lounge or shaped divan in the bathroom signal an approach to interiors uncommon in Japan.

The remaining three condominium complexes are less interesting architecturally, each for different reasons: Ishiyama's design bristles with corbels, balconies, metal frames and other clutter that overwhelm the fine detailing, while Portzamparc's arbitrarily irregular parallelograms offer odd-shaped interiors within a traditional Western and conservative design. Overall, the Nexus project evidences a range of design alternatives unusual in a single development, but the IBA provokes more thought about the directions for both housing design and urban design.

CHAPTER THREE

Reconfiguring the Urban Sphere

At the beginning of the century, Peter Behrens's decision to take on the job of designing the AEG Turbine factory in Berlin was unusual. In a time when architects often disdained to design train stations, factories, or other mundane structures, that a major designer would entertain such work was rare. That today the most prestigious firms routinely compete for such commissions is a measure of how much has changed. Whether architects manage to stay abreast of the broad social and economic forces that underlie changes in the workplace and in the configuration of cities is quite another matter.

As a case in point, one need only look at the sequence of buildings long disdained by the architectural profession, from the 20th-century American suburb to the suburban shopping mall, or even more recently, to the emergence of the minimall, or small-scale urban mall, in Los Angeles in the early 1980s. The indifference of architects also coheres with the strategy of developers to work out formulas for their projects, formulas that do not admit of the singularity of good design. While architects and critics were quick to heap scorn on the minimall, for example, usually outfitted in bold Postmodern decorations, they failed to recognize the needs it addressed. As a quick and handy place to accomplish a wide array of tasks, and as a setting where immigrant families could open small businesses dependent upon family labor, the minimall responded to growing segments of Los Angeles's population, and contractors and builders supplied the design expertise. The low prestige associated with minimalls led many architects to ignore them, just as for decades they ignored suburbs, shopping malls and gas stations. The twin losers from this obvious failure of the profession are the broad community and architects themselves. Whether the profession will be able to come to terms with the revolution being wrought by fast-developing communications and computer technologies, the changing workplace and the increasing shift to part-time and home-based employment remains an open question.

Architects have eagerly responded to the call of governments or major private corporations to revamp large areas of cities. The redesign of large parts of Paris during the second half of the 19th century is probably the most powerful instance of the modernization of a historic city, not matched even by the huge urban design programs supported by Benito Mussolini in Italy during the 1920s and 1930s. The last twenty-five years, particularly the 1980s, have been characterized by megaprojects on a scale comparable to that of Paris under Napoleon III.

INDUSTRIAL WASTELANDS

Rapidly changing technologies and the correspondingly greater mobility of capital have transformed the industrial landscapes of late 20th-century cities throughout Europe and the Americas. In their wake lay either a swath of derelict and unused structures formerly occupied by heavy industry, such as automobile or steel plants, or new manufacturing facilities inserted into Third World countries as cheap replacements for those closed down in older industrialized nations because of high labor costs, taxes, and more stringent environmental controls. Among the most obvious cases are the *maquiladora* factories producing high technology components and other manufactured goods in northern Mexico near the United States border, or gigantic new plants being planned for Poland and elsewhere in Eastern Europe. The toll on the landscape in industrialized nations has been visible for decades. But in other areas it is only beginning to emerge, in the rusting carcasses of heavy industry's stagnant plants, and in the armies of homeless and unemployed living in their cars and moving from city to city in search of work. Devastating as these convulsive changes have been for hundreds of thousands of workers, it is some measure of fin-de siècle values—and the capitalist economic system—that politicians, developers and real estate moguls dedicated the bulk of their energy to speculating on buildings rather than to addressing the plight of the under- and unemployed, to the ever freer movement of capital rather than to the needs of populations in turmoil. And there is also little pressure on behalf of the disadvantaged from other sectors of society.

As heavy industry and large corporations fled urban areas to less costly sites, cities encouraged or allied with private investors to turn empty buildings into sources of private and public revenue. Such efforts resulted in outdated structures being refashioned into specialty shopping centers —one thinks of Ghirardelli Square (1967) by Wurster Bernardi & Emmons, crafted from an aged chocolate manufacturing factory, and The Cannery (1968) by Joseph Esherick & Associates, converted from a former Del Monte cannery, both in San Francisco. Discreetly scaled and

127 Giacomo Mattè Trucco, Fiat Lingotto Factory, Turin, Italy, 1919.

favored with attractive brick structures overlooking the Bay, they proved easy for small investors to develop. Elsewhere, in decayed centers of heavy industry such as Pittsburgh, Pennsylvania, city officials tore down old steel mills or entrepreneurs reconfigured them for light industrial uses, and refashioned enormous rail yards into attractive riverside parks. For the most part, these actions were part of larger strategies of gentrification, which principally consists of the substitution of upwardly mobile urban professionals for poor or working-class families in warehouse, industrial, or inner-city zones. But other kinds of large industrial structures pose more vexing problems.

The Fiat Lingotto factory in Turin, a hulking mass of reinforced concrete and a milestone of modern architecture (by Giacomo Mattè Trucco, 1919), typifies industrial plants undergoing transformation to new uses. In many countries, such a structure would have been demolished in favor of third-rate precast concrete skyscrapers, but the architectural and historical merit of the Lingotto induced a different response in Italy. To the design of Renzo Piano, underway since 1984, its 250,000 square meters (over 2½ million square feet) of rehabilitated floor area have been subdivided into zones for industrial and commercial shows, conference center, heliport, spaces for small entrepreneurs, restaurants, gardens, bars, shops, hotels, and facilities for the science departments of

127

the University of Turin. Changing the function from a factory for industrial production to a behemoth largely dedicated to elite consumption poses proportionately mammoth problems for the city. When first built, Lingotto rose in solitary grey splendor on the urban periphery, only to be engulfed by the city's expansion in the subsequent decades. As was the case in most Italian cities, Turinese officials failed to anticipate this growth, and hence ignored the increasing inadequacy of infrastructures, roads, public transportation, parking, and other necessities. As a multinational corporation of gigantic dimensions, Fiat benefited substantially from various kinds of government subventions and favorable laws to give it an edge over foreign competitors. But Fiat corporate officials took the position that the city of Turin should cover one-third of the expenses for the transformation of Lingotto. Beyond this, they expected the Italian government to spend even greater (but as yet undetermined) sums to revolutionize thoroughly inadequate transportation systems in the surrounding district in order to accommodate the anticipated crowds for the various activities and events scheduled for Lingotto. Neither the city nor Fiat had remotely considered such improvements for a factory population of blue-collar workers forced to make their way to the plant as best they could.

The Fiat venture demonstrates the close collaboration of the government with industry, in favor of wealthier groups and at the expense of the working class. Such, indeed, has been the case almost everywhere that abandoned industrial zones have been reclaimed. The IBA or Internazionale Bau Ausstellung at Emscher Park in Germany constitutes a provocative counter example, 803 square kilometers (319 square miles) destined to be reclaimed following the departure of heavy industry, especially coal and steel, from the Ruhr in Germany. The objectives of the campaign, begun in 1988, were to achieve a fivefold renewal: ecological, economic, social, cultural, and of the built environment. What differentiated this project from others was the early determination for it to be fully collective, operationally as well as in the decision-making process. The intention was to avoid the rigid institutional hierarchies in place in the region, specifically the standard vast master plan, and instead to have the residents generate diverse responses to the region's problems. Within the first few years, eighty-seven different programs, from re-training to the development of new types of work to the institution of museums of industry, emerged. These were not ideal and broad-scale programs, but actions that could be reasonably undertaken in a brief period of time. IBA Emscher Park began the year after the Altbau IBA in Berlin concluded, governed by a desire to continue the planning attitude of recuperating the existing city through the decisive participation of residents, with a greater concern for processes than for idealized results whose success depends on forcing one group or class to make way for a different, wealthier one.

Derelict industrial plants were almost impossible to rehabilitate in remote areas, or those abandoned by industry such the old automobile manufacturing city of Flint, Michigan, or a former Kaiser Steel Plant in Fontana, California. Facilities located in cities where tourism could be expected to expand were more readily transformed. Among the various outdated industrial structures languishing in disuse throughout Europe and America in the early 1970s, harbors and ports, once entrances to fabled maritime cities, appealed to developers as promising settings for multi-use developments. In the 1960s, containerization had revolutionized the transport, loading and unloading of goods, and, in particular, affected the size of ships and the docks necessary to accommodate them. Ports that failed to adapt to the new technologies were destined for rapid obsolescence, the loss of business to up-to-date and efficient ports such as Hamburg and Rotterdam, and eventual closure. This fate befell many major ports, including Genoa, Copenhagen, Manchester, Liverpool, Baltimore and Boston, Massachusetts. Along with closures came layoffs and the attendant social disruptions, as well as considerable uncertainty about what to do with these decaying relics of an earlier era. In general, the most common solution was to turn them into shopping centers or festival marketplaces, often with housing and offices, as in Boston and Baltimore, in order to make up with tourism and consumption for the lost taxes and jobs associated with industry.

Emblematic of the late 1980s schemes is that of the city of Genoa, which engaged Genoese architect Renzo Piano to revamp its docks for the quincentennial of Christopher Columbus's voyage of discovery. Completed in the summer of 1992, this scheme envisioned converting the harbor into a luxury port for yachts cruising the Mediterranean, keeping the old Cotton Warehouse but transforming it into a temporary exhibition pavilion and then into expensive boutiques, and adding other temporary pavilions for the duration of the Columbus year celebrations. The city and port authorities also took advantage of the opportunity to liquidate the remaining activities in the oldest section of the harbor, laying off the last longshoremen and thus resolving the extended struggle for supremacy between the longshoremen's union, port authorities and private shippers in favor of the port authorities. In an ideal case of poetic justice, the Columbus exhibition turned out to be a flop, leaving financial problems on the horizon for Genoa.

London's Docklands

No one answer has emerged as satisfactory for all cities, but the redevelopment of London's Docklands proves to be one of the most telling with respect to the current role of architecture and its relation to the cataclysmic economic processes affecting the modern world. By the late 1970s a process of economic restructuring, spatially dispersed and globally integrated, was well underway. Three major world centers for control of finance and specialized financial service firms emerged. Lagging behind New York but ahead of Tokyo, London underwent enormous economic changes which also transformed it spatially and socially. Between the two world wars, manufacturing had already migrated out from the center to the periphery. Now, even though white-collar employment had long been a significant part of London's labor force, the number of jobs in this sector increased enormously in the 1980s, as banking, financial services and insurance companies came to account for one-third of all jobs. Canary Wharf in Docklands was conceived as a major node for globally integrated economic activities in the financial and specialized service industries which by 1990 had overtaken manufacturing as the leading economic sector.

What happened, and why the redevelopment took the course it did, must be understood in its historical context as well as its contemporary one. The zone now known as "Docklands" consists of the old Thamesside port area, some 8 miles (13 kilometers) long as the crow flies, stretching eastward from Tower Bridge, which coincides with the boundary of the City of London—traditionally the financial center. On the north bank it runs from Wapping as far as the Royal Docks in Beckton, with a huge loop half-way along forming the Isle of Dogs (where the Canary Wharf complex now stands). South of the river its extent is not so great, as it follows the bank eastward to the promontory formerly occupied by the timber-handling Surrey Docks.

Walking through Docklands today, with its jumble of restored warehouses, new housing developments, massive new office buildings, grandiose public spaces, a few quaint old streets and churches, unused wharves, and vast stretches of levelled empty land, it is difficult to reconstruct the history of the area from what meets the eye. For the last four centuries, the river was the key to London's apparently limitless trading empire. By the end of the 18th century, severe congestion and inadequate storage facilities were resulting in huge losses in commodities left prey to rot and thieves on the quays, and that in turn led to a demand for enclosed wet docks where ships could be unloaded in security, and for enormously increased warehouse space.

176

The age was dawning when British ships, British industry, British goods, and British force dominated the trade and economy of nations as distant as Australia and the Far East. Gradually the entire river was lined with warehouses and wharves, with even larger docks and more warehouses and sheds behind them. Three of the earliest, the West India Dock on the Isle of Dogs (begun 1799), the London Dock in Wapping (1802), and St. Katharine Dock next to the Tower (1827), consisted of uniform rows of brick shell and timber floor constructions developed with private funds by London merchants eager to capitalize on overseas trade. Typically four or five stories high, these warehouses boasted some of the most technologically advanced structural systems of the time, enormous brick buildings which combined the new materials of cast and wrought iron with an elemental classicism.

Development continued through the 19th century, moving further downriver, with the Royal Victoria (1855) and Royal Albert (1880) docks, and even into the 20th century, with the King George V Dock in 1921. All were vast, specialized, private worlds hidden from the public behind high walls. The Isle of Dogs, centred on the West India and Millwall Docks, had only a tiny fringe of population around the edges. The long-lived industrial building boom represented by the extensive dockworks fell victim by the 1960s to a later stage of the forces of technological and economic change that had initially brought the docks into being. Already in the 19th century, ships had become too big for the upriver docks; after 1945, containerization changed the pattern of goods handling. In the interim, during World War II, the docks suffered terrible devastation by German bombing, which left the area almost as ravaged as Berlin was to be: something like half the storage and warehousing was destroyed. Despite attempts at rallying, by 1971 all the upriver docks except the West India and Millwall group had closed; those followed in 1980.

The story of the redevelopment falls into two episodes, before and after the setting up of the London Docklands Development Corporation in 1981; and it covers both housing and commercial buildings.

The world of the docks had always been remote from the lives of most Londoners, inhabited as it was by people connected to shipping, from sailors to stevedores, and while its longshoremen and seamen may have helped supply necessary goods, they were hardly socially integrated into the life of the rest of the city. The area was physically isolated, too: with its self-contained economic life, it had never been linked by a direct Underground (subway) line to central London, and road access was patchy. Like many of the north-eastern inner-city boroughs, Docklands remained a stronghold of socialist politics.

In the 1970s, a series of proposals ranging from commercial development to low-income rental housing were advanced by various groups. The Greater London Council (GLC) governed London as a whole, but as it oscillated between Labour and Conservative control, plans for the area shifted too. The local boroughs resisted commercial development and instead argued for low-cost, largely rental housing. None of the various schemes put forward seemed to have much chance for success because of the prohibitively high cost of the necessary infrastructures, particularly transportation facilities. Nonetheless, bit by bit, change occurred. Parts of Surrey Docks were transformed into housing and parks, and the developers of St. Katharine Dock put up hotels, offices, and a private marina. Many riverside and river-based industries survived, and planned to stay in the area. Small-scale urban redevelopment was underway. Artists and others were moving in to warehouses and converting them to studios or apartments, and a few commercial enterprises had opened.

When the last upriver docks closed in 1980, and the former working population of 55,000 in the area was effectively unemployed and powerless, it was clear that a revival of the lost port industries on anything remotely resembling their former scale was impossible, and large tracts of unused—or underused, as developers prefer to put it—land remained available for possible development. The Conservatives had regained control of the central government in 1979, under Margaret Thatcher, and they soon settled the fate of Docklands. The London Docklands Development Corporation (LDDC) came into being in 1981: control of the area was removed from the local socialist councils and given over to market forces heavily conditioned by government investment. On the grounds that redevelopment had been paralyzed for years by squabbling

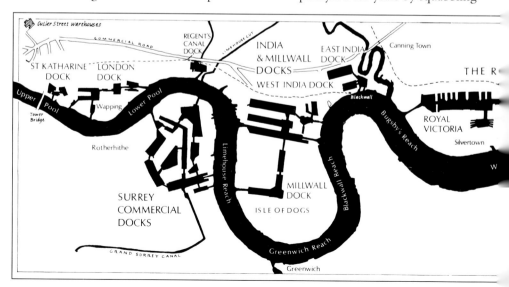

between the GLC (dismantled by the government in 1985) and local boroughs, the LDDC chose to entice private investment into the area by using government funds and other inducements.

The LDDC's chief device for minimizing development risks was the creation of an Enterprise Zone. Established in 1982 (and eventually wound up in 1991), it offered developers an apparently unbeatable package: no land tax on developments and no taxes for ten years, a 100 per cent capital allowance against tax, and, best of all, freedom from troublesome planning controls. The designated zone was in and just north of the Isle of Dogs—an uninhabited area of 8,000 square meters (860,000 square feet) on the site of the old West India, Millwall and East India

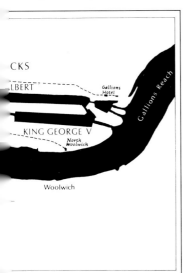

128 *left* Map showing the main areas involved in the redevelopment of Docklands, London, England.

129 *above* London's Docklands before World War II. We are looking west toward the distant City (signaled by bridges). In the foreground is the Isle of Dogs, with the three basins of the West India Dock; the quay between the two right-hand basins is now the site of Canary Wharf, that on the left of Heron Quays (cf. ill. 134). Beyond, the river curves around the many basins of the Surrey Docks, on the south bank.

Docks. The LDDC received annual allocations from the government which would help purchase and clear land, and prepare it for development by providing everything from roads to sewers. London is not the first city impelled by the loss of income from obsolete industries to craft sweetheart deals for developers. Precisely the same thing happened with the Community Redevelopment Agency (CRA) in Los Angeles and Hollywood. And as elsewhere, developers found the terms almost too good to be true, constituting real incentives for investing in the area in question. In London, however, it soon became clear that an elaborate, real life Monopoly game was underway, for the private investment that was heading for Docklands was simply being siphoned off from other potential investment sites in the City, sites without the benefit of such generous tax credits. The unimaginative response elsewhere in the City was to promote their own developments, thereby increasing the amount of office space—and vacant offices. Just how much potential tax revenue was lost is unclear, although in 1990 the Docklands Consultative Committee estimated it at £1.33 billion.

Left to the slow-paced scale of unmanaged change, over time the physical and social composition of Docklands would probably have altered considerably. Without guarantees, no one could predict how long it would take to become a pole of attraction, a process too slow and risky for the biggest developers. Downtown London had already undergone major development throughout the postwar period, and, as in the other two international financial centers, New York and Tokyo, new land for expansion was not easy to locate. Docklands offered the bonus of being inexpensive and free of the inconvenience of many residents to displace. But big developers need more than that to begin a project and, through the offices of the LDDC and the Enterprise Zone, they got it. Much of the risk was eliminated and an appalling part of the cost of large-scale development was transferred from the private sector to the public. The question was less *whether* Docklands would change, than *who* would profit, *who* would pay, *how* rapidly change would occur, *who* would control it and what role architecture would play in the enterprise. The Thatcher government's answer was that developers would profit (buying land at below market rates), the public would pay, and changes would be rapid and controlled by private, often foreign, capital.

Docklands represents a phase in a new global social and economic order, which is characterized by a polarization in income distribution and in the occupational distribution of workers: there are more high-income and more low-income jobs around, and in raw numbers more of the latter. A vast supply of low-wage jobs in London and elsewhere, often held by members of immigrant ethnic and racial minority groups, sustains the high-income residential and commercial precincts, with low-wage jobs clustered in expensive restaurants, gourmet shops and boutiques, catering firms and cleaners, and other personal services such as house cleaning and repairs, beauticians and nail salons. The downgrading of the manufacturing sector in London has led to a reduction in the number of unionized shops with union wages, and an increase in sweatshops and industrial home work, especially in the garment industry. This local dispersal of employment is linked to the global assembly line, characterized by the spatial fragmentation of work, with goods produced and assembled wherever the cost of labor and economies of scale make it cost-effective. It has the effect of neutralizing the potential political power of the workforce, who no longer work in sufficient proximity to develop effective strategies against capital.

Part of the strategy for developing Docklands involved downplaying the presence of what few residents and remaining industries there were, and rewriting the area's history. The LDDC made one of the key conditions of Docklands redevelopment the relocation of the few existing river-based industries, whether they wanted to move or not. Despite previous undertakings to the contrary, they were moved out of the area rather than elsewhere in Docklands. Ultimately unfulfilled promises were made about huge employment opportunities. Local people were promised job retraining programs through the LDDC, but so far these have received relatively little funding, and employment in adjacent residential areas is limited. A study commissioned by the LDDC (but then suppressed and not published) foresaw no more than 1,800 jobs in Docklands going to residents of the boroughs affected by the redevelopment, and many of these would be part-time. Except for low-paid service jobs, most of the new workers in Docklands were employees simply transferred by companies from their previous locations, usually elsewhere in London.

As is common in many capitalist projects, the LDDC and developers made it appear that the objections residents systematically raised during the 1980s amounted to nothing more than ignorant opposition to the forces of progress and redevelopment. They depicted opponents as attached to outdated socialist politics which called for government intervention rather than the modernizing energies of international capital and market forces. In response to these skewed presentations, resistance groups coalesced in a counter campaign of information and activism; among their most poignant observations was that the government preached against socialism, but practiced it on behalf of international corporations. The groups most aided by government intervention were the private developers who received price breaks, subsidies, and enormous favors from the public transportation network.

In fact, the favors in the transportation line have been much slower to materialize than was initially expected. Road access was improved: the Docklands Highway connecting the City with Canary Wharf cost £200 million in public money. Existing overground rail lines were extended to form the Docklands Light Railway, which reached down to new riverside housing at the tip of the Isle of Dogs—but that soon proved inadequate. The most important element, the extension of the Jubilee Line of the London Underground, was the subject of continued wrangles over funding between the government and private developers. Work did not finally begin until 1993—after the LDDC had been wound up (in 1991), and as the Canary Wharf developers went bankrupt. Coincidentally, London Transport had been induced to move their headquarters to the Canary Wharf tower shortly before work began.

The production of housing, as well as offices, in Docklands depended for its success on those transportation networks. Rental units never figured prominently in the Thatcherite agenda for Docklands development, but affordable housing for sale as well as cooperative, self-help housing association developments became part of the LDDC plans, along with a mandate to improve existing housing. Private builders received access to LDDC property so as to correct what was perceived as an imbalance in Docklands, where over 80 per cent of residential accommodation consisted of council housing, i.e. publicly owned rental units, erected largely after 1945.

The commitment to private housing, particularly for lower income groups, was not particularly strong: on the Isle of Dogs, twenty-six housing schemes were completed between 1981 and 1992, but only six on LDDC land, and of the over 15,000 units built in Docklands, just over 2,000 were for local people. Large development firms built the bulk of the flats and houses, largely in various traditional styles, with a few exceptions such as the nautically detailed Cascades apartment block by Campbell, Zogolovitch, Wilkinson & Gough (1988). Another project, Burrell's Wharf (Jestico & Whiles, begun 1987), along the southern tip of the Isle of Dogs, blended new constructions with adaptations of existing manufacturing and industrial facilities into shops, offices and flats. Unusual in working with the existing building fabric, Kentish Homes developers handsomely juxtaposed rough bricks and beam warehouse conversions with newer versions of the same type and with sleek concrete panel grids on others.

Among the groups receiving assistance from the LDDC were self-help housing associations, usually formed specifically for the purpose of building flats or terrace housing in Docklands. Three such associations (the Great Eastern, the Isle of Dogs Self-Build Housing Association, and the Second Isle of Dogs Self-Build Housing Association) consisted of local residents who purchased land from the LDDC and erected 89 three-bedroom dwellings at Maconochie's Wharf (1985–90) adjacent to Burrell's Wharf, with the help of Roy Stout of the Stout & Litchfield Architectural Partnership. Within strict LDDC standards that insisted upon uniformity in general mass and orientation, timber details, and slate roofs, residents turned out to be capable of building credible housing, modest in scale and well-constructed, with interiors suited to the needs of specific families.

Speculation drove up residential prices after 1985, until the stock market slump of October 1987 sounded the end of speculative building for units to sell. Some new council estates were built, however, including Masthead Terrace (1990–92) by the Alan J. Smith Partnership. These boldly chromatic two- to six-story blocks are, like most of the new Docklands housing, quite traditional in design, either following the earlier

130 Stout & Litchfield Architectural Partnership, Maconochie's Wharf self-build scheme, West Ferry Road, London, 1985–90.

council schemes or adapting traditional features of domestic design to new terraces. Elsewhere, faced with existing housing, a different solution was occasionally adopted. Although much was in desperate need of repair both inside and out, the LDDC's early allocation of funds for improvements to such buildings was largely limited to landscaping, followed later by cosmetic adjustments to exteriors. The Millpond Estate in Bermondsey, for instance, south of the river, was tarted up with colonnades, new doors and windows, railings, flowerboxes, strategic plantings of trees and rebuilt dock walls. As the Rotherhithe Community Planning Centre bitterly observed, the new owners of adjacent luxury units did not want a panorama of the slums. Such LDDC enterprises squarely confront the reality of uneven development with the myth of an idyllic community.

In the sphere of commercial development, several additional factors played a key role in both the character and the form of what was built. First, in 1985, the Bank of England relaxed its rule that banking firms had to have their headquarters within the City of London: the low rents and freedom from rates offered by the Enterprise Zone were now an invitation that could be accepted. Then, in 1986, the financial revolution known as 'Big Bang' led to further expansion and to a call for buildings with facilities for new technology. New technology was also a spur behind the move of major newspaper groups to Docklands, spearheaded by the relocation of News International (publishers of *The Times*) to the filled-in site of the London Dock. The result from the mid-1980s was a great expansion in height and density: projects were radically redesigned, and in some cases new buildings were demolished and replaced by something larger. Prices, which in 1981 had averaged £50,000 per acre, had by 1988 reached as much as £10,000,000 per acre for exceptional sites.

Given the enormous incentives to build and the boom economy of the time, developers stampeded Docklands. The results were predictable: many ill-conceived, indifferently designed, and poorly built projects, garbed in one of several Postmodern fashions and mostly speculative in nature, appeared, it seemed, overnight. Building fast did not necessarily mean building badly, however. Nicholas Grimshaw's steel-frame *Financial Times* Building (1988), within the Enterprise Zone on the old East India Dock site, completed in just a year, is a case in point. The client asked for a simple industrial shed, but Grimshaw saw the visual possibilities of the powerful printing presses at work, so he wrapped the building in an aluminum skin, and pulled a frameless glass skin, interrupted only by slender steel columns with brackets, over the section where the presses were, providing a spectacular sight at night when they were at work and the building was ablaze with light. (The structure's subsequent fate is illustrative of the rapid changes that affect commercial and industrial buildings in the late 20th century: in 1995 the presses had been moved out to other sites, and the *Financial Times* was giving up its purpose-built, much-praised building.) Another notable exception to the reign of mediocrity is Michael Hopkins's David Mellor Building (1991) in Shad 131 Thames, south of the river. Care and clarity of construction, quality of materials, and elegant, unadorned simplicity distinguish both buildings by contrast with the typically fussy, overdone office buildings in the area.

One of the most popular buildings in Docklands is the Storm Water Pumping Station by John Outram (1988) on the eastern shore of the Isle 133 of Dogs. Done up in bright stripes of red, yellow and purple brick with equally loud colors on the historicizing columns, capitals, pediment and roundel, the Station design takes a necessary but not particularly exciting

131 Michael Hopkins and Partners, David Mellor Building, Shad Thames, London, 1991.

132 Nicholas Grimshaw and Partners, Financial Times Building, East India Dock Road, London, 1988.

133 John Outram Associates, Storm Water Pumping Station, Isle of Dogs, London, 1988.

activity and turns it into a startling visual experience. Not all is in the eye of the beholder, however: most of the neo-Egyptian details actually double as functional elements for the pumping station.

Canary Wharf
Canary Wharf is the most important development in Docklands, and affords the best example of the development game and its connection with the architectural world. It is an overscaled version of a process repeated throughout the world. The site, within the Enterprise Zone, is significant: near the north end of the Isle of Dogs, on the quay separating two basins of the historic, but badly war-damaged, West India Dock. Whatever was built there would have to conform to a long, narrow ground-plan. And the complex would also find itself isolated—from the City by working-class districts, and on the Isle of Dogs itself within the no-man's-land of the old dock precinct. These factors go some way toward explaining both the eventual formal layout and the developers' insistence on presenting their creation as part of historic London.

English proposals for the site in 1984 called for the conversion of existing structures into dwellings, shops, offices and cafés. But in 1985 an American developer, G. Ware Travelstead, stepped in with an entirely commercial scheme that envisioned much greater density and grandiosity in architecture and urban organization.

Travelstead headed a consortium that included two American investment banks, Crédit Suisse First Boston and Morgan Stanley, both of whom wanted new headquarters buildings. Skidmore, Owings & Merrill (SOM) and Pei Cobb Freed, American firms with international practices, were called in as architects. The resulting scheme included three towers, all slightly taller than the single one eventually built. Objections from the GLC and some local boroughs—notably Greenwich, worried by the effect of skyscrapers as a backdrop to the view of Inigo Jones's and Sir Christopher Wren's famous buildings—came to nothing (Enterprise Zone status made objecting very difficult). Tower Hamlets, the borough covering the area, was in any case in favor of the scheme because of the promise of jobs for local people. By 1987 the infrastructure was complete. At this stage, however, Travelstead realized his funding was inadequate and backed out. The American developer was then followed by a Canadian developer, the Reichmann brothers' Olympia & York.

With global investments in real estate as well as many other sectors, Olympia & York claimed to be one of a handful of international developers with the ability to finance projects with their own funds. Among their notable ventures are the commercial structures in Toronto at First

136

Canadian Place and Queen's Quay Terminal, and in New York at Battery Park City, which Olympia & York took over in 1981, especially the World Financial Center there, another vast complex of office space with four towers designed by Cesar Pelli (architect of the Canary Wharf tower).

134   Olympia & York made their presence felt at once. For them, SOM reconfigured the plans on a much more ambitious scale. Conveniently bisected by the Docklands Light Railway and accessible from the west by a major existing road, the 71-acre (28.5-hectare) site of Canary Wharf was intended to contain nearly 10 million square feet (929,000 square meters) of office space and shops, not to mention an estimated 250 restaurants and other service facilities. The development site was also expanded, to include Port East on the north side of the northern dock basin (where the only early 19th-century warehouses in the entire wet-docks system still survive) and Heron Quays to the south. The armature upon which the design of Canary Wharf proper was to be hung deliberately summoned references to Baroque composition, the design strategy of choice for bastions of absolute power in the 17th and 18th centuries. The grand, tree-lined space of Westferry Circus inaugurates the sequence to the west, at the junction with the access road from central London.

135   From it, a perspectival axis extends eastward, opening into Cabot Square, then splitting into two around an island of low buildings culminating in the colossal punctuation mark of a 50-story skyscraper. In the scheme as planned before work stopped (a subject to which we shall return), the axis resumed beyond the tower to cross another square and terminate at a smaller circular piazza, Cartier Circle.

SOM supervised the design of the entire scheme and also provided some of the individual buildings. The other participating architects were similar large, well-known architectural firms with international practices—Pei Cobb Freed, Cesar Pelli, and Kohn Pederson Fox (KPF)—and also some smaller firms—Koetter and Kim, Aldo Rossi, and Hanna/Olin Landscape Architects. After protests at the absence of British architects, local offices were brought in, such as Troughton McAslan and, if the project should continue, Norman Foster Associates. Before his death, James Stirling of Stirling and Wilford received a commission to build a series of residential towers along the river side of Westferry Circus.

As Olympia & York press releases made clear, the purposes of the design were rhetorical and representational. Only with the promise of something novel and grand could potential tenants be seduced away from other locations in the City. Three straightforward design objectives characterized the buildings for Canary Wharf: homogeneity of overall appearance, variety in detail, and historicism. For leasing purposes,

Olympia & York needed enough variety for potential clients to have distinctive office buildings, but enough homogeneity for the entire complex to be a definable entity. SOM established a set of design guidelines to cover everything from set-backs to materials and facade details. Along with the urban plan itself, their professed goal was to distill the rich texture of London's older neighborhoods in a new setting, with individual and massively scaled "signature" buildings designed by different architects to add limited variety.

The elevations of Westferry Circus, by SOM and by Koetter & Kim, are in a stripped-down classical style, with cornices and an arcade of paired piers. The arcade theme runs through the whole development, establishing a traditionalist note. From Westferry Circus, West India Avenue leads to Cabot Square, where at the corners two restrained, pedestrian variations on familiar Modernist models face one another: to the north, Pei Cobb Freed's building for CS First Boston compressed 500,000 square feet (4,650 square metres) into stacks of granite panels in a trabeated pattern, while to the south for Morgan Stanley SOM glazed a giant box and added tapering mullions. KPF's two buildings at 20 Cabot Square and 30 South Colonnade are slicked-up versions of 1930s streamlined generic government classicism, alternating vertical panels of glazing and grey granite between heavy bases and high attics, and a full-height cylindrical tower at one corner. The tower is echoed symmetrically on what is the most overtly historicist and eclectic building in the group, 10 Cabot Square, by SOM, which combines in the by now familiar Postmodern collage manner allusions to a range of architectural modes. The dominant flavor is, however, American, including sub-Louis Sullivan Celtic interlace decoration. Further along, prompted by Olympia & York who wanted greater stylistic variety, Troughton McAslan rejected such heavy-handed historicism in favor of a tautly wrapped Modernist granite-and-glass-skinned block. Bands of different glazing and slender columns running from the portico to the third floor constitute only a faint attempt to engage any of the historical sources proposed by SOM. Such design strategies characterized many smaller urban developments in the 1980s, where memory was carefully refabricated to simulate the diversity of a city constructed over time rather than in a few months.

Signature architecture serves as an important instrument for two related goals: marketing office space and focusing criticism on form. Not surprisingly, Cesar Pelli's skyscraper at One Canada Square generated the most spirited discussion. Clad in stainless steel panels, the 800-foot (244-meter) obelisk is the tallest building in Britain and the second tallest in Europe. It towers over everything else in London, performing the

134

135

134–136

134 Skidmore Owings & Merrill, early project for Canary Wharf, London, begun 1988, looking east. Beyond Westferry Circus (foreground), the axis leads to Cabot Square and the pyramid-topped tower of One Canada Place. Some changes were made to the designs, and the two towers at the end of the site are also unbuilt.

136 Cesar Pelli, One Canada Square, Canary Wharf, London, seen across Inigo Jones's Queen's House and Wren's Royal Hospital, Greenwich, in 1991.

obvious function of a skyscraper—an emblem of power. The Prince of 136 Wales was only the best-known of those who complained that its scale was out of proportion with the rest of the city, let alone with the Isle of Dogs. Well-paid and well-published, Pelli could afford to disdain criticisms, since the great bonus of the Enterprise Zone for developer and architect is that it operates entirely outside of the public control exercised through planning commissions or citizen's review boards.

The most idiosyncratic of all the designs are as yet unrealized: two buildings by Aldo Rossi, intended to form the corner of a public square on one side and on the other frame the corner of an old lock. They pick up some of the chromatic richness familiar from Rossi's Hotel Il Palazzo 124 in Fukuoka, with pink and red stone facing and an enormous green copper barrel vault on what is called the Basilica structure. By way of contrast, along the edge of the docks the two facades appeal to the local warehouse tradition with their cast iron colonnades and metal panel revetments, the sole homages in Canary Wharf to the earlier building tissue. Olympia & York's financial problems halted construction at little

135 *opposite* Looking down on Cabot Square, Canary Wharf. On the left, buildings by SOM and Troughton McAslan are separated by the Docklands Light Railway. On the right is a corner of SOM's Morgan Stanley building, followed by two KPF facades. Pelli's tower rises beyond the station.

more than the foundation, so the way they will fit into the development remains to be seen.

In view of the galaxy of foreign architects employed, and remoteness of the site on the Isle of Dogs, it is perhaps not surprising that Olympia & York elected to promote Canary Wharf to its audience as having a 'normal and natural appearance'. The pitch to prospective British and overseas clients stressed the architects' efforts to study the urban fabric of historic London, and presented the open spaces as thoroughly local in type—London squares for today. In fact, to the average British visitor the complex feels completely alien, provoking bafflement or exhilaration according to the individual. Norman Tebbit, Secretary of State for Trade and Industry, had excitedly predicted in 1986 that the area of the West India and Millwall docks would become "Manhattan-on-Thames," and that is the effect, whatever the verbal suggestions of Regent Street, Georgian squares, or the heyday of the British Empire.

And what of the nature of the new urban spaces? As in similar developments elsewhere in the late modern world, the notion of the public embodied in the new streets and squares was limited from the outset, for the so-called public space, without exception, was in fact private, as Olympia & York retained the prerogative to control both access and activities. Security police patrol the private streets; at the gated entrances visitors are scrutinized and access is carefully limited. (To be sure, the IRA bomb in 1996 at nearby South Quay was a potent reminder that in eras of political and economic unrest such theaters of rampant capitalism as Canary Wharf will be targets of dissidents and terrorists.) The developers' publicity continually asserted that Canary Wharf would be for that indistinct category, "people." But the kinds of facilities the developers pointed to as being available to these people were those typically favored by office workers and not necessarily those of interest to blue-collar workers living in the adjacent areas: chiefly expensive restaurants, shops selling designer clothes, wine bars and cafés.

By 1985–86, in the midst of England's economic boom, 1.8 million people lived at or below the poverty line, twice as many as in 1960, and in 1991, an estimated 75,000 were homeless. Homelessness in Docklands nearly quadrupled between 1979 and 1987, and the price of new housing built under the auspices of the LDDC far exceeded the meager resources of these families, at least until after the recession had taken effect. Against these masses of new poor, Canary Wharf and much of Docklands offered an isolated oasis. The many hypothetical images distributed by Olympia & York portray well-dressed office workers eating lunch outdoors, visiting art galleries, swinging out of their cars, or shopping in upscale shops. They do not envision people washing windows, patrolling parking, vacuuming offices or repairing copy machines—let alone setting up ad hoc ball games on the lawn at the center of Westferry Circus, engaging in political activity in the streets, or clutching beer or cider cans, pushing grocery carts full of belongings, or sleeping overnight on benches.

In Canary Wharf and the rest of Docklands, the struggle is not between public and private sectors, but *which* public and *which* private will control the future of the area. In the United States and most capitalist countries where land is a commodity, property owners develop their property and public bodies attempt to mediate between private interests and the welfare of the community. In Docklands, the private property owners allowed to participate in development are huge international conglomerates, and the public interests were represented by the Secretary of State for the Environment and the LDDC, meeting in secret and in service to market-driven development. Smaller private property owners, such as low- and moderate-income residents displaced by transportation thoroughfares, or river-based industries whose operations failed to conform to the image the LDDC had in mind for Docklands, were systematically left out of the equation. The LDDC was likewise enabled by the terms of its creation to ignore the desire of local government, in the form of democratically elected boroughs and neighborhood and community groups, to participate in planning and overseeing the enormous changes being wrought to their communities.

But although in 1990 the LDDC and private developers seemed to be winning, only two years later many Docklands developers, thrashed by the spiraling recession, were out of business, and the office real estate market had plunged. Even Olympia & York struggled with the sword of Damocles hanging overhead, forced by the threat of bankruptcy to sell off properties at bargain prices, default on some interest payments, and reorganize where possible in order to salvage their investment in Canary Wharf, losing control of the enterprise in the process. By 1993 Olympia & York's total indebtedness amounted to $20 billion, and receivership and the forced sale of some properties were inevitable. At Canary Wharf in 1994 empty offices stretched on forever, empty trains pulled in and out of the station, partially built structures emerged awkwardly from the ground, and car parks stood vacant. At the time of writing, however, ten years after the great boom in Docklands began, Canary Wharf is back in Reichmann hands, and while much of the accommodation is still untenanted, four-fifths of the flagship tower are let.

Canary Wharf poses a number of questions, not least of which concerns the role of architects. Given the level of detail in SOM's master plan and the design guidelines, the individual firms were left to do a little facade, lobby and roof work. In fact, Olympia & York adopted the title "conceptual architects" for the firms participating, giving them no responsibility beyond the initial design concept. This makes it possible for architects from the most avant-garde to the most institutional to have large international practices, by the simple expedient of having little to do with the actual building. They need only provide the kind of acceptable cultural image that will encourage tenants to rent, visitors to come, and criticism to fix on facade studies and the Baroque urban plan rather than confront the social and political implications of the project.

URBAN INTERVENTIONS IN SPAIN AND FRANCE

Docklands epitomizes the contradictions and tensions in the structure of the contemporary workplace, as well as the worst aspects of decision-making politics in the misuse of public lands and spaces. It is also the physical realization of the contemporary configuration of the workplace. The examples to be considered below fall roughly into three broad groups, defined by architectural language and hence the understanding of specific social and built environments. Generally, designing new workplaces in existing urban areas entails either sprucing up what is there already through the adroit deployment of a dramatic new architectural language, or inserting a striking new element without substantially altering the character of the surroundings. A third solution, by far the easiest of all, is to insist on employing one architectural language in any place, at any time, with little regard for other factors. While this approach allows the designer to use a personal repertoire of tried and true techniques, it also usually grossly simplifies the myriad problems associated with building.

Two recent airports, one by Rafael Moneo and the other by Renzo Piano, illustrate the point. Located deep in the countryside far to the northeast of the city, Seville's new San Pablo Airport (1991) by Moneo follows a standard organizational schema. But Moneo's particular solution demonstrates that architects can render the most complicated functional programs clear and compelling. Although constructed rapidly in anticipation of Expo '92 in Seville, the airport also looked forward to accommodating future expansion, for its life expectancy extends well beyond the end of the fair. Rather than succumbing to the facile and often banal appeal of high-tech imagery deployed in a multi-purpose shed, typical of Renzo Piano's airport in Osaka (1994) or of Ricardo Bofill's reflective glass box for Barcelona Airport (1991), Moneo deftly summoned elements drawn from Spanish–Moorish architecture. The

137

138

137 Rafael Moneo, San Pablo
Airport, Seville, Spain, 1991.

138 Renzo Piano Building Workshop,
Kansai International Airport, Osaka,
Japan, 1994.

concrete block facing, fabricated of a local, warm yellow sand, and the roof covering of brilliant blue ceramic tile together appeal to ancient vernacular traditions.

Instead of the expansive, monotonous transparency of the other two airports, Moneo's San Pablo became a fortress-like refuge against the searing Seville sun in the manner of more traditional Spanish buildings, relying on the thermal properties of the materials, orientation, and fenestration patterns to cool interiors. Inside, the traveler meets not the tedious and anonymous spaces standard in regional shopping malls, but a setting defined by natural light gently diffused through a long row of double cupola skylights, each of which tops a large arch springing from robust, flared concrete columns. Tectonic elements and materials together emphasize the continuity of present functions, however technologically advanced, with those of the distant past.

138 Renzo Piano's response halfway round the world in Japan could hardly be more different: a steel and glass structure engineered to perfection, monotonous perfection. Its chief claim to fame may be that it survived the 1995 Kobe earthquake. Even when it is realized with skill and sensitivity, the limitations of the multipurpose shed are obvious: endless repetition of the same motif producing environments that may well be clear and calm, but are of mind-numbing and irritating sameness.

The flowering of architecture in Spain during the late 1970s and 1980s is comparable to similar bursts of creativity in Germany in the 1920s, Italy in the 1930s, and Japan in the 1970s. In each case, political and economic conditions were essential components. The situation in Spain was fueled by pent-up demand from years of strict control under Francisco Franco. His death in 1975 liberated suppressed architectural creativity as the country hastened to install a vast new infrastructural network to compensate for decades of neglect. Although the 1960s and 1970s saw the despoiling of the country's magnificent coastline by an orgy of speculative building and mountains of cement poured on pristine landscapes— Spain was hardly the only victim of such reckless development—a reversal began in the late 1970s. Throughout the 1980s, under the guidance of a socialist administration, the state and the private sector launched a vast public and private building campaign: commissions for railroad stations, museums, air terminals, schools and universities, rehabilitation and reconstruction of historic buildings, housing and commercial and retail space, not to mention preparations for the Olympics in Barcelona and Expo in Seville. This public building gave a generation of Spanish architects opportunities to blossom, and employed thousands of workers in the construction industry. But not even pent-up demand could resist

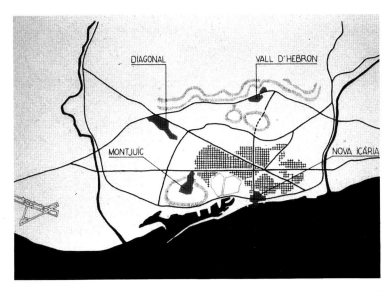

139 MBM Arquitectes (Martorell, Bohigas, Mackay y Puigdomènech), plan of Barcelona, Spain, showing the four Olympic areas, 1992.

the pressure of international economic conditions. By mid-1992, the Spanish government's economic boom abruptly terminated, and as the speculation, tourism and foreign investment which initially concealed the extent of public and private indebtedness began to fade, the structural inadequacies of the Spanish economy—inflation, deficit and balance of trade—became more apparent. Although major industries benefited handsomely from the economic boom of the 1980s, the plan of Spanish Premier Felipe González for resolving the country's economic woes involved slicing unemployment funds for the 17 per cent of the population without work and cutting medical care (a privilege only recently extended to the entire population), as well as increases in value-added tax and income tax, all of which affect primarily the poor. Wracked by the international financial crisis and further weakened by overextension during the 1980s, employment prospects for Spanish architects suddenly dimmed by 1992.

Prior to this, however, they had managed to produce a rich assemblage of striking works. Emblematic of the flowering of Spanish architecture were the cities of Seville and Barcelona, which acquired major buildings from the mid-1980s onward to accommodate two international events, Expo '92 in Seville and the 1992 Olympics in Barcelona. Long neglected

140 Vittorio Gregotti and Correa & Mila, Olympic Stadium, Barcelona, 1992.

by the Franco regime in retaliation for republican resistance during the Spanish Civil War, Barcelona used the Olympics to compress a vast infrastructural campaign that was decades overdue into a few short years, and under the direction of Oriol Bohigas, four zones of development were designated for Olympic facilities, with the goal of enriching existing urban areas instead of eradicating them or moving outside of the city to create an Olympic Village.

A breathtaking variety of facilities were planned to endure long after the Olympics. As the airports by Moneo and Bofill demonstrated, architectural languages and approaches ranged from High Tech to historicizing, with most falling somewhere in between. In the Montjuic area of Barcelona alone the designs range from Santiago Calatrava's crisp and elegantly engineered Telecommunications Tower to the remodeling of the Olympic Stadium by Vittorio Gregotti with Correa & Mila, where a

139

140

busy modern truss and cantilevered canopy were set atop the baroque domed stadium of 1929. Ricardo Bofill's Montjuic sports facility, with its 141 pedimented facade in precast concrete, faces away from the Esplanade of the Olympic Ring and the other sports venues. Although Bofill scaled down the overblown rhetorical use of classical elements typical of his French projects, it still leaves a disquietingly heavy and monumental impression. There is nothing fresh in his design, such as can be found in Calatrava's engineering feats, nor any attempt at a sensitive reinterpretation of a historical architecture as in Moneo's Roman Art Museum in 44, 45 Mérida. Bofill's project epitomizes the formulaic repetition of a personal arsenal of architectural elements heedless of site or tradition.

Bohigas summoned a diverse group of architects, both foreign and Spanish, to produce the Olympic Village, a new area carved out of unused rail and shipping facilities along the shores of the Mediterranean. In addition to new port facilities and 3 miles (5 kilometers) of freshly refurbished beaches, Bohigas's master plan called for thousands of new housing units to be designed by different architects. Liberally interspersed with green spaces, these were intended to replicate the urban consistency and architectural diversity of traditional cities: the brick facing and perimeter blocks lend regularity to the urban tissue, while the many different treatments by architects as diverse as Esteve Bonell and

141 Ricardo Bofill Taller de Arquitectura, I.N.E.F.C. (National Institute of Catalonia for Physical Education), Montjuic, Barcelona, 1991.

Francesc Rius on the one hand, and Oscar Tusquets and Carlos Díaz on the other, prevent the cityscape from becoming one of monotonous replications. Unfortunately, the whole complex is dominated by two skyscraper hotels, one by Bruce Graham, senior partner of Skidmore Owings and Merrill, and the other by the Barcelona firm of Inigo Ortiz Díez and Enrique León García. Completely out of scale with their seven-story neighbors, the hotels represent the typical exploitation of urban centers and beachfront property throughout Western cities more than they do a Barcelonan urbanism.

Happier additions are over one hundred small interventions in public spaces dispersed throughout the city and around its edges, a modest, inexpensive program to add small urban parks, sculpture and murals to neglected sections, such as the powerfully understated memorial next to the church of Santa María del Mar by Carme Fiol (1983).

Along with the construction of new buildings, Spanish architects engaged in the preservation of older ones. The sudden spurt of economic growth during the 1960s led to the destruction of many historic centers, but beginning with the death of Franco, a new attitude and a more focused involvement by architects transformed the field of preservation. For the first time, even busy firms with large portfolios of new buildings began to work with historic preservation under the guidance of local and provincial governments. Exemplary in this respect is Josep Lluis Mateo's transformation of the old Catex Factory (1990) in Barcelona's Poble Nou area, the city's cradle of industrialization. Instead of tearing down the empty factory, the city, with the encouragement of neighborhood residents, elected to develop it as a community facility where the children and grandchildren of former laborers could come to play sports or participate in the cultural center. Mateo's design navigated between the severe classical facade and the elegant riveted iron frame and Catalan-vaulted interiors by inserting brightly colored panels and new flooring inside, and a slender, partially glazed access tower outside. Nearby, José Antonio Martínez Lapena and Elías Torres remodeled a magnificent factory from the 1950s into workshops for fledgling companies. The exposed concrete frame, with its round windows, rational detailing, and streamlined massing, received a new finish and sunshades over the windows, in addition to subdivided interior bays with yellow chain-link fencing as security canopies.

During the same period, from the 1970s through the early 1990s, the city of Paris became the setting for an ambitious group of buildings, collectively dubbed the *Grands Travaux* (large-scale works), that afford an instructive counterpoint to the Spanish example. The impulse for the

142

French scheme came not from an international exhibition or sporting event, but from the desire of French presidents from Georges Pompidou to François Mitterrand to increase massively the art and cultural facilities in Paris. The tales of the individual buildings also reveal shifts in French politics, as some constructions were halted at certain points, government funding withdrawn from others, and earlier decisions were reversed as different political parties came to power. Despite the grand aspirations and the lavish sums of money expended, many of the buildings of the Grands Travaux are undistinguished architecturally. The Pompidou Center, 51, 52 launched in 1969 and opened in 1977, was the first of a series of major undertakings that included the transformation of the old Gare d'Orsay into a museum, designed by Gae Aulenti (1986), the Institut du Monde 147, 148 Arabe, by Jean Nouvel (1987), the Opéra de la Bastille, by Carlos Ott (1989), the Arche de la Défense, by Johan Otto von Spreckelsen (1989), 145 the New Louvre, by I. M. Pei (1993), the new Finance Ministry, by Paul 143, 144 Chemetov and Borja Huidobro (1993), the series of projects for La 146 Villette, master-planned by Bernard Tschumi (parts opened beginning in 1989), the transformation of the zoology gallery at the Natural History Museum into a Gallery of Evolution, by Chemetov and Huidobro (1994), and the Bibliothèque de France, by Dominique Perrault (begun 1990).

The range of the projects varies from the reconfiguration and adaptation of the 19th-century Orsay rail station and parts of the Natural History Museum to brand new buildings such as the Institut du Monde Arabe and the Bastille Opéra. Projects such as Pei's expansion of the Louvre, with the addition of over 60,000 square meters (650,000 square feet) of underground space, were intended to obtain maximum additional area with minimum visible disruption to the historic center. The glazed pyramid in the Cour Napoléon raised a hue and cry throughout 143 the world, but turned out to be modest in scale and only minimally disruptive aesthetically, far less so than many opponents feared. Indeed, the pyramid provided a fresh entrance to the new underground facilities for 144 visitors, bathed the entrance area in natural light, and signaled the departure of the hundreds of automobiles connected with the Finance Ministry that formerly occupied the site. Surely even the staunchest traditionals would prefer the pyramid to an autopark and its fumes, even if it has led to insufferably long queues.

Other projects share the same goal of maximum size, but with less felicitous results. With the Arche de la Défense, the Géode Theater at La 145 Villette, and the Finance Ministry, the government clearly sought maxi- 146 mum visual "bang for the buck." Situated at the terminus of the Grand Louvre–Place de la Concorde–Champs-Elysées–Arc de Triomphe axis,

142 Josep Lluis Mateo, remodelled Catex Factory, Barcelona, 1990.

143, 144 *below and opposite* Pei Cobb Freed & Partners, Grand Louvre, Paris, France, 1993: exterior and interior views of the pyramid.

145 Johan Otto von Spreckelsen (competition winner) and Paul Andreu, Grande Arche de la Défense, Paris, 1989.

145   the Arche de la Défense is a gigantic marble-sheathed cube with a vast hollow core, looming above the new financial district on the western edge of the city. Of staggering constructional complexity—among other things, the building's constant movement had to be allowed for through the pre-stressed concrete structural frame and a vast array of suspension cables—the design was selected from among four hundred entries by President Mitterrand in 1982 and was the work of an unknown and inexperienced Danish architect, Johan Otto von Spreckelsen. Loosely based on the historical precedent of the triumphal arch (and thus alluding to Paris's own Arc de Triomphe), the Arche was to be the communications center for the adjacent financial district and appears to have been designed to make a visual impact on the city comparable to that of the

Eiffel Tower. Alas, it does indeed make a visual impact, but not a particularly favorable one. Where the Eiffel Tower boldly expressed the optimism of the 19th century, this silent, unexpressive, monolithic mass sounds nothing so much as the overwhelming predominance of financial bureaucracies, a sad commentary on the end of the rich and diverse urban fabric of Paris and other historic cities from which increasing spatial segregation progressively drains away much of their liveliness.

Just as the New Louvre design respected the urban area, so the Arche and other projects disdained it. The new Finance Ministry on the eastern rim of Paris adjacent to the Seine, however ingeniously partitioned internally to facilitate circulation and endow each office with a window, meets the city far less efficaciously. The 216,000-square-meter (180,000-square-foot) mass, framed by undeniably routine elevations, spans a site bordered by rue de Bercy, quai de la Rapée and boulevard de Bercy, with one wing extending out over the highway into the Seine and dubbed a "gateway" to the city. It bears comparison to the toll gates erected by Claude-Nicolas Ledoux around Paris during the 1780s that represented a last attempt by the monarchy to replenish the depleted state treasuries. Decisive in the expression of state power and bold in modifying the classical tradition, Ledoux's toll stations so symbolized authoritarian power to his contemporaries that he landed in prison during the Revolution. The new gateway, with its bland austerity and monotonous facades, understates a power no less strong today than two hundred years ago. Along with La Défense on the other side of Paris, it fittingly brackets a

146 Paul Chemetov and Borja Huidobro, Finance Ministry, Paris, 1993.

147, 148 Jean Nouvel, Institut du Monde Arabe, Paris, 1987: entrance front, and elevation with light-sensitive panels.

city dominated by state bureaucracies. But it will probably be remembered chiefly for having finally enabled the liberation of the Louvre from another state agency. The Ministry is a reminder that the story of the Grands Travaux is also one of painfully squandered opportunities, such as Rem Koolhaas's competition design for the Bibliothèque de France (1989), which envisioned richly luminous and sensuous façades of varying degrees of transparency in opposition to the heavy monolith of the Finance Ministry.

Of all the buildings of the Grands Travaux, Jean Nouvel's Institut du 147, 148 Monde Arabe (Arab World Institute) has been the most aesthetically successful. Urbanistically, the lightweight skin and slender metal cage of the structure maintain the scale of the surrounding buildings and directly confront what amounts to a degraded urban area, even opening a generous public square toward the city. The institute is a center for research on and dissemination of information about Arab culture, so Nouvel made several references to Arab motifs, especially the 240 glass and aluminum panels with light-sensitive openings that maintain a constant intensity. They recall the mushrabiya, or window with latticework screen, found in some traditional Arab housing. Here they are rendered in industrial materials with uncommon poetic force.

Fascination with high technology as a source of aesthetic image is common to several of the projects, most successfully resolved in the Institut du Monde Arabe, but seen also in the garish Bastille Opéra and in Adrien Fainsilber's rehabilitation of a meat-packing plant for the Museum of Science and Industry (1986). Unusually among governments in postwar Europe, the French state has been identified with a representative architectural style, just as various French monarchs in the past elected their emblematic architectural aesthetics. High Tech—not only in the Grand Travaux, but in numerous other works, such as those of Rem Koolhaas for Lille and housing by Renzo Piano on the periphery of Paris—and the mammoth overscaled classicism of Ricardo Bofill appear to have been the state architecture of choice since the 1970s. The state is no less prominent and pervasive in other countries, so the decision to affiliate with a particular style is not simply the expression of its power, but a clear decision by the French government to render its presence emphatically apparent wherever it occurs.

In both Spain and France, government funds were poured into major building projects during the last two decades, but to very different effect. Sleek buildings which foreground steel, glass, and visibly complex technologies dominate the skylines of Paris and other cities, radically differentiated from the surrounding urban fabric. Mutely standing in splendid isolation, these buildings are simply objects, as appropriate or inappropriate in France as in Hong Kong, Rio de Janeiro or Melbourne. By contrast, the majority of buildings erected in Spain are deeply rooted in the culture and its architectural traditions, and there is no effort to affirm one style as the exclusive representation of the state. Additionally, the Spanish interventions more consistently sought to recuperate existing but abandoned or outmoded industrial structures.

THE WORLD OF WORK

More than anything else, the reconfiguration of industrial buildings for other uses and urban restructuring schemes remind us how the world of work has changed in the last decades of the 20th century. The decline of heavy industry in Western Europe and the United States and the transfer of production and jobs to less highly paid labor forces elsewhere in the world have led to an increasing polarization, with a growing share of opportunities only for part-time employment, and the concomitant loss of benefits and protections that often come with full-time jobs. All indications are that the trends toward service, part-time, home-based and minimum-wage employment, particularly piece work and sweatshop labor in garment and other industries, will rise rather than fall in future decades. At the same time, greater awareness of the negative environmental impact of many industries continues to propel small and large manufacturers away from urban settings, to depressed rural areas or to Third World nations, where the spectre of unemployment outweighs environmental concerns.

What this means for future architecture and urban design is unclear, but some of the changes that have already occurred left a strong impact on the urban territories of industrialized nations, from the creation of Barcelona's Olympic Village from the ruins of old railroad yards to the transformation halfway round the world of the Los Angeles harbor from a multi-use facility to a modern containerized port. Perhaps the first changes occurred in two parallel movements. Corporations moved out of downtown areas into suburban or semi-rural areas, often called office parks. And cities enticed corporations into the center through the use of tax and financing incentives.

Industrial and business or office parks can be found throughout the world. From Silicon Valley on the San Francisco peninsula to the suburbs of Paris, a strong, decentralizing trend has characterized the development of office and industrial districts. For obvious reasons having to do with pollution, noise and expense, heavy industry gradually migrated out of urban centers during the 19th century. At the same time, people with access to new means of transportation likewise began to move, in a process known as suburbanization. Beginning in the second half of the 20th century, the impulse to move non-industrial business operations out of urban cores strengthened and gathered speed. Propelled by the automobile, trucks and highways, the trend toward the suburbanization of business kept pace with the growth of residential suburbs. With heavy industry already moving out, light industry, warehousing and related activities, and ultimately white-collar employment followed, particularly defense industries during World War II, and the trend accelerated after the war. The planned industrial areas to which they moved, unlike the urban areas they left behind, were usually spacious, designed for ease of traffic circulation and utilities servicing, and were often lavishly landscaped.

The office park followed the industrial park as a means of taking advantage of new roads, cheaper land and ample parking, not to mention lower taxes and fewer big city problems. It is worth remembering that the appeal of the new, park-like settings grew in direct proportion to the increase of crime and poverty in urban cores. Office parks were also cheaper locations for fledgling industries that depended upon low overheads to survive. In Houston, Texas, a classic example of this pattern is the development of the Post Oak area west of the city center. Although a few strip centers (commercial shopping aligned along a roadway) had already migrated to Post Oak by 1970, the development that ignited subsequent office development was Gerald Hines's Galleria, designed by Hellmuth, Obata and Kassabaum with Neuhaus and Taylor (1969–71). Covering 45 acres (18 hectares) and containing nearly 4 million square feet (370,000 square meters) of mixed-use development, the Galleria was intended by Hines to be a center for Houston. The core was the shopping mall, 149

149 Hellmuth, Obata and Kassabaum with Neuhaus and Taylor, Galleria, Houston, Texas, 1969–71.

done up in grand Texas style with ice rinks and skylights. Hotels and office towers by local firms such as 3D/International, S.I. Morris, and Morris★Aubry, and by such internationally known architects as Philip Johnson and Cesar Pelli, were added within a few years, realizing Hines's dream of a new downtown with all of the benefits of suburbia, including acres of parking, cheaper land, and plenty of landscaping. The Docklands development along the Thames to the east of London is yet another example, but business park suburbs ring cities from Hong Kong to San Francisco, Atlanta to Milan, São Paulo to Istanbul.

The second trend—upgrading old central business districts in order to attract business back—grew in tandem with the office and industrial parks. Deserted by the middle classes and by business, city administrations virtually gave away land in order to entice corporations and international capital to reinvest there. Preceded by massive slum clearance projects in the 1950s and 1960s to bulldoze away not only dilapidated housing stock but also their inhabitants, inner-city redevelopment was invariably marked by some or all of the following: attempts at gentrification, upgraded marinas and festival marketplaces, urban shopping malls, sometimes sports stadiums, new parking facilities and even the insertion of new parks or the refurbishing of old ones, such as the colorful but

150   emphatically exclusionary redesign of Pershing Square in Los Angeles by Legorreta Arquitectos with landscaping by Laurie Olin (1994). In the end, city centers took on many of the features of the suburban office parks, which in turn in the United States came increasingly to resemble old centers in terms of traffic problems, pollution, crime, and other big

150 Legorreta Arquitectos and Laurie Olin, Pershing Square Project, Los Angeles, California, 1994.

city problems. The happy language associated with this process (variously referred to as revitalization, gentrification, renewal) emphasizes the transformation from something negative—"dead," poor, unproductive—to something positive, reintroducing the "gentry," that is, more prosperous, educated, middle-class people in areas that are now "alive." Through language as well as design, diverse, often chaotic cities which included the working poor are dismissed, and instead what amount to highly segregated spaces are celebrated as proper urban settings.

Dominated by tight economic constraints, cheap materials, and a functionalist impulse, much of the architecture for office and industrial parks has been uninspired, usually governed by the fact that most of the buildings are structural skeletons onto which architects drape various types of cladding. The variety of materials—precast concrete, bronze-anodized aluminum, stone panels, stainless steel, silver, bronze or green reflective glass—typically stands in inverse proportion to the imaginativeness of the design and the variety of interior spaces. Even the classicizing impulse of 1980s Postmodernism failed to offer much opportunity for dressing up an essentially monotonous building type, usually only a few stories lower than the skyscrapers in central redevelopment areas. A few designers have been successful in devising new solutions for office and industrial spaces that set them apart from the majority and are unusual in the vast market of commercial and industrial building.

The pathbreaking Centraal Beheer Building in Apeldoorn, the 151, 152 Netherlands (1972), by Herman Hertzberger carried into the sphere of the workplace some of the ideas found in housing that stress the ability of occupants to make spatial decisions. Hertzberger argued that in both realms architects needed to develop prototypes that made it possible for individuals to interpret spaces as they chose. In the Centraal Beheer, Hertzberger slotted differentiated working platforms into a regular orthogonal grid with light wells that illuminated offices even on the lowest floors. Instead of the standard open-plan warehouse type of spaces designed for maximum flexibility with the use of partitions, Hertzberger's building complemented visual variety with a three-dimensional grid of spaces susceptible to modification by moving furniture, much as is possible in the warehouse unit. The entire plan is comparable to a small city linked by a variety of passageways and visual connections that radically challenge traditional notions of office space. A more recent Hertzberger project for the Ministry of Social Welfare and Employment in The Hague (1990) provides office space for two thousand state employees, following the principles articulated at Apeldoorn to maximize natural light and spatial variety.

151, 152 Herman Hertzberger,
Centraal Beheer Building,
Apeldoorn, Netherlands.
Above Air view, with the 1972
building in the centre and the
new building of 1995 on the left.
Left One of the light wells in the
1972 building.

The advantages of Hertzberger's organization are readily visible when pitted against Arata Isozaki's Team Disney Building in Orlando, Florida 153 (1991), a classic warehouse spatial type with staircases and internal galleries framing a central atrium. Painted gun-metal gray, the grid of relentlessly identical modular office units extends from the interior corridor to the exterior walls throughout the building, with virtually no natural light and no differentiation from one unit to the next except for the hierarchy of size and nearness to the atrium. The impression is of overwhelming order and control, rendered explicit by the enormous sundial, an image of the corporate measurement of time. By contrast, Hertzberger's building offers a variegated sequence of well-lit spaces 152 modified by their occupants for functional purposes and for decoration. Instead of the Taylorized units of the Disney scheme, the Centraal Beheer challenges the dictates of assembly-line rationality in the workplace by insuring that far more control visibly remains in the hands of the occupants.

Niels Torp's SAS Airline Headquarters in Stockholm, Sweden (1988), is 154 a worthy successor to the Centraal Beheer. Like Hertzberger's client, the chief executive officer of SAS, Jan Carlzon, dispensed with the conventional elements of corporate hierarchy and bureaucratic control typically institutionalized in office buildings and their furnishings. Instead, he envisioned a building in which creative and casual interaction would be encouraged without having to sacrifice privacy. To accomplish this, he abandoned the dogmas of contemporary real estate regarding the ratio of net usable space to gross area in favor of a custom-designed building. Thus while nearly everyone who works in the building has a private

153 Arata Isozaki & Associates, Team Disney Building, Orlando, Florida, 1991.

154 Niels Torp, SAS Airline
Headquarters, Stockholm, Sweden, 1988.

office with individual controls for lighting, windows, and power as well
as personal furniture, the building also offers an uncommon number of
possibilities for informal meetings in many kinds of settings.

154   Torp laid out the complex as if organizing a multi-block street.
Although it is an atrium space, the "street" bears only minimal resem-
blance to such garish but yawningly empty spaces as the atrium of Jon
Jerde's Westside Pavilion in Los Angeles (1985) or the lobby of Johnson/
Burgee's AT&T Building in New York (1978–84). Adorned with trees,
with a view out to an adjacent man-made lake, small cascades and
bridges, the SAS street is framed by building masses ranging from four to
seven stories in height and articulated by varied elevations. Seats and
benches of different types dot the internal street, as do cafes and restaurants, serving as settings for casual encounters and supplemented by a
gym, saunas, swimming pool and squash courts. In its suburban office
park setting, the exterior of the SAS building may not make a distinguished contribution to urban design, any more than Hertzberger's does,

214

but the successful resolution of the interior spaces more than compensates for this. Conversely, the arresting facade of Isozaki's Team Disney Building will never compensate for the drab, suffocating interiors for those who work there.

Of quite a different stamp is Álvaro Siza's Borges & Irmão Branch 155 Bank at Vila do Conde, Portugal (1985). This modest insertion into the cityscape emphasizes its public presence through a series of perspectival vistas opened up in strikingly original ways from the lobby, interior and exterior stairs. While the offices are partitioned in fairly standard ways, the marble revetted lobby and stairs offer a stunning variation of the traditional banking setting. Although the building reveals Siza's Modernist roots, his sensitivity to the topographical and urban context makes the bank more than a Modernist exercise. Oblique passages, sliced vistas into other parts of the building or the surroundings, and other devices are the tools with which Siza transformed the typically mundane setting for financial transactions into an aesthetic delight on a par with that of his museums, in effect reminding us that the workplace deserves as much thoughtful attention as a place to display art.

Equally compelling is the Museum of Fine Arts Administration and Junior School Building in Houston, Texas (1994), by Carlos Jiménez, a combination office building and art school for youngsters. Jiménez rejected the tyranny of the elevator-centered loft tray of tiers of undefined space wrapped in a skin, the archetypal speculative office building,

155 Álvaro Siza, Borges & Irmão Branch Bank, Vila do Conde, Portugal, 1985.

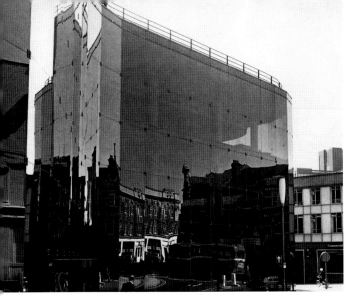

156 Foster Associates,
Willis–Faber and Dumas
Building, Ipswich,
England, 1974.

for a fundamental spatial reconfiguration of the clerical workplace. His resolution of this problem demonstrates how a fine architect can envision new spaces and solutions when given the opportunity.

The limited number of projects that successfully wed architectural accomplishment with humane, individualized and non-Taylorized office settings testifies to the exponentially greater difficulties of such an enterprise. The most common response to programmatic complexity and to the problems associated with inserting a bulky building into an urban or suburban setting has been either a skyscraper with varied facade articulations, or an office block with a glass curtain wall inertly reflecting its surroundings rather than constituting a compelling addition in its own right. Many well-known slick-skinned buildings fall into this category, most notably Cesar Pelli's Pacific Design Center in West Hollywood, California, and Norman Foster's Willis–Faber and Dumas Building at Ipswich in England (1974). The centers of many Asian, European and United States cities own their share of similar buildings, as do suburban office parks throughout the developed world. Postmodern variations combine such oversized, vaguely historicizing details as fan-shaped aedicules with several hues of transparent and reflective surfaces, nowhere more crassly than in Anthony Lumsden's Marriott Hotel (1989), a garish, overwrought addition to the skyline of San Francisco.

Kenneth Frampton lucidly outlined the principles of Productivism: the provision of a neutral and maximally flexible shed, rendered possible by an integrated service network; and the vivid expression of the building's structure and services as well as the process of production itself.

216

Component production and the expression of production processes as well as structural principles in the building are the ideas that underlie many of Norman Foster's buildings, such as the Sainsbury Centre at Norwich in England, and the Hong Kong and Shanghai Banking Corporation headquarters in Hong Kong. His speculative office building in Tokyo, Century Tower (1991), revealed these principles in clear fashion: two towers with eccentrically braced frames, services tucked into opaque projections, and such technological features as lighting,

157

157 Sir Norman Foster and Partners, Century Tower, Tokyo, Japan, 1991.

158 Richard Rogers, Lloyd's Building, London, England, 1978–86.

sprinklers, heating and cooling systems slotted into the interstices between floors and elsewhere. Foster emphasized the structural system by color coding the elements in dark gray, light gray, silver and white. Whatever its merits, this technologically sophisticated, beautifully constructed building could quite literally have been built anywhere, even though the design was conditioned by local site constraints.

The design style pioneered by Foster and Richard Rogers, known as High Tech, comprised a combination of straightforward, uncomplicated plans, factory-produced materials, and a tendency to exposed structural frames. Foster never succumbed to the temptation to expose a building's innards on the exterior as did Rogers. Rogers spent eight years on the

218

design and construction of Lloyd's of London (1978-86), located in the 158
heart of the capital's financial district. This unusual institution, which consists of syndicates of underwriters, is one of the oldest insurance companies in the world (if not necessarily the most stable, as recent actions to collect money from its Names suggest). Business is done as if in a great marketplace, the underwriters meeting in an enormous room to decide on risks to be insured. Rogers's design included this grand room at the core of the building, surrounded by the perimeter development of all other spaces, as indicated by six service towers, and concealed behind the exposed, free-standing structural frame. The maximum flexibility and purity that this scheme supposedly provides also results in fundamentally anonymous, even boring spaces. This is particularly true of the rooms to which are consigned the staff responsible for the care and maintenance of this technological feat: mean, bare, nasty rooms and corridors below ground level, bereft even of natural light. Not surprisingly, neither architect nor client seemed to care much about them.

Despite the emphasis on technological sophistication, the surface of Lloyd's is aging as rapidly and devastatingly as that of the Pompidou Cen- 51 ter, which leads directly to a major problem of emphatically High Tech architecture: the strident application of technological appendages evinces a view of technology as aesthetic scenography rather than a type of architectural knowledge bound up within a broad and continuing research project. On the whole, Foster's more controlled and subtle designs have stood the test of time better, and forthcoming projects such as the sleekly engineered Hong Kong Airport promise even greater refinement.

Since most office buildings are insipid and monotonous, it would be naive to hope for greater richness with industrial building. The larger and

159 Julie Snow of James/Snow, Phillips Plastics Factory, New Richmond, Wisconsin, 1991.

more complex the program, the more difficult it is to work with all the variables in an architectonically and programmatically convincing fashion. Although factories that express in the mode of production and the division of labor into repetitive mindless tasks on the one hand, and creative activity on the other, are few, occasionally an opportunity arises to circumvent the norm with a different approach to manufacturing. With her Phillips Plastics Factory in the prairie outside of New Richmond, Wisconsin (1991), Julie Snow of James/Snow harmonized the company's manufacturing processes with an unusual building. Work is divided among different teams, each of which follows the entire process of producing plastic products, from molding to painting and assembling. Each team enjoys complete control over and responsibility for the artifacts it manufactures. Snow housed the operations in a steel-frame structure bounded by masonry walls and insulation panels and spanned by 160-foot (49-meter) long trusses to keep the interior space as open as possible. While the company deliberately rejected hierarchy and bureaucratic separation, noise considerations dictated that offices and production sections be separated. To reduce the impact of this division, Snow designed a transparent glass wall of 4-foot (1.22-meter) square panels. The same kind of arrangement of open space within a shed is also a convenient tool for absolute control and visibility. At Phillips the management insisted that its goals were entirely the opposite.

160, 161   Another manufacturing plant, the Herman Miller Western Region Manufacturing and Distribution Facility in Rocklin, California (1989), in the Sierra Nevada foothills, embodies another approach to participative management and significant employee involvement in the company, in this instance a long-established, global organization which produces office furniture. Herman Miller's participatory management strategy evolved until by the 1980s every employee had become a shareholder with a personal stake in the quality of the products and the success of the company, a strategy that contributed to its singular economic success. Frank Gehry designed the complex as a series of warehouse, or shed, structures disposed asymmetrically around a central common area which he envisioned as a reduced town square. Set atop a rocky berm and clad in galvanized steel panels, the assembly and storage buildings appear to have quilted surfaces. Like the similarly quilted copper panels of the huge trellis structure that dominates the center of the complex, they are alive with movement and sensuality. Perhaps because the company produces high-quality, carefully detailed furniture, officials encouraged Gehry to use high-quality materials and exacting construction techniques. Although employees will spend most of their time inside the shed

160, 161 Frank Gehry, Herman Miller Western Region Manufacturing and Distribution Facility, Rocklin, California, 1989: assembly and storage buildings (*above*), and "town square."

161 buildings, Gehry dedicated the bulk of his design energy to the town square in the center, where a skylit employee cafeteria with a conical protrusion is tucked into the trellis. The final contribution to the plaza is a thoroughly anomalous folly by Tigerman-McCurry Architects, a domed auditorium sunk into a grassy picnic area rendered in a language that could not be more remote from that of Gehry.

The other strong feature of the Herman Miller project is the landscaping by Martha Schwartz. Instead of planting expanses of lawn around another aluminum-paneled office building as is typical of office parks, Schwartz restored meadows of California wildflowers and native grasses on most of the 156-acre (63-hectare) complex. She added formal lawns and trees only in the plaza itself. Someday this will be the only reminder of the original landscape of the area, an oasis within a depressingly insensitive landscape of ruthless and wasteful suburban and office development. Rocklin residents may not remember Gehry's name, or even that of Herman Miller, but they readily distinguish between the architect-designed building and its boxy, nondescript industrial park neighbors: it is, in the language of several of them, "the funny-looking building on the hill outside town."

Gehry's design strategy of tossing building masses apparently randomly on the plot finds an appropriate collocation in this windswept, once remote site. Just a few years ago the land in this area was agricultural, but population pressure and the increasing cost of land adjacent to major cities spurred developers to assemble the Stanford Ranch Business Park, an office park of gigantic proportions. The same kind of pressures led to thousands of acres of land in and around Rocklin being bulldozed to make way for the kind of badly planned suburban wastelands common throughout California. Such sites as Rocklin are attractive to companies not only because land and labor are cheap, but also because the stringent environmental impact studies and controls characteristic of more prosperous counties in the San Francisco Bay Area or in Southern California have not been enacted or are ignored because of the economic problems that local governments hope to eradicate with the arrival of more jobs.

162 The Houston Fine Art Press in Houston, Texas (1988), designed by Carlos Jiménez, houses an even more limited, more highly refined kind of activity. The Press produces extremely high quality prints and books, and like any factory needed light, ample workspace and some differentiated but non-hierarchical spaces for different kinds of activities. Located on a long, thin lot in one of the city's industrial suburbs, the building accepted and improved upon its neighbors' industrial shed typology. After enveloping the site with a 10-foot (3-meter) high pale gray

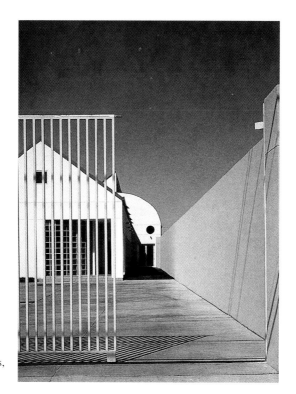

162 Carlos Jiménez,
Houston Fine Art Press,
Houston, Texas, 1988.

concrete wall, Jiménez organized the interior in two large sections, one for public activities and the second for production, as an enfilade of rooms, a sequence leading from the curved glass wall of the small exhibition gallery to the reception and office area. The production zone follows the offices with an abrupt shift of scale and light, the shape changing to that of a combination gable and barrel-vaulted shed split apart at the top to provide extensive daylight. Above all the interiors are articulated by different qualities of light, from the curved glass block wall at the entrance to the high window in the small upper-level work station at the other end, from the clerestory level to the row of windows opposite the office area. Printing demands clear light, hence the interiors have pale cream plastered walls. The pink stucco shed nestles accommodatingly among its neighbors but demonstrates with striking power that even the most utilitarian building or building type can be transformed into compelling architecture. The opposite also holds true. Even the most culturally significant building type can be rendered dull and boring.

Among the most daunting types of building are those for health care, an area in which firms tend to specialize. They demand some of the most

223

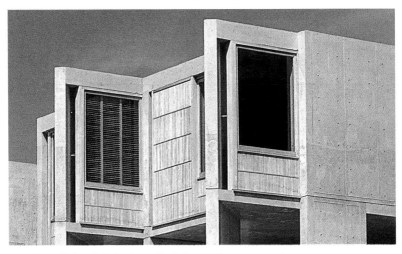

163 Louis Kahn, Salk Institute, La Jolla, California, 1959–65.

164 Machado and Silvetti, parking structure, Princeton University, Princeton, New Jersey, 1991.

complex architectural programs and the participation of many different experts and consultants. Nonetheless, even smaller practices with considerably varied projects manage to take on this type of work successfully. Two buildings designed during the 1980s, both located in busy urban settings, point up radically opposed attitudes toward the architecture of the genre. In 1988, Morphosis (Thom Mayne and Michael Rotondi) completed the Comprehensive Cancer Clinic connected to Cedars– 165 Sinai Medical Center, Los Angeles. Constrained by hospital height requirements, most of the Center sinks one level underground, even though the high water table demanded regular pumping and foundations comparable to those of a skyscraper. The low profile of the building on the outside and the understatement of the entrance and parking arrangements were unusual in the work of this firm, normally known for their distinctive industrial aesthetic. The designers missed few opportunities to express their vision of architecture and, judging both from the actual interiors and from interviews, their attitudes about disease. Throughout the center, Morphosis foregrounded technology and technological instruments, usually against stark white backgrounds, including specially designed lamps, an abstract painting of the building design, a technological folly in the waiting area, and the metal pins and rods affixed to translucent panels. Instead of the harsh, often rusted or boldly black-painted metal fixtures in much of their work, Morphosis diluted the impact of the metal by painting it white, but this only slightly diminished the Rube Goldberg (in English terms, Heath Robinson) quality of the apparently aimless contraptions. With these gestures the architects were perhaps suggesting the limited knowledge medicine has about cancer, not a particularly cheering vision for the afflicted patients.

165 Morphosis, Comprehensive Cancer Clinic, Los Angeles, California, 1988.

166 Tadao Ando, Fukuhara Arthritis Clinic, Setagaya, Tokyo, Japan, 1985–87.

166 In the Fukuhara Arthritis Clinic in Tokyo (1985–87), Tadao Ando projected an entirely different attitude about wellness. True to his previous architectural strategies, Ando produced a robust building of remarkable poetic power out of such potentially uninspiring materials as exposed concrete and grey paint. Where the spatial organization of the Comprehensive Cancer Center was driven by axes and rigid geometries, Ando's sequence followed the traditional Japanese principles of *mujokan*, a pattern of discontinuous and deflected movement reflecting the notion of changeability and transformation. He expressed this by offering spatial volumes that are distinct from one another and, in a sort of architectural promenade, connected or traversed by steps, bridges, and ramps organized to emphasize the climaxes and tensions so important to his conception of building. The seven-story structure presents a half-round volume of alternate bands of concrete and ribbon windows which, apart from their serene but emphatic urban presence, also make for dazzling sunlit spaces and expansive panoramas over Tokyo, for the entrance hall, physiotherapy unit, cafeteria, and inpatient rooms. Another point of

226

contrast with the Cancer Center's white walls and busy sequence of metal members jutting from the walls or bristling about the technological folly are Ando's sensuously rich and warm concrete surfaces, set within spaces on a domestic scale.

Research facilities constitute an essential aspect of health care, and Louis I. Kahn's Salk Institute in La Jolla (1959–65) is perhaps the most famous research facility of the last twenty-five years. Located in a breathtakingly beautiful setting in Southern California, Kahn's design took full advantage of the site by opening up a broad plaza between two research and lab wings overlooking a magnificent panorama of the Pacific Ocean and the coastline. The plan is a study in deceptive simplicity. From the long bars of the lab wings, separate studies for researchers jut into the plaza, each with its own vista over the ocean and each a setting for quiet thought and reflection away from the bustle of the labs. Kahn carried out the motif of the interlocking volumes on multiple scales, all the way down to details of the furniture. Sensuous concrete surfaces are complemented by slowly weathering wood that ages toward the same gray. Such infrastructures as heating and ventilation are tucked out of site in easily accessible spaces between the floors as deftly as in Norman Foster's buildings, but without relying on High Tech imagery to define the overall aesthetic. As in many of his buildings, Kahn planted a grove of trees along the main entrance to the site, and water is an integral element of the design, particularly in the channel running through the center of the plaza.

Within the world of work, there are many other types of building. Factories, parking structures, small office buildings, airports and other light industrial structures are often designed by engineers according to strictly functional considerations precisely because few architectural offices demonstrate either willingness or ability to tackle the technical and aesthetic problems involved. Parking facilities, for example, constitute a vexing design problem to which architects usually respond either by going underground or by tacking an unattractive addition behind an otherwise interesting building almost as an afterthought, typically leaving an ugly frontage on at least part of the site. Elsewhere, as in many office towers in downtown Los Angeles and shopping centers such as the Beverly Center, parking facilities occupy the street and the first few levels precisely in order to discourage street activity.

When taken as a serious architectural problem, however, even such a humble building type can become a noble achievement. Machado and Silvetti's parking structure at Princeton, New Jersey (1991), the first of several planned by the University, exemplifies the possibilities.

Doubly restricted by the building type itself and by University officials' requirements for a design in harmony with the historic campus, the architects adopted the materials and dimensions of an existing McKim, Mead and White masonry wall (1911), extending it around the site as a frame for the first two levels of the parking structure. Organized on five floors with a central circulation ramp, the garage is of simple concrete column, beam and horizontal slab construction. The surface treatment of the upper three floors distinguishes this from other parking structures, for along the garden side a steel screen is to become an ivy-covered trellis, while along the other three sides the architects arranged a bronze double lattice screen. Confined within a double rectangular grid and formed of two different-sized lattices, the screen curves at the top into a projecting cornice. With these three deceptively simple design solutions—lattice screen, masonry wall and trellis—the parking structure acquired an austere elegance in keeping with its context. At the same time it challenged recent additions to the campus that fail to match its understated grandeur.

The small, individual projects presented in the second half of this chapter are overwhelmingly distinguished works of architecture, which are elegantly inserted into their surroundings. In contrast, the massive urban interventions in London, Paris, "renovated" ports and degraded industrial areas throughout the world often testify to infusions of public and private funds, but afford dismal pictures of what can only be seen as future cities with less democratic aspirations: highly segregated and controlled, with an unabated destruction of the natural landscape, a greater polarization of wealth and greater concentrations of power in the hands of anonymous financial institutions, and an architecture that expresses that power unambiguously and usually unimaginatively.

Notes on Architects

The following list gives life-dates (where known), location of the architectural practice, training, and, where applicable, academic position. Architects associated with larger firms are listed separately in cases where the firm no longer exists or major changes have taken place.

Aida, Takefumi b. 1937
Tokyo, Japan
B.Arch., M.Arch., D.Arch., Waseda Univ., Tokyo. Professor, Shibaura Institute of Technology, Osaka

Ando, Tadao b. 1941
Osaka, Japan
Self-educated in architecture

Appleton, Marc b. 1945
Venice, Calif.
B.A., Harvard Univ.; M.Arch., Yale Univ.

Arquitectonica
Miami, Fla.
  Bernardo Fort-Brescia b. 1951
  B.A., Princeton Univ.; M.Arch., Harvard Univ.
  Laurinda Spear b. 1950
  B.A., Brown Univ.; M.Arch., Columbia Univ.

Architectenbureau Alberts & Van Huut
Amsterdam, Netherlands
  Anton Alberts b. 1927
  Ecole Nationale Supérieure des Beaux-Arts, Paris; Dip.Arch., Academy of Architecture, Amsterdam
  Max van Huut b. 1947
  Dip.Arch., Academy of Architecture, Amsterdam

Aymonino, Carlo b. 1926
Rome, Italy
Dip.Arch., Univ. of Rome. Professor, Architectural Institute, Univ. of Venice

Baracco, Juvenal b. 1940
Lima, Peru
Dip.Arch., National Univ. of Engineering, Lima

Barragán, Luis 1902–88
(Guadalajara, Mexico)
Dip.Eng., Univ. of Guadalajara

Bausman, Karen b. 1958
New York, N.Y.
B.Arch., Cooper Union, New York

Bawa, Geoffrey b. 1919
Colombo, Sri Lanka
B.A., Univ. of Cambridge; barrister-at-law, Middle Temple, London; Dip.Arch., Architectural Association, London

Binder, Rebecca b. 1951
Playa del Re, Calif.
B.A., M.Arch., Univ. of California, Los Angeles

Bofill, Ricardo b. 1939
Barcelona, Spain / Paris, France
Dip.Arch., Escuela Técnica Superior de Arquitectura, Barcelona; Geneva School of Architecture

Calatrava Valls, Santiago b. 1951
Zurich, Switzerland
Dip. Civil Engineering, D.Arch., ETH, Zurich

Calthorpe, Peter b. 1949
Berkeley, Calif.
B.A., Antioch College, O.; M.Arch., Yale Univ.

Casasco, Victoria b. 1956
Venice, Calif.
B.F.A., Rhode Island School of Design; M.Arch., Columbia Univ.

Cavaedium
Los Angeles, Calif.
  James Bonar
  B.Arch., Univ. of Southern California; M.Arch., Massachusetts Institute of Technology
  Kathleen FitzGerald
  B.F.A., B.Arch., Rhode Island School of Design; M.Arch., Harvard Univ.
  Kenneth Kuroe
  B.A., Yale Univ.; B.Arch., Southern California Institute of Architecture

Chemetov, Paul b. 1928
Paris, France
Dip.Arch., Ecole Nationale Supérieure des Beaux-Arts, Paris

Ciorra, Pippo b. 1955
Rome, Italy
Laurea, Univ. of Rome; D.Arch., Univ. of Venice. Professor, School of Architecture, Univ. of Ascoli Piceno

Coop Himmelblau
Vienna, Austria / Culver City, Calif.
  Wolfgang Prix b. 1942
  Dip.Arch., Akademie für Angewandte Kunst, Vienna. Professor, Akademie für Angewandte Kunst, Vienna
  Helmut Swiczinsky b. 1944
  Dip.Arch., Technische Univ., Vienna; Dip.Arch., Architectural Association, London. Visiting Professor, Architectural Association, London

Correa, Charles b. 1930
Bombay, India
B.Arch., Univ. of Michigan; M.Arch., Massachusetts Institute of Technology

Cruz, Antonio b. 1948
Seville, Spain
Dip.Arch., Escuela Técnica Superior de Arquitectura, Seville

Dam, Cees b. 1932
Amsterdam, Netherlands
Dip.Arch., Academie van Bouwkunst, Amsterdam. Dean, Faculty of Architecture, Technical Univ. of Delft

Doshi, Balkrishna Vithaldas b. 1927
Ahmedabad, India
Ferguson College, Poona; Dip.Arch., J. J. School of Art, Bombay

D/PZ
Miami, Fla.
  Andres Duany b. 1950
  B.Arch., Princeton Univ.; M.Arch., Yale Univ.
  Elizabeth Plater-Zyberk b. 1950
  B.Arch., Princeton Univ.; M.Arch., Yale Univ. Dean, Univ. of Miami

Dubnoff, Ena
Santa Monica, Calif.
B.Arch., Univ. of Southern California; M.Arch., Columbia Univ.

Duinker, Margreet
Amsterdam, Netherlands
Dip.Arch., Technical Univ. of Delft. Professor, Amsterdam Art School

Eisenman, Peter b. 1932
New York, N.Y.
B.Arch, Cornell Univ.; Ph.D., Univ. of Cambridge. Professor, Cooper Union, New York

Erskine, Ralph b. 1914
Drottningholm, Sweden
Dip.Arch., Regent Street Polytechnic, London

Fathy, Hassan 1900–1990
(Cairo, Egypt)
Dip.Arch., School of Engineering, Cairo

Foster, Sir Norman b. 1935
London, England
Dip.Arch., Univ. of Manchester; M.Arch., Yale Univ.

Franciosini, Luigi
Rome, Italy
Laurea, Univ. of Rome

Galí, Beth b. 1950
Barcelona, Spain
Dip.Arch., Escuela Técnica Superior de Arquitectura, Barcelona. Professor, Escuela Técnica Superior de Arquitectura, Barcelona

Gehry, Frank b. 1929
Santa Monica, Calif.
B.Arch., Univ. of Southern California; M.Arch., Harvard Univ.

Gill, Leslie b. 1957
New York, N.Y.
B.Arch., Cooper Union, New York. Professor, Parsons School of Design, New York

Graham, Bruce b. 1925
Chicago, Ill.
B.Arch., Univ. of Pennsylvania

Graves, Michael b. 1934
Princeton, N.J.
B.Arch., Univ. of Cincinnati; M.Arch., Princeton Univ. Professor, Princeton Univ.

Gregotti, Vittorio b. 1927
Milan, Italy

229

Laurea, Polytechnic of Milan.
Professor, Polytechnic of Milan
Grimshaw, Nicholas b. 1939
London, England
Dip.Arch., Architectural Association,
London
Gruen, Victor 1903–80
(Los Angeles, Calif.)
Dip.Arch., Akademie für
Angewandte Kunst, Vienna
Gwathmey, Charles b. 1938
New York, N.Y.
B.Arch., Univ. of Pennsylvania;
M.Arch., Yale Univ.
Hadid, Zaha M. b. 1950
London, England
B.Sc., American Univ., Beirut,
Lebanon; Dip., Architectural
Association, London
Hejduk, John b. 1929
New York, N.Y.
B.Arch., Univ. of Cincinnati;
M.Arch., Harvard Univ.
Hellmuth, Obata and Kassabaum
St. Louis, Mo.
George Hellmuth b. 1907
B.Arch., M.Arch., Washington
Univ., St. Louis; Dip.Arch., Ecole
des Beaux-Arts, Fontainebleau,
France
Gyo Obata b. 1923
B.Arch., Washington Univ., St.
Louis; M.Arch., Cranbrook
Academy of Art, Mich.
George Kassabaum b. 1920
B.Arch., Washington Univ.,
St. Louis
Hertzberger, Herman b. 1932
Amsterdam, Netherlands
Dip.Arch., Technical Univ. of Delft.
Professor, Technical Univ. of Delft
Hilmer & Sattler
Berlin / Munich, Germany
Heinz Hilmer b. 1936
Dip.Eng., Technical Univ., Munich
Christoph Sattler b. 1938
Dip.Eng., Technical Univ., Munich;
M.Arch., Illinois Institute of
Technology, Chicago
Thomas Albrecht b. 1960
Dip.Eng., Technical Univ., Munich;
M.Arch., Illinois Institute of
Technology, Chicago
Hodgetts and Fung
Santa Monica, Calif.
Craig Hodgetts b. 1937
B.A., Oberlin College, O.; M.Arch.,
Yale Univ. Professor, Univ. of
California, Los Angeles
Hsin-Ming Fung b. 1953
B.A., California State Univ.,
Dominguez Hills; M.Arch., Univ. of
California, Los Angeles. Professor,
California State Polytechnic Univ.,
Pomona
Holl, Steven b. 1947
New York, N.Y.

B.Arch., Univ. of Washington;
Dip.Arch., Architectural Association,
London. Professor, Columbia Univ.
Hollein, Hans b. 1934
Vienna, Austria
Dip.Arch., Akademie für
Angewandte Kunst, Vienna;
M.Arch., Univ. of California,
Berkeley. Head, School and Institute
of Design, Akademie für
Angewandte Kunst, Vienna
Holzbauer, Wilhelm b. 1930
Vienna, Austria / Amsterdam,
Netherlands
Dip.Arch., Akademie für
Angewandte Kunst, Vienna
Hopkins, Michael b. 1935
London, England
Dip.Arch., Architectural Association,
London
Ishiyama, Osamu b. 1944
Tokyo, Japan
Dip.Arch., Waseda Univ., Tokyo.
Professor, Waseda Univ., Tokyo
Isozaki, Arata b. 1931
Tokyo, Japan
Dip.Arch., Architectural Faculty,
Univ. of Tokyo
Jahn, Helmut b. 1940
Chicago, Ill.
Dip.Eng./Arch., Technische
Hochschule, Munich
Jerde, Jon b. 1940
Venice, Calif. / Hong Kong
B.Arch., Univ. of Southern
California
Jiménez, Carlos b.1959
Houston, Texas
B.Arch., Univ. of Houston
Johnson, Philip b. 1906
New York, N.Y.
B.A., M.Arch., Harvard Univ.
Kahn, Louis 1901–74
(Philadelphia, Pa.)
B.Arch., Univ. of Pennsylvania
Karmi-Melamede, Ada b. 1936
Tel Aviv, Israel
Dip.Arch., Architectural Association,
London; Dip.Arch., School of
Architecture, Technion, Haifa, Israel.
Professor, Columbia Univ.
Kleihues, Josef Paul b. 1933
Berlin, Germany
Dip.Eng., Technische Hochschule,
Berlin
Koetter, Kim and Associates
Boston, Mass.
Fred Koetter b. 1938
B.Arch., Univ. of Oregon; M.Arch.,
Cornell Univ. Dean, Yale Univ.
Susie Kim b. 1948
B.Arch., Cornell Univ.; M.Arch.,
Urban Design, Harvard Univ.
Kohn Pederson Fox (KPF)
New York, N.Y. / Berlin, Germany /
London, England
A. Eugene Kohn b. 1930

B.Arch., M.Arch., Univ. of
Pennsylvania. Professor, Graduate
School of Fine Arts, Univ. of
Pennsylvania
William Pederson b. 1938
B.Arch., Univ. of Minnesota;
M.Arch., Massachusetts Institute of
Technology
Sheldon Fox b.1930
B.Arch., M.Arch., Univ. of
Pennsylvania; M.Arch., Real Estate
Development, Harvard Univ.
Robert Cioppa b. 1942
B.Arch., Pratt Institute, Brooklyn,
N.Y.
Lee Polisano
B.A., LaSalle College, Philadelphia,
Pa.; M.Arch., Virginia Polytechnic
Institute
David M. Leventhal
B.A., M.Arch., Harvard Univ.
Koning Eizenberg Architects
Santa Monica, Calif.
Hank Koning b. 1953
B.Arch., Univ. of Melbourne,
Australia; M.Arch., Univ. of
California, Los Angeles
Julie Eizenberg b. 1954
B.Arch., Univ. of Melbourne,
Australia; M.Arch., Univ. of
California, Los Angeles. Adjunct
Professor, Univ. of California, Los
Angeles
Koolhaas, Rem b. 1944
London, England / Rotterdam,
Netherlands
Dip.Arch., Architectural Association,
London. Visiting Professor, Harvard
Univ.
Koolhaas, Teun b. 1940
Almere, Netherlands
Dip.Arch.Eng., Technical Univ. of
Delft; M.Arch., Urban Design,
Harvard Univ.
Krier, Rob b. 1938
Vienna, Austria
Dip.Ing.Arch., Technische
Hochschule, Munich. Professor,
Technische Hochschule, Vienna
Kroll, Lucien b. 1927
Brussels, Belgium
Dip.Arch., Institut Supérieur
d'Urbanisme, Ecole Normale
Supérieure, Brussels. Professor,
Institut Supérieur d'Urbanisme,
Ecole Normale Supérieure, Brussels
Lapena and Torres
Barcelona, Spain
José Antonio Martínez Lapena
b. 1941
Dip.Arch., Escuela Técnica Superior
de Arquitectura, Barcelona.
Professor, Escuela Técnica Superior
de Arquitectura, Barcelona
Elías Torres Tur b. 1944
Dip.Arch., Doctorate, Escuela
Técnica Superior de Arquitectura,

Barcelona. Professor, Escuela Técnica Superior de Arquitectura, Barcelona

Legorreta, Ricardo b. 1931
Mexico City, Mexico
Dip.Arch., Univ. Nacional Autonoma de México

Lumsden, Anthony b. 1928
Los Angeles, Calif.
B.Arch., Univ. of Sydney, Australia

Machado and Silvetti
Boston, Mass.
  Rodolfo Machado b. 1942
  Dip.Arch., Univ. of Buenos Aires, Argentina; M.Arch., Univ. of California, Berkeley. Professor, Harvard Univ.
  Jorge Silvetti b. 1942
  B.A., Univ. of Buenos Aires, Argentina; M.Arch., Univ. of California, Berkeley. Professor, Harvard Univ.

Mack, Mark b. 1949
Venice, Calif.
Dip.Arch., Akademie für Angewandte Kunst, Vienna. Professor, School of Architecture, Univ. of California, Los Angeles

Mateo, Josep Lluis b. 1949
Barcelona, Spain
Dip.Arch., Escuela Técnica Superior de Arquitectura, Barcelona

MBM Arquitectes S.A.
Barcelona, Spain
  Oriol Bohigas b. 1925
  Dip.Arch., D.Arch., Escuela Técnica Superior de Arquitectura, Barcelona
  Josep Martorell b. 1925
  Dip.Arch., D.Arch., Escuela Técnica Superior de Arquitectura, Barcelona
  David Mackay b. 1933
  Dip.Arch., Northern Polytechnic, London
  Albert Puigdomènech b. 1944
  Dip.Arch., Escuela Técnica Superior de Arquitectura, Barcelona

Mechur, Ralph b. 1949
Santa Monica, Calif.
B.Sc., Univ. of Pennsylvania; M.Arch., Univ. of California, Los Angeles

Meier, Richard b. 1934
New York, N.Y. / Los Angeles, Calif.
B.Arch., Cornell Univ.

Mockbee, Samuel
Greensboro, Ala. / Canton, Miss.
B.Arch., Auburn Univ., Ala. Professor, Auburn Univ.

Moneo, Rafael b. 1937
Madrid, Spain
B.Arch., D.Arch., Escuela Técnica Superior de Arquitectura, Madrid. Professor, Harvard Univ.

Moore, Charles 1925–94
(Los Angeles, Calif.)
B.Arch., Univ. of Michigan; M.Arch., Ph.D., Princeton Univ.

Morphosis
Santa Monica, Calif.
  Thom Mayne
  B.Arch., Univ. of Southern California; M.Arch., Harvard Univ.
  Michael Rotondi
  B.Arch., M.Arch., Southern California Institute of Architecture, Los Angeles. Head, Southern California Institute of Architecture, Los Angeles

Murcutt, Glenn b. 1936
Mosman, N.S.W., Australia
Dip.Arch., Univ. of New South Wales

Nouvel, Jean b. 1945
Paris, France
Dip.Arch., Ecole Nationale Supérieure des Beaux-Arts, Paris

Nylund/Puttfarken/Stürzebecher
Berlin, Germany
  Kjell Nylund b. 1939
  Dip.Eng., Technische Hochschule, Berlin
  Christof Puttfarken b. 1949
  Dip.Eng., Technische Hochschule, Berlin
  Peter Stürzebecher b. 1943
  D.Eng., Technische Hochschule, Berlin. Professor, Technische Hochschule, Berlin

Olin Partnership
Philadelphia, Pa.
  Laurie Olin b.1939
  B.A., Univ. of Washington, Seattle; Civil Eng., Univ. of Alaska. Lecturer, Univ. of Pennsylvania

OMA (Office for Metropolitan Architecture)
London, England / Athens, Greece
  Elia Zenghelis b. 1937
  Dip.Arch., Architectural Association, London
  Matthias Sauerbruch b. 1955
  Dip.Arch., Architectural Association, London

Outram, John b. 1934
London, England
Polytechnic of Central London; Architectural Association, London

Patkau Architects
Vancouver, B.C., Canada
  John Patkau
  B.A., B. Environmental Studies, M.Arch., Univ. of Manitoba
  Patricia Patkau
  B. Interior Design, Univ. of Manitoba; M.Arch., Yale Univ. Professor, School of Architecture, Univ. of British Columbia
  Michael Cunningham
  B.A., M.A., Environmental Design, Univ. of Calgary

Pei, Ieoh Ming b. 1917
New York, N.Y.
B.Arch., Massachusetts Institute of Technology; M.Arch., Harvard Univ.

Peichl, Gustav b. 1928
Vienna, Austria
Dip.Arch., Akademie der Bildenden Künste, Vienna

Pelli, Cesar b. 1926
New Haven, Conn.
Dip.Arch., Univ. of Tucuman, Argentina; M.S.Arch., Univ. of Illinois, Champaign–Urbana

Piano, Renzo b. 1937
Genoa, Italy
Laurea, Polytechnic of Milan

Portman, John C., Jr. b. 1924
Atlanta, Ga.
B.Arch., Georgia Institute of Technology

Portoghesi, Paolo b. 1931
Rome, Italy
Laurea, Univ. of Rome. Professor, Univ. of Rome

Portzamparc, Christian de b. 1944
Paris, France
Dip.Arch., Ecole Nationale Supérieure des Beaux-Arts, Paris

Predock, Antoine b. 1936
Albuquerque, N.M.
B.Arch., Columbia Univ.

Quintana, Marius b. 1954
Barcelona, Spain
Dip.Arch., Escuela Técnica Superior de Arquitectura, Barcelona. Professor, Escuela Técnica Superior del Vallés, Barcelona

Rogers, Sir Richard b. 1933
London, England
Dip.Arch., Architectural Association, London; M.Arch., Yale Univ.

Rossi, Aldo b. 1931
Milan, Italy / New York, N.Y.
Laurea, Polytechnic of Milan. Professor, Institute of Architecture, Univ. of Venice

Saggio, Antonino
Rome, Italy
Laurea, Univ. of Rome

Santos, Adèle Naudé
Philadelphia, Pa. / San Diego, Calif.
Dip.Arch., Architectural Association, London; M.Arch., M. Planning, Univ. of Pennsylvania; M.Arch., Urban Design, Harvard Univ.

Scheine, Judith
Los Angeles, Calif.
B.A., Mathematics, Brown Univ.; M.Arch., Princeton Univ. Professor, College of Environmental Design, California State Polytechnic Univ., Pomona

Schwartz, Martha b. 1950
Cambridge, Mass.
B.F.A., M. Landscape Architecture, Univ. of Michigan. Professor, Graduate School of Design, Harvard Univ.

Siza, Álvaro b. 1933
Porto, Portugal

Dip.Arch., School of Architecture, Univ. of Porto. Professor, Univ. of Porto
Skidmore, Owings & Merrill
Chicago, Ill. / London, England / and other offices
 Louis Skidmore 1897–1962
 Nathaniel Owings 1903–84
 John Merrill 1896–1975
 In Chicago:
 Raymond J. Clark
 B.Sc., Mech.Eng., M.Sc., Mech.Eng., Purdue Univ.
 Thomas K. Fridstein
 B.Arch., Cornell Univ.; M.B.A., Columbia Univ.
 Joseph A. Gonzalez
 B.Arch., Oklahoma State Univ.; Loeb Fellowship, Harvard Univ.
 Jeffrey J. McCarthy
 B.Arch., Univ. of Illinois, Champaign–Urbana
 Larry K. Oltmanns
 B.Arch., Univ. of Illinois, Champaign–Urbana
 Adrian D. Smith
 B.Arch., Univ. of Illinois, Chicago
 Richard F. Tomlinson
 B.Arch.Eng., Pennsylvania State Univ.; M.Arch., Univ. of Illinois, Champaign–Urbana
 Robert L. Wesley
 B.Sc., Arch.Eng., Tennessee State Univ.; B.Arch., M.Arch., Univ. of Oklahoma
 In London:
 Roger G. Kallman b. 1944
 B.Arch., Miami Univ., Fla.; M.Arch., Urban Design, Univ. of Minnesota; M. Regional Planning, Univ. of North Carolina
 Peter J. Magill
 B.Arch., Univ. of Illinois, Champaign–Urbana
 Robert L. Turner b. 1947
 B.Arch., Virginia Polytechnic Institute
Snow, Julie b. 1948
Minneapolis, Minn.
B.Arch., Univ. of Colorado. Adjunct Professor, Univ. of Minnesota
Solanas, Antonì b. 1946
Barcelona, Spain
Dip.Arch., Escuela Técnica Superior de Arquitectura, Barcelona

Steidle, Otto b. 1943
Munich, Germany
Dip.Arch., Akademie der Bildenden Künste, Munich. Professor, Akademie der Bildenden Künste, Munich
Stern, Robert b. 1939
New York, N.Y.
B.A., Columbia Univ.; M.Arch., Yale Univ.
Stirling, Sir James 1926–94
(London, England)
Dip.Arch., Liverpool School of Architecture
TEN Arquitectos (Taller de Enrique Norten Arquitectos)
Mexico City, Mexico
 Bernardo Gómez-Pimienta
 b. 1961
 B.Arch., Anahuac Univ., Mexico City; M.Arch., Cornell Univ.
 Enrique Norten b.1954
 B.Arch., Iberoamerican Univ., Mexico City; M.Arch., Cornell Univ.
Tigerman McCurry Architects
Chicago, Ill.
 Stanley Tigerman b. 1930
 B.Arch., M.Arch., Yale Univ.
 Margaret McCurry
 B.A., Vassar College, N.Y.; Loeb Fellowship, Harvard Univ.
Torp, Niels b.1940
Oslo, Norway
B.Arch., NTH, Trondheim; and further studies
Troughton McAslan
London, England
 James Troughton b. 1950
 M.A., Dip.Arch., Univ. of Cambridge
 John McAslan b. 1954
 M.A., Dip.Arch., Univ. of Edinburgh
Tschumi, Bernard b. 1944
New York, N.Y.
Dip.Arch., Federal Institute of Technology, Zurich. Dean, School of Architecture, Columbia Univ.
Tusquets, Oscar b. 1941
Barcelona, Spain
Dip.Arch., Escuela Técnica Superior de Arquitectura, Barcelona
Ungers, Oswald Mathias
b. 1926

Düsseldorf, Germany
Dip.Arch., Technical Univ., Karlsruhe
Venturi, Scott Brown and Associates
Philadelphia, Pa.
 Denise Scott-Brown b. 1931
 A.B., Univ. of Witwaterswand, Johannesburg, South Africa; Dip.Arch., Architectural Association, London; M.City Planning, M.Arch., Univ. of Pennsylvania
 Robert Venturi b. 1925
 B.A., M.F.A., Princeton Univ.
El-Wakil, Abdel Wahed
b. 1943
Miami, Fla.
B.Sc., Ains Shams Univ., Cairo, Egypt
Waldhör, Ivo b. 1931
Malmø, Sweden
Dip.Arch., Akademie der Bildenden Künste, Vienna. Lecturer, School of Architecture, Lund Univ.
Weinstein, Edward b. 1948
Seattle, Wash.
B.Arch., Univ. of Washington; M.Arch., Urban Design, Harvard Univ.
Werkfabrik
Berlin, Germany
 Hendrikje Herzberg b. 1952
 Dip.Arch., Technical Univ., Berlin
 H. P. Winkes b. 1946
 Dip.Arch., Technical Univ., Berlin
 Margarete Winkes b. 1947
 Dip.Arch., Technical Univ., Berlin. Guest Professor, Technical Univ., Berlin
Wilford, Michael b. 1938
London, England / Singapore / Stuttgart, Germany
Kingston Technical School, Mx.; Northern Polytechnic School of Architecture, London; Regent Street Polytechnic Planning School, London
Wu, Liangyong b. 1922
Beijing, China
Dip.Eng., National Central Univ., Chongqing; M.Arch., Urban Design, Cranbrook Academy of Art, Mich. Professor, Institute of Architectural and Urban Studies, Tsinghua Univ.

Selected Bibliography

General

Airahmadi, Hooshang, and Salah S. El-Shakhs, *Urban Development in the Muslim World* (New Brunswick, N.J.: Center for Urban Policy Research 1993)

Amin, Ash, ed., *Post-Fordism: A Reader* (New York and Oxford: Basil Blackwell 1994)

—, and Nigel Thrift, "Living in the Global," in A. Amin and N. Thrift, eds. , *Globalisation, Institutions and Regional Development* (Oxford: Oxford University Press 1994), 1–22

Archigram (Paris: Editions du Centre Pompidou 1994)

Berkeley, Ellen Perry, and Matilda McQuaid, *Architecture: A Place for Women* (Blue Ridge Summit, Pa.: Smithsonian Institution Press 1989)

Bluestone, Barry, and Bennett Harrison, *The Deindustrialization of America: Plant Closings, Community Abandonment, and the Dismantling of Basic Industry* (New York: Basic Books 1982)

Cantacuzino, Sherban, *Architecture in Continuity: Building in the Islamic World Today. The Aga Khan Awards in Architecture* (London: Academy Editions/New York: Aperture 1985)

Cook, Peter, et al., eds., *Archigram* (New York: Praeger 1973)

Correa, Charles, *The New Landscape: Urbanisation in the Third World* (Sevenoaks, Kent: Butterworth Architecture 1989)

Dear, Michael J., and Jennifer Wolch, *Landscapes of Despair: From Deindustrialization to Homelessness* (Cambridge, Mass.: Polity Press 1987)

De Seta, Cesare, *L'architettura del Novecento* (Turin: UTET 1981)

Fathy, Hassan, *Architecture for the Poor; an experiment in rural Egypt* (Chicago, Ill.: University of Chicago Press 1973)

Frampton, Kenneth, *Modern Architecture: A Critical History*, 3rd edn., rev. (London and New York: Thames and Hudson 1992)

Fuller, R. Buckminster, *Ideas and Integrities: A Spontaneous Autobiographical Disclosure* (Englewood Cliffs, N.J.: Prentice-Hall 1963)

—, *Critical Path* (New York: St. Martin's Press 1981)

Gilbert, Alan, *Cities, Poverty and Development: Urbanization in the Third World* (Oxford and New York: Oxford University Press 1992)

Harvey, David, *The Condition of Postmodernity* (Oxford: Basil Blackwell 1989)

Holod, Renata, *Architecture and Community: Building in the Islamic World Today. The Aga Khan Awards in Architecture* (London: Academy Editions/Millerton, N.Y.: Aperture 1983)

Huyssen, Andreas, *After the Great Divide* (Bloomington: University of Indiana Press 1986)

Jackson, Anthony, *Reconstructing Architecture for the Twenty-First Century: An Inquiry into the Architect's World* (Toronto, Ont.: University of Toronto Press 1995)

Jacobs, Jane, *The Death and Life of Great American Cities* (New York: Vintage Press 1961)

Klotz, Heinrich, *The History of Postmodern Architecture*, transl. Radka Donnell (Cambridge, Mass.: MIT Press 1988)

Larson, Magali Sarfatti, *Behind the Postmodern Facade: Architectural Change in Late Twentieth Century America* (Berkeley, Los Angeles, and London: University of California Press 1993)

Lash, Scott, *Sociology of Postmodernism* (London and New York: Routledge 1990)

McLeod, Mary, "Architecture," in Stanley Trachtenberg, ed., *The Postmodern Moment: A Handbook of Contemporary Innovation in the Arts* (Westport, Conn.: Greenwood Press 1985), 19–52

—, "Architecture and Politics in the Reagan Era: From Postmodernism to Deconstructivism," *Assemblage* 8 (1989), 23–59

Nanji, Azim, ed., *The Aga Khan Award for Architecture: Building for Tomorrow* (London: Academy Editions 1994)

Rossi, Aldo, *L'architettura della città* (Padua: Marsilio Editori 1966), English edn. *The Architecture of the City* , transl. Diane Ghirardo and Joan Ockman (Cambridge, Mass.: MIT Press 1982)

Serageldin, Ismail, ed., *Space for Freedom: The Search for Architectural Excellence in Muslim Societies. The Aga Khan Awards in Architecture* (London and Boston, Mass.: Butterworth Architecture 1989)

Sieden, Lloyd S., *Buckminster Fuller's Universe: An Appreciation* (New York: Plenum Press 1989)

Smith, Neil, *Uneven Development: Nature, Capital and the Production of Space* (Oxford: Basil Blackwell 1984, 1990)

Steele, James, ed., *Architecture for a Changing World* (London: Academy Editions 1992)

—, ed., *Architecture for Islamic Societies Today* (London: Academy Editions 1994)

Storper, Michael, and Richard Walker, *The Capitalist Imperative: Territory, Technology and Industrial Growth* (New York and Oxford: Basil Blackwell 1989)

Sudhir, Ved Dan, ed., *The Crisis of Changing India* (Delhi: National Publishing House 1974)

Terry, Quinlan, *Quinlan Terry: Selected Works* (London: Academy Editions 1993)

Tzonis, Alexander, and Liane Lefaivre, *Architecture in Europe since 1968: Memory and Invention* (London: Thames and Hudson/New York: Rizzoli 1992)

Venturi, Robert, *Complexity and Contradiction in Architecture* (New York: Museum of Modern Art 1966)

Wilson, Elizabeth, *The Sphinx and the City: Urban Life, The Control of Disorder and Women* (Berkeley: University of California Press 1991)

Chapter One: Public Space

Ando, Tadao, "On Designing," *Domus* 738 (May 1992), 17–24

Arango, Silvia, *Modernidad y Postmodernidad en América Latina* (Bogotà: Escala 1991)

Beard, Richard, *Walt Disney's Epcot: Creating the New World of Tomorrow* (New York: Abrams 1982)

Blomeyer, Gerald, "Learning and Stirling," *Architectural Review* 1105 (Mar. 1989), 28–41

Bolton, Richard, "Figments of the Public: Architecture and Debt," in M. Diani and C. Ingraham, *Restructuring Architectural Theory* (Evanston, Ill.: Northwestern University Press 1988), 42–47

Brannen, Mary Yoko, "'Bwanna Mickey:' Constructing Cultural Consumption at Tokyo Disneyland," in Joseph J. Tobin, *Remade in Japan: Everyday Life in Consumer Taste in a Changing Society* (New Haven and London: Yale University Press 1992), 216–34

Cantacuzino, Sherban, *Charles Correa* (Singapore: Concept Media 1984)

Ciorra, Pippo, Botta, Eisenman, Gregotti, Hollein: *Musei* (Milan: Electa 1991)

Cole, B. C., and Ruth E. Rogers, comp., *Richard Rogers* (London: Academy Editions/New York: St. Martin's Press 1985)

Correa, Charles, "Mystic Labyrinth," *Architectural Review* 1139 (Jan. 1992), 20–26

Crawford, Margaret, "The World in a Shopping Mall," in M. Sorkin, ed., *Variations on a Theme Park: The New American City and the End of Public Space* (New York: Hill and Wang 1992), 3–30

Crosbie, Michael, "Ace of Clubs,"

Architecture 80 (June 1991), 90–93

Davis, Mike, "The Redevelopment Game in Downtown Los Angeles," in Diane Ghirardo, ed., *Out of Site: A Social Criticism of Architecture* (Seattle, Wash.: Bay Press 1991), 77–113

Walt Disney Company, "Port Disney: Preliminary Master Plan, Executive Report," July 1990

Dixon, John Morris, "Learning from London," *Progressive Architecture* (Aug. 1991), 80–85

Ellis, Charlotte, "Disney Goes to Paris," *Landscape Architecture* 80 (June 1990), 38–41

EuroDisney, Press Information Packet (Apr. 1992)

Forster, Kurt W., "Shrine? Emporium? Theater? Reflections on Two Decades of American Museum Building," *Zodiac* 6 (1991), 30–74

Ghirardo, Diane, "Two Museums," in D. Ghirardo, ed., *Out of Site: A Social Criticism of Architecture* (Seattle, Wash.: Bay Press 1991), 114–28

Gutiérrez, Ramón, and Adriana Irigoyen, *Nueva Arquitectura Argentina: Pluralidad y Coincidencia* (Bogotá: Escala and the University of the Andes 1990)

Habermas, Jürgen, *The Structural Transformation of the Public Sphere: An Inquiry into a Category of Bourgeois Society* , transl. Thomas Burger (Cambridge, Mass.: MIT Press 1991)

Irace, Fulvio, "Radiant Museum: Museum für Kunsthandwerk," *Domus* 662 (July 1985), 2–11

Ivy, Robert, "The New City as a Perpetual World's Fair," *Architecture* 76 (Apr. 1987), 50–55

Khan, Hasan Uddin, *Charles Correa: An Architect in India* (London: Concept Media 1987)

Kleinberg, Benjamin, *Urban America in Transformation: Perspectives on Urban Policy and Development* (Thousand Oaks, Calif.: Sage 1995)

Laurenzi, Laura, "Viaggio nel paese dei balocchi," *La Repubblica*, 12–13 Apr. 1992, pp. II–III

Legorreta, Ricardo, "Mexican Lexicon," *Architectural Review* 1139 (Jan. 1992), 37–41

Maitland, Barry, *Shopping Malls: Planning and Design* (Harlow, Essex: Longman Scientific & Technical 1985)

Moore, Rowan, "National Gallery," *Architectural Review* 1133 (Nov. 1991), 30–37

Pease, Victoria, "Children's Museum, Hyogo, Japan," *Architectural Review* 1134 (Aug. 1991), 55–60

Peckham, Andrew, "A Critique of the Sainsbury Centre," *Architectural Design* (1978) 2–26

Robbins, Bruce, ed., *The Phantom Public Sphere* (Minneapolis: University of Minnesota 1993)

Rykwert, Joseph, "The Cult of the Museum: From the Treasure House to the Temple," *Museos Estelares. A & V Monografía de Arquitectura y Vivienda* 18 (1989), 81–83

Sandercock, Leonie, *Gender: A New Agenda for Planning Theory* (Berkeley, Calif.: Institute of Urban and Regional Development 1990)

Seling, Helmut, "The Genesis of the Museum," *Architectural Review* 141, no. 840 (Feb. 1967), 103–14

Snyder, Susan Nigra, "Mapping a New Urban Realm: Consumption Sites and Public Life," unpublished paper presented at American Cultural Landscape Symposium, Syracuse University, N.Y., Mar. 1993

Sorkin, Michael, "See You in Disneyland," in M. Sorkin, ed., *Variations on a Theme Park. The New American City and the End of Public Space* (New York: Hill and Wang 1992), 205–32

Stephens, Suzanne, "Future Past," *Progressive Architecture* (May 1977), 84–88

Vilades, Pilar, "Mickey the Talent Scout," *Progressive Architecture* 69 (June 1988), 104–7

La Villa Olimpica, Barcelona 92: Arquitectura, Parques, Puerto Deportivo (Barcelona: Gustavo Gili 1992)

Walker, Derek, *Animated Architecture* (London: Academy Editions 1982)

Zukin, Sharon, *Landscapes of Power: From Detroit to Disneyland* (Berkeley and Los Angeles, Calif.: University of California Press 1991)

Chapter Two: Domestic Space

Acevedo, Mauricio P., ed., *Togo Díaz: El Arquitectura y su Cuidad* (Bogotá: Escala and University of the Andes 1993)

Albenaa, vol. 6, No. 34 (Apr./May 1987): special issue on Abdul Wahed El-Wakil

Architecture and Urbanism 5 (1987): special issue on the IBA, Berlin

"The Ark," *A + U* 276 (Sept. 1993), 76–95

Baracco, Juvenal, and Pedro Belaunde, *Juvenal Baracco: un universo en casa* (Bogotá: Escala and the University of the Andes/Miami: University of Miami Press 1988)

Bergdoll, Barry, "Subsidized Doric," *Progressive Architecture* (Oct. 1982), 74–79

"Berlin as Model," *Architectural Review* 1076 (Sept. 1984), 18–119

Blake, Peter, "Berlin's IBA: A Critical Reassessment," *Architectural Record* 181

(Apr. 1987), 50–52

"Brant House," *Architectural Design* 5/6 (1980), 33–34

Bristol, Katharine G., "The Pruitt Igoe Myth," *Journal of Architectural Education* (May 1991), 163–71

Capuzzeto, Rita, *Berlino: La nuova ricostruzione. IBA 1979-1987* (Milan: CLUP 1992)

Croset, Pierre Alain, "Berlino '87: la costruzione del passato," *Casabella* 506 (Sept. 1984), 4–25

Davey, Peter, "Berlin: Origins to IBA," *Architectural Record* 181 (Apr. 1987), 22–106

De Rossi, Pietro, "In the Circuit of Representation: The Nexus World Operation in Fukuoka," *Lotus* 71 (1992), 36–40

Dixon, John Morris, "Seaside Ascetic," *Progressive Architecture* (Aug. 1989), 59–67

—, "Layers of meaning," *Progressive Architecture* (Dec. 1979), 66–71

Doshi, B. V., "Aranya Township, Indore," *Mimar* (June 1988) 24–29

uany, Andres, and Elizabeth Plater-Zyberk, *Towns and Town-Making Principles* (New York: Rizzoli/Cambridge, Mass.: Harvard University Graduate School of Design 1991)

Duffy, Frances, "SAS Co-operation," *Architectural Review* 1105 (Mar. 1989), 42–51

Dunlop, Beth, "Coming of Age," *Architectural Record* 177 (July 1989), 96–103

Egelius, Mats, *Ralph Erskine, Architect* (Stockholm: Byggförlaget 1990)

Fathy, Hassan, *Gourna: A Tale of Two Villages* (Cairo: Ministry of Culture 1969), republished as *Architecture for the Poor* (Chicago and London: University of Chicago Press 1973)

Firth, Simon, and Jon Savage, "Pearls and Swine: The Intellectuals and the Mass Media," *New Left Review* 198 (Mar.–Apr. 1993), 107–16

Fisher, Thomas, "The Private and the Public," *Progressive Architecture* (Nov. 1991), 70–74

—, "A Literary House," *Progressive Architecture* (Dec. 1988), 62–67

Frampton, Kenneth, "The Adventure of Ideas," *Progressive Architecture* 66 (Jan. 1985), 25–27

Frank, Suzanne, *Peter Eisenman's House VI: The Client's Response* (New York: Whitney Library of Design 1994)

G. L., "Emilio Ambasz, Prefecture International Hall, Fukuoka," *Domus* 738 (May 1992), 38–41

Garreau, Joel, "Edge Cities," *Landscape Architecture* 78 (Dec. 1988), 48–55

Ghirardo, Diane, "Carlos Jiménez, Tests of Stability," *Lotus* 77 (1993), 47–57

—, "Entre el terremoto y la sequía: Las dos últimas décadas," *A & V* 32 (1991), 16–25

—, *Mark Mack* (Tübingen: Wasmuth 1994)

—, "Peter Eisenman: Il camouflage dell'avanguardia," *Casabella* 613 (June 1994), 22–27

Hayden, Dolores, *Redesigning the American City: The Future of Housing, Work and Family Life* (New York: Norton 1984)

Hoffman, Peter, "Report from West Berlin," *Architectural Record* 173 (Feb. 1985), 87

Hogben, Gavin, "Synthesis," *Architectural Review* 1085 (Feb. 1985), 26–39

—, "Vernacular," *Architectural Review* 1104 (Feb. 1989), 80–86

Holl, Steven, *Anchoring* (New York: Princeton Architectural Press 1989)

Isozaki, Arata, "Project in the Renga Form: The Game of Individual Expressions," *Lotus* 71 (1992), 41–75

Jones, Peter Blundell, "Ecolonia," *Architectural Review* 1141 (Mar. 1992), 64–67

Kleihues, Josef Paul, et al., *Das NEUE Berlin: Konzepte der Internationalen Bauausstellung 1987 für einen Städtebau mit Zukunft* (Berlin: Mann 1987)

Krier, Leon, *Leon Krier: Architecture and Urban Design 1967–1992* (London: Academy Editions 1992)

Kroll, Lucien, *An Architecture of Complexity* (Cambridge, Mass.: MIT Press 1987)

Loomis, John, "Ralph Erskine Arkitekt," *Progressive Architecture* 72 (Oct. 1991), 101, 153

Lucan, Jacques, "Rem Koolhaas, Villa Dall'Ava, Paris," *Domus* 736 (Mar. 1992), 25–35

McCamant, Kathryn, and Charles Durret, *Co-housing. A Contemporary Approach to Housing Ourselves* (Berkeley, Calif.: Ten Speed Press 1994)

Mead, Christopher, *Space for the Continuous Present in the Residential Architecture of Bart Prince* (Albuquerque: University of New Mexico Art Museum 1989)

—, *Houses by Bart Prince: An American Architecture for the Continuous Present* (Albuquerque: University of New Mexico Press 1991)

Miller, Wallis, "IBA's Models for a City: Housing and the Image of Cold War Berlin," *Journal of Architectural Education* 46 (May 1993), 202–16

Mohney, David, and Keller Easterling, *Seaside: Making a Town in America* (New York: Princeton Architectural Press 1991)

Morales, Carlos, "Juvenal Baracco of Peru," *Mimar* 40 (Sept. 1991), 70–75

Morton, David, "Venturi & Rauch," *Progressive Architecture* (Aug. 1976), 50–53

Nexus World, *The Imagination of Nexus World* (Fukuoka: Fukuoka Jisho 1991)

"Il nuovo aeroporto di Seviglia," *Domus* 736 (Mar. 1992), 36–47

Peters, Paulhans, "Mixed Reviews for Berlin's International Building Exhibition," *Architecture* 76 (Sept. 1987), 18–19

Quantrill, Malcolm, "Century Symbol," *Architectural Review* 1133 (Nov. 1991), 27–37

Schuman, Tony, "Utopia Spurned: Ricardo Bofill and the French Ideal City Tradition," in Diane Ghirardo, ed., *Out of Site: A Social Criticism of Architecture* (Seattle, Wash.: Bay Press 1991), 220–49

Sprague, Joan Forrester, *More than Housing: Lifeboats for Women and Children* (Stoneham, Mass.: Butterworth–Heinemann 1991)

Strobel, Roland, "German City Planning and the International Building Exhibition Berlin 1987," unpublished paper, University of Southern California, Los Angeles, Apr. 1991

Takiguchi, Noriko, and Makoto Murata, eds., *Architecture and the Contemporary City* (Fukuoka: Fukuoka International Architects' Conference '89 and Fukuoka Jisho 1989)

Venturi, Robert, and Denise Scott Brown, *A View from the Campidoglio: Selected Essays 1953–1984* (New York: Harper & Row 1984)

Waisman, Marina, "Two Arcades by Two Architects Meet and Meld," *Architecture* 73 (Sept. 1984), 182–84

Waldhör, Ivo, "Process and Product," *Architectural Review* 1141 (Mar. 1992), 25–29

Wallis, Brian, ed., *If You Lived Here: The City in Art, Theory and Social Activism. A Project by Martha Rosler* (Seattle, Wash.: Bay Press 1991)

Warren, James A., *Ricardo Bofill, Taller de Arquitectura: Buildings and Projects* (New York: Rizzoli 1988)

Wheeler, K. V., P. Arnell, T. Bickford, eds., *Michael Graves: Buildings and Projects 1966–1981* (New York: Rizzoli 1982)

Woodbridge, Sally, "Nexus Cultural Concert in the Far East," *Progressive Architecture* (Aug. 1991), 60–79

Chapter Three: Reconfiguring the Urban Sphere

Anderton, Frances, " Docklands Double Act," *Architectural Review* 1106 (Apr. 1989), 28–38

Appelbaum, Eileen, *The New American Workplace: Transforming Work Systems in the United States* (Ithaca, N.Y.: ILR Press 1994)

Association of London Authorities and the Docklands Consultative Committee, *10 Years of Docklands: How the Cake was Cut* (London 1991)

Barna, Joel Warren, *The See Through Years: Creation and Destruction in Texas Architecture and Real Estate 1981–1991* (Houston 1992)

Bird, Jon, "Dystopia on the Thames," *Art in America*, July 1990, 89–97

Blakeley, Edward James, *Changing Places: American Urban Planning Policy for the 1990s* (Berkeley, Calif.: Institute of Urban and Regional Development 1992)

Brownhill, Sue, *Developing London's Docklands: Another Great Planning Disaster?* (London: Paul Chapman Publishing Ltd. 1990)

Buchanan, Peter, "Quays to Design," *Architectural Review* 1106 (Apr. 1989), 39–44

Cox, Alan, *Docklands in the Making: The Redevelopment of the Isle of Dogs, 1981–1995* (London and Atlantic Highlands, N.J.: The Athlone Press for the Royal Commission on the Historical Monuments of England 1995)

Crilley, Darrell, "Canary Wharf, " unpublished paper, London 1991

Cruickshank, Dan, "Gwilt Complex," *Architectural Review* 1106 (Apr. 1989), 55–58

Davey, Peter, "What to do in the Docks," *Architectural Review* 1106 (Apr. 1989), 27

Docklands Consultative Committee, *Six Year Review of the LDDC* (London 1988)

—, *The Docklands Experiment: a Critical Review of Eight Years of the London Docklands Development Corporation* (London 1990)

Gabetti, Giovanni, "Il fantasma dei Docklands," *La Repubblica*, 12 June 1992

Ghirardo, Diane, and Ferruccio Trabalzi, "Piano Quays," *Architectural Review* 1106 (Apr. 1989), 84–88

Harvey, David, *The Condition of Postmodernity* (Oxford: Basil Blackwell 1989)

Hatton, Brian, "The Development of London's Docklands: The Role of the Urban Development Corporation," *Lotus* 67 (Dec. 1990), 54–89

Henderson, George, *Cultural Diversity in the Workplace: Issues and Strategies* (Westport, Conn.: Quorum Books 1994)

235

Carlos Jiménez, with essays by Aldo
Rossi and Kurt Forster (Barcelona:
Gustavo Gili 1991)
MacCormac, Richard, "Canary Wharf
Options," *Architects' Journal* (4 Dec.
1985), 32–33
Herman Miller Inc., *Rocklin, California*
(Grand Rapids, Mich.: Herman Miller
1989)
Minister für Stadtentwicklung, Wohnen
u. Verkehr des Landes Nordrhein-
Westfalen (1989), *Internationale*

*Bauausstellung Emscher Park:
Memorandum zu Inhalt und
Organisation* (Düsseldorf 1989)
Olmsted, Barney, *Creating a Flexible
Workplace: How to Select and Manage
Alternative Work Options* (New York:
AMACOM 1994)
Olympia & York, London, *Canary
Wharf: The Untold Story*; *Canary
Wharf: Vision of a New City District*;
The Tower, No. 1 Canada Square; and
Ogilvy & Mather, No. 3 Cabot Square,

Canary Wharf (London: Olympia &
York 1990)
Williams, Stephanie, *Docklands*
(London: Architecture Design and
Technology Press 1990)
Wynne, Richard, *Under Construction:
Building for Health in the EC Workplace*
(Shankill, Co. Dublin: European
Foundation for the Improvement of
Living and Working Conditions
1992)

Illustration Credits

Index

Figures in *italic* type indicate pages
on which illustrations appear.

238